Follow Your Leader

The memoir of a Newmarket trainer

Gavin Pritchard-Gordon

Foreword by Brough Scott

Copyright © 2023 Gavin Pritchard-Gordon

The right of Gavin Pritchard-Gordon to be identified as the author of this work has been asserted in accordance with the Copyright, Design and Patents Act 1988

All rights reserved. No part of this book may be reproduced or used in any manner without written permission of the copyright owner except for the use of quotations in a book review.

*

This book has been generously sponsored by
CAR COLSTON HALL STUD in Nottinghamshire,
which is held in high regard by all those involved
with the Racing and Breeding Industry.

I would like to dedicate this book to my father and mother, Bill and Lesley Pritchard-Gordon; to my four siblings, Giles, Grant, Tessa and Amanda, and their respective families; to my four wonderful offspring, Rupert, Paddy, Rosanna and Charlie; and to Billy (Diana) Thompson, whose inspiration, encouragement and support has been immense throughout my endeavours.

Table of Contents

Foreword	9
1. What Might Have Been	11
2. Self-Examination	13
3. Parental Disbelief	14
4. A Ray of Light	16
5. The Cub Reporter	19
6. A Sojourn In Paris	21
7. My First Time in Newmarket	26
8. My Mentor, Harvey Leader	29
9. The Pupil Trainer	31
10. A Heaven-Sent Opportunity	39
11. Joys of The Emerald Isle	57
12. With PTW at Seven Barrows	65
13. My Return to Newmarket	75
14. The Start of My Training Career	79
15. My Training Days at Shalfleet	92
16. Ardoon, Record Run and King Pele – Happy Days	102
17. The Move to Stanley House Stables and Fairway	120
18. Happy Humans Make Happy Horses	129
19. Noalcoholic	132
20. Wis	134
21. Spanker	137
22. A Far-Eastern Odyssey	139
23. The Derby Dinner	141
24. Ladbrokes Lunch	144
25. Princess Genista	146
26. Ayr Races	148
27. Doncaster Bloodstock Sales	150
28. Quick Review	155

29. Moments in Sport	158
30. Rugby	163
31. Footnotes on Football	168
32. Newmarket Trainers Federation	170
33. Manager and Boom Patrol	174
34. Staff at Stanley House Stables	177
35. Young Assistant Trainers in Newmarket	185
36. Ben Hanbury	188
37. Coral	193
38. Divorce	203
39. Graham Place/Trillium Place	204
40. Yorkshire and Garrowby	209
41. NH Jockeys – The Bravest of The Brave	213
42. More about National Hunt Racing and SSE	216
43. Racing at Perth	219
44. The Joys of Brighton	221
45. Pheasant Shooting – Not My Strong Point!	225
46. Midwood	228
47. Billy Cahill at The Police Station	234
48. Giles William	237
49. The End of My Training Career	248
50. BHB	251
51. TBA	254
52. Walk Up Memory Lane in Newmarket	260
53. The Epilogue	271
Photographs	275
Index	315
Acknowledgements	323

Foreword

We only have one life. It is best lived with humour, energy, affection and enthusiasm. It is even better if you manage to capture those qualities in print. Hats off to our new author.

His is a great achievement in three different ways. Firstly in being one of the very, very few of the very, very many who say they are going to write a memoir and finally overcome all the effort and grind to publication.

Second, for providing such a vivid and unique chronicle of an age that is gone. That some of it may seem out of date or even order these days is not the point. The assorted triumphs and disasters did actually happen, including the brilliant early one when the euphoria of saddling a first winner was clouded by a major bollocking from the titled owner who wanted the horse "to have a 'joey'" and wait for another day.

What's more the writing is very often a delight. The leading players who walk through these pages are described with loving and almost Dickensian detail and some very welcome wit. "The morals of the upper classes," concludes one passage of our hero escaping the clutches of an over amorous owner, "left much to be desired in that era."

But the third achievement is the greatest. It is the warmth it spreads as he leads us along his journey. "Training racehorses was our passion," he says and chapter after chapter this shines through. The game has its share of bad guys and bad times have hit Gavin too, yet he never dwells on the negative. His is a tale of gratitude for the gifts he was given, a love letter to the game that enthused him, and especially to Newmarket, the very heartbeat of it all.

The book is a good deed in an often naughty world. When I finished I felt uplifted by the reading of it. You will too.

Brough Scott

1.
What Might Have Been

"You are not doing very well at this interview, Mr Pritchard-Gordon," booms the small, bespectacled Dean of Christ Church, who is sitting immediately opposite me in the middle of a long, narrow mahogany table in the magnificent library of this famous Oxford College. The two learned and belligerent dons at either end of the table, who had marked my English and History exam papers, had finished their lengthy and detailed interrogation of an unsuspecting 18-year-old.

"What do you want to do, when you come to this College?" continues the Dean, in a menacing and demeaning tone.

Sensing my opportunity and recalling the advice given to me by my Headmaster before my departure, I reply, "I love all sports, and my ambition is to get a Rugby Blue, in line with the sporting traditions of the College."

"There is the door, Mr Pritchard-Gordon. That is the end of the interview. We need people with academia in this College," exclaimed the Dean, gesticulating frantically to make himself understood.

I am numbed, speechless and crestfallen. Now riveted to my chair.

"The door is behind you, Mr Pritchard-Gordon – we have others to interview. Thank you for attending. Goodbye."

I left the library, and descended the dimly lit spiral staircase to the cloisters below – my mind in neutral, my confidence totally shattered. It had been a crucifying and embarrassing experience – and one, in hindsight, which changed the course of my life, at one fell swoop. Without doubt for the better.

I would have read Law at Oxford for three years, struggling to keep up with my contemporaries, and hamstrung by my limitations. Going on to be a sedentary solicitor in Sinchinhampton – or a bumbling, boring barrister in Bickeringborough, perhaps.

Instead, I have spent 55 years in the world of Horse Racing and Breeding, and enjoyed my life enormously as a trainer in Newmarket for 23 years, and 14 years as Chief Executive of the Thoroughbred Breeders' Association (TBA), meeting a multitude of like-minded people, from all walks of life, who are passionate about our wonderful sport.

2.
Self-Examination

The train journey from Oxford, back to our home in Mid Sussex, was not a happy one. I sat huddled in a crowded carriage, shocked, disillusioned, and very angry. Finding it very difficult to fathom, and believe, what had happened – and incensed at the way that I had been treated.

I had been led to believe by my Headmaster, himself an alumnus of the College, that my place at Christ Church was a fait accompli, and that my interview with the Dean would be cordial and friendly in his study, with tea and crumpets. He could not have been more wrong. It later transpired that, unbeknown to my Headmaster, remarkably, a new Dean, an American academic, had been appointed – his brief being to raise the intellectual profile of the College, thereby diluting the games playing image it had acquired previously.

By the time the train had reached Three Bridges, our local station, and after a great deal of soul searching and self-examination, my mind was firmly made up. I did not want to go to University – of any description, and whatever might be offered to me. Decision made – and I was not going to be persuaded otherwise. But I was dreading the thought of telling my parents. They would be flabbergasted and furious. How right I was.

3.
Parental Disbelief

My father and mother were waiting for me in the drawing room – they had already had a couple of drinks, in anticipation of my return.

I loved my parents, for whom I had the greatest respect, but was also in awe of them, like so many of my generation.

My father served in the Royal Marines, ending the Second World War as a full major, at the tender age of 22. He was now a successful shipbroker with H. Clarkson and Co in the City of London.

My mother was a Wren in wartime – and, before the war broke out in 1939, had qualified as a lady barrister, at the Middle Temple, being one of the youngest ever to do so.

They were a loving and fair-minded pair, but formidable nonetheless.

"How did it go today in Oxford, Gavin?" enquires my father, excitedly.

"Not very well, Dad, unfortunately," I reply.

"What do you mean, Gavin – I was under the impression that gaining a place at Christ Church was a done deal?" says my father.

"I failed the interview, Dad, and that is that." I reply, giving a brief outline of my nightmare day.

"I just can't believe this, Gavin. What are you going to do in your life?" he retorts despairingly.

"I don't know, Dad – but, one thing is for certain, I do not want to go to University, any University. Full stop." I reply emphatically.

"Well, you'd better make your mind up very quickly. Is there anything you would like to do?" enquires Dad.

"As you know, I am passionate about horseracing but have had very little experience with horses," I say.

"As a thought, you could write about Racing for a newspaper, perhaps. You contributed a racing column for the School Magazine, I seem to remember. I would suggest that you make some enquiries, and contact a couple of Fleet Street editors to see whether there might be any vacancies." says Dad.

"That is very sound advice, Dad. I have taken note and will make amends for today, I promise." I add.

The atmosphere at supper was decidedly frosty – and I was very early to bed afterwards, needless to say.

4.
A Ray of Light

I was up with the lark the next morning – having spent a troubled and almost sleepless night agonising about the ghastliness of my day in Oxford, and trying, in vain, to be positive about the future.

By midday, my letters to the editors of two well-known London national newspapers had been penned and posted, and I was feeling a little more relaxed. Much to my surprise, I had a reply to one of these missives, by return of post – from Bill Hicks, the Sports Editor of the *Daily Mail*, asking me to ring him with regard to an interview. I was over the moon – the more so when we spoke, as he agreed to meet me in his office in Fleet Street on Monday of the following week.

Towards the end of the interview, he asked, "Please give me one very good reason why I should employ an 18-year-old with no journalistic experience on my Racing Desk?"

This was my chance, I thought my possible joker, as I took from the inside pocket of my jacket a photocopy of my latest racing column "P-G Tips" in the School Magazine. A preview of the Grand National at Aintree, earlier in the year, analysing the form and chances of the twenty most fancied horses in the race, and giving my final selection. Kilmore, ridden by Fred Winter, and trained by Ryan Price – THE WINNER at 33 to 1! Truth be told, I was probably a little influenced by the fact that Fred Winter and Ryan Price were my two idols in Racing – but fortuitous, nonetheless. I handed it to him gingerly adding, "I would like you to have a brief look at this, Mr Hicks."

"I am very impressed, Gavin," replied Mr Hicks, after a swift perusal. "You have an excellent knowledge and flair for Racing and are very enthusiastic about the sport. I would like you to come to my office for a second interview one day next week to meet members of my Racing Team".

"Regrettably, that will not be possible." I reply, "As I am going into hospital for a complicated operation on my left eye, which will necessitate having bandages around my head and eyes for five days."

"Where will you be having the operation, Gavin?" asks Mr Hicks.

"In London, at Bart's Hospital," I reply.

"Great, that will work well. Bart's is only round the corner from Fleet Street. I will come and read to you every evening when I leave the office. Daily Racing articles from the *Mail* and excerpts from the *Sporting Life* to keep you updated." says Mr Hicks.

I had the operation, as planned – and, true to his word, Bill Hicks called in my room on a regular basis. And he was genuinely delighted on the day the bandages were removed to hear that the surgeon considered the operation to have been a success.

"That is wonderful," he exclaimed, "and I have more good news for you. I would like you to join our Racing Team – but with one proviso. There are three specific things to be done before you come. First, I want you to spend a year on a local newspaper, to get a basic grounding in journalism," says Mr Hicks. "Secondly, you must spend six months in Paris, getting to know as much as possible about French Racing and learning the language, given that our Racing rivals on the *Daily Express*, Peter O'Sullevan and Clive Graham speak French fluently and know most of the leading owners, trainers and jockeys in their Racing Industry. We have to compete with them in the future – that is vitally important. And thirdly, I am determined that you go to Newmarket to work for a trainer for a year, to learn about the training and breeding of racehorses, and the organisation and regulation of Racing. And get to know the major players in the industry. This will be invaluable."

"Thank you so much Mr Hicks, you have been so kind, helpful and supportive," I reply, taken totally by surprise by his offer and now brimming with glee and excitement.

"I will send you a letter of confirmation and will also contact the Editor of the Mid Sussex Times in Haywards Heath, which must be close to where you live in Sussex, to see whether he has a vacancy for a young cub reporter," concludes Mr Hicks.

Looking back on my life, Bill Hicks was my inspiration – the man who introduced me to Racing, and gave me my first break, for which I will always be immensely grateful.

My respective interview experiences in Oxford and in Fleet Street could not have been more different. Poles apart, chalk and cheese, indeed. But, as it happened, the Dean of Christ Church did me an enormous favour!

5.
The Cub Reporter

Thanks to the helping hand and introduction of Bill Hicks, I was granted an interview with the Editor of the Mid Sussex Times – an old-fashioned but much-loved local newspaper based in Boltro Road in the delightful market town of Haywards Heath. He was an elderly, dishevelled looking man with long grey tousled hair, bushy side whiskers and a flowing, grey beard. He reminded me of Mr Pickwick and was very genial. We chatted together affably for half an hour, and I was duly given a position as junior of the junior reporters on the paper starting immediately. I was exceedingly happy – mission accomplished, a foot on the journalists' ladder, and a weekly wage packet to boot – basic wages, however, needless to say.

My duties included attendance in this role at the Magistrates' Court, local Council meetings, fetes, funerals and the town cattle market – and other mundane gatherings. I was allotted a tiny little office on the third and top floor of this dilapidated building, which had not seen a duster, a brush or a mop in ages to my mind. A rabbit warren of very odd shaped and musty rooms accessed by two narrow, dimly lit, wooden spiral staircases, and interconnected with the ancient printing works that produced our weekly newspaper.

A month after my start in Boltro Road, the Sports Editor gave his notice – and I was made his replacement, which pleased me. And relieved me of my previous responsibilities. My weekly brief was to fill two full pages of the newspaper each week, with results, reports and future fixtures, of all sports and matches, in a 15-mile radius of Haywards Heath. Mostly village Football, Cricket, Rugby, Hockey, dependent on the season – but to include Stoolball, Darts, Cribbage, Billiards and Pigeon racing, which were equally popular with our readers, surprisingly. I was later given permission by the

Editor, to start a column on Racing at Plumpton, which was located on our patch.

It was a rewarding experience, which taught me a work ethic, gave me an insight into local Government and politics, and the grounding in journalism required by Bill Hicks. Furthermore, I also saw more of my parents and family, having previously spent ten years of my life at boarding school.

But looking back in time, I was ready to move on to my second project at the end of the year in Haywards Heath. The thought of six months in Paris was a lot more appetising!

6.
A Sojourn In Paris

Despite being somewhat bemused by my career choice in journalism, my father was pleased that I was meaningfully employed at the Mid Sussex Times, but was adamant that when I went to Paris, I had to find another job, pay my own living expenses and not sit idle in cafes, restaurants and nightclubs. He suggested that I might spend my six months helping out in H. Clarkson and Co's Paris office, Sociéte Asmarine, thereby becoming acquainted with the day-to-day running of a shipbroking office, and keeping myself constructively occupied. This appealed to me, and arrangements were then made for me to become telex operator and Assistant to Philippe Fauresson, one of the two young French Directors, who were in joint charge of the business. The office was in Rue de Miromesnil, in the epicentre of Paris, just off the Rue St. Honorée, round the corner from the President's Elysees Palace – and only a stone's throw from the Louvre, Champs Elysees, and Place de la Concorde. The average age of the ten people at Asmarine was only 23 – and there were some very good-looking secretaries to keep us motivated! Our office hours were eight till five – with two hours for lunch, which was brilliant and very French. I learnt the basics of shipbroking, was always busy, had fun, and had to speak French at all times. And was partial to a little social life in Paris of an evening!

Every weekend, I made a point of going racing – either to Longchamp, St Cloud or Auteuil. I was at Longchamp when the majestic Sea Bird won the Prix de l'Arc de Triomphe – a magnificent racehorse, and a very special moment in the history of racing. And it was on my birthday, furthermore!

My father had a devilish sense of humour, and as my first lodgings in Paris, he booked me into a minuscule room in the Hotel Pretty situated in a drab and sleazy little street in Les Invalides, across the River Seine via Pont de la Concorde, and only a twenty-minute walk from the office. It was dark, unwelcoming and very basic – but unbelievably cheap and somewhere to lay my head. I was immediately struck by the steady stream of very attractive, scantily dressed young females, who frequented the hotel, on a permanent basis – and it soon dawned on me that it was a haven, and a haunt, for "Ladies of the Night", who were so much a part of nightlife in Paris.

In fairness, the Hotel Pretty was not ideal, and I later found more comfortable and conducive lodgings with an aristocratic family, who lived in a smart top floor apartment in the 16th Arrondissement, a very chic part of Paris. It belonged to a splendid widowed lady, in her late seventies, who had been part of the French Resistance in the Second World War. Baroness Roger was proud, principled and formidable – but very kind and hospitable to her young English paying guests. An accomplished cook, and a lover of fine wine, she lived in a grand French style, and made us speak in French, before, during and after dinner. Very frustrating for us at the time – but just the discipline that was needed.

While I was in Paris, I was told about an advertisement in the *Sporting Life*, seeking applications for the position of BBC Television Racing Correspondent. I immediately dispatched a response and, miraculously, received a written reply inviting me to go to Broadcasting House in London for an interview – with instructions to book a return ticket from Paris to London, all expenses paid.

Nothing ventured, nothing gained, I thought – and having been given two days' leave by Asmarine, I made my way post haste to London. Everything went well, and on my return to Paris, I received another letter from the BBC summoning me to a second interview at Broadcasting House, ten days afterwards, all expenses paid once more. Again, luck was on my side. I pleased the judges and was put through to the final stages of the selection process. I had been chosen as one of six thus far successful candidates from an original total of 600 applicants who were to travel to Newbury Racecourse for a day of commentary trials "to camera" on a Friday afternoon, when there was no live racing on TV – prior to BBC's regular coverage of racing on the Saturday. Our trial commentaries would be relayed back to Broadcasting House in London to be examined, assessed and compared.

I travelled back to Paris in a state of shock and elation – but apprehensive and concerned, as I was very much out of touch with racing in the UK. And I was now aware that my five competitors were already employed in Racing journalism.

On the day in question, the six candidates were asked to meet the BBC production team at Departure Gate No 13 at Paddington Station at 8.30am. Five of us assembled half an hour before departure and introduced ourselves. The other four, at that stage, being Jack Millan (*Daily Mail*), Tim Richards (*The Sun/Mirror*), David Philipps (Racing Pay TV) – and yes, one Michael Stoute, recently arrived from Barbados. All had third-class tickets. But there was no sign of the sixth contestant – until two minutes before the departure of the train, when Peter Dymock, Head of Outside Broadcasting at the BBC, hurried down the platform to an awaiting first-class compartment with a dapper, thin-faced young man beside him, who turned out to be Julian Wilson – his godson, as it happened!

On reaching Newbury Racecourse and after an instructional briefing from Peter Dymock, each one of us was asked to give a virtual Grandstand Preview, as if before racing, followed by a Paddock Commentary, and finally, a commentary on one of the six races, which had been allotted to us the day before, once final declarations had been made.

I was extremely nervous, but to my surprise my Grandstand preview and my Paddock commentary, appeared to be well received. On then to my race commentary – the fifth race on the card, a novice chase, over two miles with 19 runners. One of the major problems was that by this stage of a horrible November afternoon a thick fog had descended on Newbury Racecourse necessitating a Steward's Inspection to see whether racing could continue. This was not good for my nerves, as I ascended the steep wooden ladder to the Commentary Box on the main Grandstand, where Peter O'Sullevan was waiting to greet, help and advise me.

"Hello, Gavin. I'm Peter O'Sullevan," beams the master commentator. "The good news is that the Stewards have given the go-ahead for racing to continue – but it will make your commentary more difficult. Visibility is now down to only 200 yards, so you will have to rely upon the monitor while the runners are out of your vision. And then pick them up, with your binoculars, as they jump the final fence."

"Thank you, Mr O'Sullevan," I spluttered, now quaking in my boots. "But what is a monitor?"

"It is the screen in the corner of the Commentary Box," he replies knowingly. "But there is no colour, just black and white."

The race begins, and I warm to my task. Picking up the leaders, with my binoculars, as they go over the last fence, coming to the crescendo of my commentary as they pass the post and giving the final result.

"That was great, Gavin," concludes Peter O'Sullevan, as I put my binoculars back proudly in their case. "There is only one problem, however – the two horses that you called first and second have not yet finished!"

I did not get the job, needless to say – but the BBC, in their follow-up letter, did ask me to inform them before accepting another position, which made me feel better.

The contest was duly won by Julian Wilson, who went on to become an outstanding and very professional BBC Racing Correspondent and a fund of knowledge and information on all matters relating to our sport.

Michael Stoute was another "also ran" on this occasion – the Fates steering him fortuitously down another road. Strange to think that, had he been successful that day, he would never have become the Champion Trainer that he now is.

On then to my next assignment in Newmarket.

7.
My First Time in Newmarket

I only received one reply from the five letters that I wrote to Newmarket trainers – this coming from Harvey "Jack" Leader – a very popular and much respected man, whose Shalfleet stables were half-way up the Bury Road. A charming, two-sided letter inviting me to meet him at Shalfleet, after racing and Evening Stables, on the first day of the Craven Meeting on the Rowley Mile Racecourse. It was a filthy early April afternoon, a bitterly cold wind and rain billowing across Newmarket Heath from Siberia. Mr Leader had a couple of runners on the card, but no winners. Grey Venture, hot favourite for the first race, a two-year-old maiden, having been beaten into second place in a photo finish.

As bidden, I arrive at Shalfleet at 6pm and knock on the office door. There is no answer – despite the fact that I could see two elderly gentlemen, dressed in racing suits, huddled round a roaring open fire. I knock again – and this time, the smaller of the two gentlemen, whom I instantly recognise as Mr Leader, opens the front door.

"What do you want, young man? Can't you see that I am busy, and it is bitterly cold out here," he shouts.

"Good evening, Mr Leader, you wrote me a letter last week, asking me to come to Newmarket to meet you, after racing and Evening Stables," I plead.

"I have no recollection of this – please go away," continues Mr Leader. Fortunately, I had Mr Leader's letter in my jacket pocket, and hand it to him firmly, at the same time very bravely taking a step forward over the threshold of the office.

"Well, I suppose you'd better come in. Lord Willoughby de Broke and I are studying possible entries for his horses – go and sit over there in the corner until we have finished," he says.

Half an hour later, they are still in earnest discussion – and at seven o'clock get up from their comfortable chairs, put on their coats, and head for the door.

At this stage, I make a feeble plea from my darkened corner, as they depart "Could I please speak to you, Mr Leader, before you go?"

"No you can't. I am very late for dinner – Lord Willoughby and I must return immediately to my home in Denston. Come back in the morning. Be here for first lot. I will speak to you then," he says, as they disappear into the night.

I am flabbergasted, distraught and very angry. Debating my next move and deploring the way I had been treated, luckily finding overnight accommodation at short notice at a pub in Newmarket. The next morning, I return to Shalfleet at 7am, as requested, and am standing by the office, admiring the first lot of horses gathering in the collecting ring, as Mr Leader and Lord Willoughby come down the short drive. They both look a little the worse for wear, to my mind, having had a late alcohol-fuelled evening no doubt. Not a good omen, I note. Paying no attention to my presence, they stand by the paddock fence, taking stock of the horses, as they trot round the asphalt ring – and Mr Leader issues a series of instructions to the lads, before they make their way across the Bury Road to the Heath.

At this point, knowing that this would be my final chance, I make my approach, and stutter a garbled "Good morning, Mr Leader".

"What do you want, young man?" replies Mr Leader, tersely.

"I just want to speak to you about the letter you wrote to me last week," I reply, almost at the end of my tether.

"Well, do you drive, young man? You could take Lord Willoughby and me out to the gallops," he now suggests, motioning me to the driving seat of his little grey mini.

Could my luck be turning, against all the odds, I think, as I jump aboard, and drive these two worthies down the Bury Road and on to the Waterhall gallop, on this hallowed turf. And now actually speaking to the former Senior Steward of the Jockey Club, and one of Newmarket's leading trainers, one-on-one, about the minutiae of Racing. To my surprise, I am invited to join Mr Leader and Lord Willoughby for breakfast afterwards – and then to repeat my chauffeuring role for second lot, as well. And later to partake of a glass or two of champagne in the office at the end of the morning. Seizing my opportunity, Mr Leader finally and very kindly agreed that I could spend a year with him at Shalfleet, as a Pupil Trainer starting on the following Monday. From the very jaws of despair and disaster to the realms of joy and elation. Fate and destiny, to be sure. That morning in Newmarket shaped the future course of my life – and little did I know what might lie in store. Another twist in the tale, perhaps.

8.
My Mentor, Harvey Leader

Looking back in time, my first ever morning in Newmarket, with Mr Leader and Lord Willoughby de Broke, proved to be a sneak preview and a microcosm of my upcoming year. I could not wait to return. After a frantic three days planning, packing up, and getting myself prepared. The thought of spending a year with a top trainer at Racing's headquarters mingling with the cream of the thoroughbred crop, put a spring in my step and filled me with verve and excitement.

Harvey Leader was a legend of the Turf, a master amongst trainers, and an exceptional horseman. One of the very few trainers to saddle a winner of the Grand National, Jack Horner in 1929 – and a Classic on the Flat, Diomedes, who won the St. Leger at Doncaster. He was also a past Master of the Newmarket and Thurlow Foxhounds, about which he was passionate.

He had an empathy with horses, fillies in particular – both of the four-legged and two-legged variety! He loved to lay horses out for big Handicaps – the Cambridgeshire on the Rowley Mile being his speciality. He was also one of the greatest judges of a yearling – and never consulted his catalogue before making an inspection, preferring to judge them as individuals and athletes, paying particular attention to their action, balance, personality and conformation. He never went to see yearlings in their boxes at the sales – just waited, leaning on the rail, for them to come to the pre-parade ring so that he could compare them with their peers, and wait till a potential star caught his eye.

Training horses was his passion, but he loved people almost as much. He worked hard and played hard – his motto in life – and few enjoyed a party more than he did. Having a horse in training with Harvey Leader was a privilege and a pleasure. Not only was your horse trained with skill and to perfection – you had fun, and were lavishly entertained as well.

Although his stables were in Newmarket, Harvey Leader actually lived at Denston Hall, twelve miles away, between Clare and Bury St. Edmunds. He was married to Miry Dunn-Gardner, whose family owned swathes of land in Suffolk and Norfolk, and one of the finest private collections of Racing paintings in the country. Denston Hall was, and still is, a magnificent Georgian mansion, with a sizeable estate, standing proudly in stunning park and woodland. He and Miry lived in grand style and were the most hospitable hosts. For the record, Stanley, the butler at Denston Hall, had one very important task every evening. He had to position himself in Mr Leader's bedroom, looking furtively out of the window, and turn on the hot and cold bath taps, with precision, as soon as he saw his Guv'nor's little grey mini pass through the lodge gates at the bottom of the drive on his return from Evening Stables at Shalfleet. And place a large gin and tonic, with loads of ice and lemon, at the end of the bath, with a piping hot towel at the ready. Enough said!

Not knowing the geography of Newmarket, and because time was of the essence, finding accommodation at such short notice was of major concern. But, fortunately, Tim Preston, a close friend of mine since our early prep school days in Brighton, came to my rescue. He was working in Racing in Newmarket at the time – but, as luck had it, was leaving to take up a new position in the USA that very weekend. He very kindly suggested to Bunty Richardson that I might take his place as an inmate in her lodgings – Bury Hill, at the bottom of the Bury Road, adjacent to the Severals, and only 200 yards from the top of Newmarket High Street. Deal done.

Everything was now sorted, and my life in Racing was about to begin.

9.
The Pupil Trainer

Truth be told, I landed on my feet when given the opportunity to be a Pupil Trainer with Harvey Leader. His Shalfleet stables ran like clockwork, and everything was done to the highest standards. It was the perfect environment for me to become acquainted with the day-to-day running of a Newmarket stable, which Bill Hicks quite rightly thought could be such an advantage when writing for the *Daily Mail* afterwards.

The twenty-five stable staff employed at Shalfleet were all skilled and capable horsemen in their own right, having served either a three or five year apprenticeship with a licensed trainer after leaving school. Taffy Williams, Head Lad at Shalfleet, was diligent and much respected and a dab hand at feeding horses – while Jean Short was a meticulous and very experienced Racing Secretary, having been with Harvey Leader for a number of years. Jock Halsey had been Salaried Assistant to Harvey Leader for some time, in charge of day-to-day organisation of the yard, and in command, when Harvey Leader was away. A delightful man, in his sixties, Jock was not ambitious, however, and never wanted to hold a trainer's licence in his own right. All Veterinary visits and treatments were dealt with by Crowhurst, Leader and Day, the leading Equine Practice in Newmarket – and the Curtis family, renowned for their expertise in this field throughout the country, did all the farriery work on a daily basis. In summary, I was learning the basics of Racehorse Training with the best possible tutors.

My role evolved, and my duties were to take HL to the gallops every morning in his mini; to drive him to all "day trip" race meetings; to accompany him to sales in Newmarket and Doncaster; to go round Evening Stables with him compiling a list of things to be done to specific horses; to study individual horse's handicap ratings in the weekly Racing Calendar; to help HL with the entertaining of his owners, both at Shalfleet and at the races; and to go to Denston Hall every Sunday morning to discuss suitable entries for the horses for inclusion on the weekly Weatherbys entry form. He was genuinely interested in my progress, giving me sound and useful advice at all times, all the while treating me in a fatherly way, but not slow to rebuke or reprimand me, if there was a need.

A stickler for keeping to time, he was also very particular about dress and appearance, insisting that I wore a cap and tie at all times, and a trilby hat at the races. I remember driving him one Saturday afternoon from Shalfleet to the July Racecourse for racing on a fiendishly hot July day, when the temperature was in the low nineties. As we arrived in the car park, and were about to walk to the Members Entrance, he shouted to me "Where's your hat, Gavin?"

"It is back at Shalfleet, Mr Leader – I thought that it would be too hot for hats," I reply.

"Too hot be damned – go back to the yard and fetch it. You are not coming into the paddock with me without it," he concluded sharply. Later in the afternoon the Stewards of the meeting made an announcement over the public address system, decreeing that "shirt sleeve order" would be permitted in all enclosures, on account of the excessive heat. But I still had to wear my hat – believe it or not!

*

Two Saturdays later, England were playing Germany in the Final of the Football World Cup at Wembley. The country was in a state of frenzy and expectation, never seen before. There was also a race meeting on the July Course that day, attended by a large crowd, keen to watch the racing, but also hoping to keep abreast of what was happening at Wembley. Fifteen minutes before the end of the match, with the scores level, there was nobody to be seen on the stands – everyone packed into the bars, screaming at the television. The 4.30 race, in which we had a runner, had no spectators at all. A very strange and eerie sensation – but thankfully England triumphed in the World Cup, and we also won the race!

*

Towards the end of the season, Shalfleet was gripped by Cesarewitch fever – as Sayfar, a doughty and very talented stayer, belonging to Sidney Grey, was a short-priced favourite for this famous autumn marathon. He had his "prep" race in the Gordon Carter Stakes (handicap) at Ascot, ten days before – and, ridden by stable jockey Brian "Haynie" Taylor, won in a common canter. Very unwisely, however, Brian pulled up far too quickly, after the winning post – and worse still, yanked Sayfar round in a tight circle, and trotted him back to the Winners' Enclosure. Harvey Leader was incensed, no words of congratulation uttered. Shouting in a loud voice so that the Racing Press and spectators could hear "You stupid boy, Haynie – what did you think you were doing? How many times have I told you that you have to give horses time to pull up at the end of their races? He will be lame tomorrow, for certain."

There was a stunned silence around the Winners' Enclosure – press and bookmakers now in a quandary about Sayfar's participation in the Cesarewitch, his price drifting in the market, despite his facile and effortless success.

The next morning Sayfar was perfectly sound when led out to stretch his legs – but if there was any damage to his forelegs this would only become apparent when HL felt his legs at Evening Stables. HL was in a foul mood all day, and approached his box cautiously – bending down to run his left hand down Sayfar's tendons and ankle joints, as he did every night at Evening Stables. His near fore tendon was fine – but the horse flinched, gave a snort and half reared when he felt his off fore tendon.

"He's sore – I told you that he would be. That stupid Haynie. He won't be able to run in the Cesarewitch. It's a disaster – what am I going to say to Mr. Grey?" exclaims HL, alarm bells now ringing.

Sayfar was confined to light trotting exercise, his front legs bandaged, for the rest of the week, and continued to resent having his off fore tendon felt by HL at Evening Stables. Omens were not good for his participation in the Cesarewitch.

HL never came to Shalfleet on a Saturday and Sunday evening, spending the rest of his weekends at Denston, once work was done on the Saturday morning – Taffy Williams overseeing Evening Stables and responsible for feeling the horses' legs in the Guv'nor's absence. On both Saturday and Sunday evening, Sayfar's front legs were ice cold with no soreness in his off fore tendon, no sign of a flinch, a snort or a half rear. Taffy duly relayed this news back to HL in their telephone conversations – and it was agreed that Sayfar would resume his preparation on the Monday morning. Back to cantering with the string – the plan being to give him a "sharp blow out" over five furlongs on the Friday morning to put him spot on for the Cesarewitch on the Saturday, as long as he had no ill-effects afterwards.

Everything went to plan through the week – but Sayfar's price continued to drift in the market. The racing Press were adamant in their columns that there was something amiss with the favourite. How wrong could they have been. On the day he finished second, beaten in a photo, running a very brave race in defeat, which did not surprise HL one little bit, I might add!

A fortnight later, when the Cesarewitch was but a distant memory, we were going round Evening Stables, when the heavens suddenly opened and rain bucketed down in torrents. "Go and get my raincoat, Gavin, and bring it to me ASAP." shouted HL. I ran into the office and retrieved his coat, which was hanging on the hook, behind the door – thinking quickly that it would be more sensible to wear, and not carry it, back to the Guv'nor. As I walked down to the Bottom Yard, I put my hand in the pockets of the coat – and let out a yelp when the index finger of my left hand made contact with a very sharp little object. This turned out to be a drawing pin, no less.

I said nothing to anyone at the time – and have kept this secret to myself ever since. But the significance of that drawing pin has never been lost on me. HL was a very, very shrewd trainer – and knew exactly what he was doing.

*

Time flies by, when you are enjoying yourself, so they say – and my year at Shalfleet passed in the twinkling of an eye. I was very happily immersed in the atmosphere and ambiance of life in Newmarket, and soaked up as much pertinent information about the Racing Industry as my motley brain could absorb.

Apart from a riotous 21st birthday party and a very happy Christmas at home in Sussex, I was very much confined to the daily routine at Shalfleet. And I experienced my first Tattersalls December Sales, when owners, breeders and trainers come from all over the world to buy the very best British and Irish Bloodstock. And to party and have fun at Newmarket's biggest social event of the year.

The yearlings, both homebred and bought at the Sales, were all broken in, ridden away, and cantering, by Christmas – and then restricted to trotting exercise on the roads, kitted out in knee boots and hoods, for the months of January and February along with all the older horses, when HL went away for his customary winter holiday to South Africa.

At the beginning of January, I wrote a long and informative letter to

Bill Hicks, giving him a summary of my year in Newmarket – and received a very upbeat and positive response. Asking me to report for my first day at the *Daily Mail* office in Fleet Street in the first week of March in time for the start of the Flat Season.

All that I now had to do was to inform HL of my plans on his return from South Africa. I waited for the right moment, and brought up the subject when we were alone together in his office one night, after Evening Stables.

"Could I please have a word with you, Mr Leader, of a personal nature," I ask. "Of course you can, Gavin – is there something wrong?" he replies.

"No, Mr Leader, I could not be more happy here at Shalfleet, and cannot thank you enough for all that you and your staff have done for me. But, as I told you when we first met, I have to go to the *Daily Mail* in London, in March, to start work as a Racing Correspondent," I explain.

"I have absolutely no recollection of this, Gavin – and the answer is that you cannot," continues Mr Leader. "I have decided to retire from training in five years' time, and you are going to take over my stable. We will have a role reversal – you will hold the licence, and I will become your Assistant. I gave this serious thought, while I was on holiday with Mrs Leader in South Africa. I will speak to all my owners, in due course, and I know that they will all agree. You will stay another three years with me at Shalfleet – and I will then arrange for you to go to two leading trainers, away from Newmarket, spend a year with each, so that you can have an all-round perception of the training of racehorses. And then return to Newmarket and take over."

I was stunned, speechless, unable to take in what I was hearing.

"I am overawed, Mr Leader, and just don't know what to say," I stutter. "I am very flattered that you have so much confidence in my ability – but I have a long standing commitment to go and write about Racing for the *Daily Mail*. I must have a little time to properly consider this before making a decision. It has all come as an enormous shock."

"Well, think about it very seriously this evening, Gavin – and let's speak tomorrow after Morning Stables. I really want you to accept my offer – and it will be a wonderful opportunity," adds HL.

I return to Bury Hill in a daze, unable to think straight, and ring my father for advice, explaining my predicament.

"Well Gavin, you will have to make your own mind up. Your mother and I have spent a lot of money on your education, and the final decision must be yours. But I must say that you have two excellent options, for which I congratulate you," says my father.

"Thanks Dad, that is really helpful. I will do exactly what you have suggested," I reply, before retiring to bed for a sleepless night of contemplation.

The next morning, after Morning Stables, Mr Leader calls me into his office and opens a bottle of champagne, as was his daily habit.

"Have you made your mind up, Gavin, about the conversation we had last night?" he asks.

"I have, Mr Leader – I would love to accept your offer. It is beyond my wildest dreams," I reply immediately.

"That is wonderful news – we will finish the bottle to celebrate!" he concludes.

That afternoon, I wrote at length to Bill Hicks, explaining to him what had happened, out of the blue, and apologising profusely for my change of plan. He responded, by return of post, a delightful and very understanding letter, congratulating me on my appointment and wishing me the very best of luck in my training career.

Looking back, Bill Hicks was indeed a charming person, a gentleman in every sense of the word and a very kind and considerate human being. We always kept in touch and I had so much to thank him for.

Another chapter in my life was now about to begin – and one which I could never have expected.

10.
A Heaven-Sent Opportunity

In fairness, nothing changed after my momentous conversation with HL, with regard to my future in Racing. The chain of command at Shalfleet remained exactly the same, and my duties likewise. HL had a private and quiet word with Jock Halsey, Taffy Williams and Jean Short about the role reversal that would be enacted in five years' time – and, no doubt this would have permeated through to the staff in the yard, and to other racing lads and lasses in the pubs in Newmarket in time. There was no press announcement in either the *Newmarket Journal*, or the National Press – but HL did assure me that he would write to all his owners, before I went to the two other trainers for further experience.

My father and mother came to Newmarket shortly afterwards to thank HL for his kindness to me, and to take him and Miry Leader to lunch at the Bedford Lodge Hotel to celebrate this auspicious occasion. HL informed my parents that he would lodge a letter of intent with Rustons and Lloyd, his solicitors in Newmarket, outlining our intended role reversal agreement.

HL had the best possible circle of owners, all of them close friends, who had been with him for years. The unofficial leader of this loyal band was Lord Willoughby de Broke, whose home was in Warwickshire – a formidable, forthright older gentleman, very much from the "old school" with whom one did not disagree or argue. He had very strong views and opinions, did not suffer fools, and wanted everything done properly. He was a former Senior Steward of the Jockey Club, Chairman of Warwick and Wolverhampton Racecourses, and a very much revered figure in the world of racing. He was passionate about hunting, and a former Master of the Warwickshire Foxhounds. He had a couple of horses in training at Shalfleet every season, and loved them to be mapped out meticulously for specific race targets, mostly handicaps – given that he was an avid and notorious punter.

Lord Willoughby came to all the major race meetings in Newmarket – and particularly enjoyed going round the formal presentation of horses with HL at Evening Stables. Not just casting his eye over his own horses, but being briefed about the other horses in the yard, as well. The staff at Shalfleet were very fond of Lord Willoughby (known to them affectionately as Lord Willoughby de Crook) but dreaded the days he came to look round Evening Stables. He was extremely lame, and moved very laboriously – and always wanted to spend at least five minutes inspecting every horse. HL's "tour" of the horses normally took one hour – but this could become two hours when Lord Willoughby was in attendance.

The lads were thrilled when Lord Willoughby was one of the first ever to have a hip operation – it made all the difference and they were all home on time for their high tea!

*

Every big Racing stable in the country had a "stable jockey" in those days, and we were lucky to have Brian Taylor – a charismatic, fun-loving man, and also a very capable rider. He was apprenticed to HL, but had never sat on a horse before arriving at Shalfleet. The nearest he had been to an equine was riding a donkey on the beach at Southend-on-Sea, where he was brought up and lived. He was nicknamed "Haynie" by HL – the reason being that, when asked by HL early in his apprenticeship what his father did for a living, replied "He works in the ironmongery business. Going round the streets of Southend, knocking on people's doors enquiring whether they had "aynie old iron" to part with."

Brian's closest friend was Lester Piggott, with whom he had a lot in common. They were the same age, looked similar, and were both taller than most other jockeys. Brian copied Lester's very individual jockey's style – riding with exceptionally short stirrups and his "bum in the air". At the time, they were the only two in the Weighing Room – the majority of their jockey colleagues continuing to ride with a lot longer length of leg and sitting more upright in the saddle.

HL took a fatherly interest in Brian when he became stable jockey – not only promoting his ability to other trainers but also enhancing his life and social skills, as well. He introduced Brian to golf and shooting, to which he took like a duck to water, excelling at both. He got down to a golf handicap of four – and became a superb shot, and as good a trainer of gun dogs.

Joe Mercer and Jimmy Lindley, fellow jockeys and close friends of Brian's, were always invited to shoot every year with Jim Joel, one of the leading owners of the day – and engineered an invitation for Brian to join them and stay with Jim Joel at Childwick Bury the night before. Prior to dinner, being cheeky and inquisitive by nature, Joe, Jimmy and Brian went down to the kitchen to see what culinary delights were awaiting them, and calling in to inspect the port in the Butler's pantry. At the end of dinner, when the ladies had departed from the dining room table to have coffee in the Drawing Room, the port went round the table at pace – Mr Joel a connoisseur of fine port in his element and enjoying every minute. At that point, Brian was sitting next to Mr Joel, who, choosing his moment, asked Brian what he thought of his port. "It is superb, Mr Joel – I love port, and have never tasted better," replies Brian.

"Would you by any chance happen to know who produces it, and what vintage it is, Brian?" continues Mr. Joel.

Brian pauses, thinking long and hard, as if an expert, before answering. "I think it might be a Taylors 1937, Mr Joel, but I could be wrong."

"I am astounded, enormously impressed, Brian – you are absolutely right, and I would like to reward you for that, accordingly. I have recently given up shooting, as you will have heard, and would like to give you my pair of Purdeys" says Mr Joel.

The port orbits the table for another three-quarters of an hour before it is time for bed. Brian is sharing a bedroom with Joe, and, before turning off his bedside light, tells Joe about his conversation with Mr Joel about the pair of Purdeys. Joe is indignant and extremely jealous. "You can't do that, Brian – you know full well that you could only name the brand, and the vintage, because you, Jimmy and I had a sneak preview before dinner. You must tell Mr Joel the truth in the morning. Promise me," says Joe.

At breakfast the next morning, while casting his bleary eyes over the scrambled eggs, sausages, and bacon, laid out on the sideboard, Brian finds his moment to come clean with Mr Joel, who is now standing beside him.

"Good morning, Mr Joel," says Brian. "I have something to confess. Joe, Jimmy and I went to the Butler's pantry before dinner last night and spied on your vintage port. It would be totally wrong for me to accept the gift of your pair of Purdeys."

"Well actually Brian, I am going to insist that you take them. You used your charm, your initiative, and your devilish cheek – and deserve to be rewarded."

Brian was later offered a large retainer to ride as stable jockey for Ryan Price, in Findon – but always had a few rides for HL when he could. He went on to win the Epsom Derby for Peter Nelson on Snow Knight – and it was a tragedy when he was killed in the most horrific fall at Happy Valley Racecourse in Hong Kong.

Racing was deprived of a very talented and charming jockey – and we all lost a dear and very special friend.

*

In order to broaden my overall knowledge of the Racing Industry, HL very wisely suggested that I should spend a little time on one of the many stud farms situated around Newmarket during the breeding season. Indicating that the hours during the afternoon between the end of Morning Stables and Evening Stables would present an excellent opportunity. The next morning, HL saw Sir Noel Murless on the Heath, and he very kindly agreed that I could go to Beech House Stud, which he managed for Sir Victor Sassoon, one of his leading owners. This arrangement worked perfectly and, thanks to Michael McFarlane, one of the most respected Stud Grooms in Newmarket, I was able to tap into his vast experience and knowledge, and accompany the vets on their afternoon rounds of the stud. I was also able to watch the stallions, when they covered their mares – and mucked out my fair share of mares' boxes to show willing!

The three resident stallions were Crepello, St. Paddy and Twilight Alley, all of whom had been trained by Sir Noel at Warren Place. Crepello and St. Paddy were both winners of the Epsom Derby – and Twilight Alley was one of the best stayers of the day. They were a formidable trio.

Sir Noel Murless was Champion Trainer, and one of the most prolific trainers of a Classic horse in the history of our sport. He was a very shy and retiring man, however and preferred the company of horses to humans. That said, he went out of his way to make me welcome at Beech House and had a word of encouragement whenever we met. It was a privilege to speak to him about the stallions and mares at Beech House – and the Racing and Breeding Industry, in general.

*

Life at Bury Hill was fun – and ten times more comfortable than when I first set foot in Newmarket! I had been very grateful when Tim Preston originally offered me his digs at Bury Hill – but astounded and very unhappy about where I was to sleep. It transpired that the last lodger to arrive had to live in the loft above the courtyard, which was only accessed by a vertical wooden ladder. It had no carpet, just bare boards, a camp bed, one ceiling light, up in the rafters, with no shade – and no heating. To wash, and clean teeth etc, you had to climb down the ladder, and go across the courtyard to the downstairs loo in the main house. It was almost unbearable – and the rats didn't like it either. Thank God I was not there in the winter!

Bury Hill was one big happy family – Bunty Richardson, her son Jeremy, three sisters Marianne, Judith and JoJo, and us eight paying guests. Breakfast was "get your own, when you can" – and we had supper all together in the kitchen. Lunch was a beer or two in The Horseshoe pub at the bottom of the Moulton Road – or, if you had backed a winner, a three-course meal at the Chinese restaurant in Old Station Road, which was remarkably good value at two shillings and sixpence!

Bunty and I "got on" – but had a frosty relationship. The reason being that, as last lodger in, and therefore being deputed as "lodgers' spokesman", I made the mistake of making a complaint about the paucity of food at supper, confronting her bravely in the passage outside the kitchen. Bunty was furious, picked up the door stopper, and threw it at me with intent. Fortunately, I ducked – but, less fortunately, it smashed the family plate glass window behind me. I was never forgiven – but, we were pals again soon afterwards.

When Tim Preston came back from the USA, he, Jeremy Richardson, David Houston, Anne "Scrivvy" Scriven (who was Secretary to Sir

Cecil Boyd-Rochfort) and I moved into the flat in Bury Hill. They were very happy times, and we have all remained close friends ever since.

*

As previously stated, HL was one of the finest thoroughbred yearling judges ever – his fame and prowess recognised and revered by all and sundry at yearling sales in Newmarket, Doncaster and Dublin. He bought countless yearlings that went on to be successful racehorses for very small money. His maximum bid in those days was a paltry 2,000 guineas! In the late Sixties, he bought and then trained three consecutive winners of the Yorkshire Oaks, within this price bracket Exchange (by Tudor Jinks), Bringley (by Poaching) and Palatch (by Match III). All by very unfashionable sires and standing at very small stud fees. He hated to be reliant upon bloodstock agents, preferring to make all yearling selections and purchases for his owners on his own judgement.

However, there were two consequences relating to his yearling buying – the first of which frustrated and annoyed me enormously, at the time. Because he was such an astute judge, others less able would wait for HL to slam shut his catalogue at his maximum bid of 2000 guineas, and carry on bidding in their own right. In so doing they often picked up a bargain in the process – which had been previously rubber stamped by a recognised genius.

The second consequence was that HL's fortunate owners became accustomed to buying good horses for 2000 guineas, or less – and expected me to do the same, and spend no more, when I first started training. That put me at an enormous disadvantage with my fellow trainers, who had much more ammunition to hand.

I loved going to the yearling sales with HL in those late Sixties, and tried desperately hard to get into his mindset when looking at and assessing yearlings in the pre-parade ring. But, I just could not propel myself to his wavelength, which frustrated my mentor massively. He would do his best to explain and impart his wisdom – but, in essence, he had a very special and intuitive gift, and I lacked experience with horses, which was a further handicap.

One day, after Evening Stables, HL came up with a brainwave. "I am trying very hard to pass on my knowledge of yearlings to you but am not succeeding. You have the basics but need to grasp much more about conformation, which is so desperately important. Tomorrow, after Morning Stables, I am going to take you in the car to Hyperion's statue, along Snailwell Road at the entrance to Lord Derby's Woodland Stud. You will bring some sandwiches and a couple of bottles of beer and sit and stare at Hyperion for two hours until I pick you up for Evening Stables. Hyperion was one of the finest racehorses in the history of racing and a phenomenal stallion. He was only 15.2 hands in height, but had the most perfect conformation and balance. If you do what I have suggested, and concentrate really hard, you will then have in your mind the vision of the perfect racehorse. And this will help you enormously when you judge yearlings in the future."

These were wise words, indeed. I did as bidden, did not go to sleep, and benefited massively from the experience. For the record, the same statue of Hyperion was later transferred from Woodland Stud to the Jockey Club Rooms in Newmarket. He now stands, in all his majesty and glory, in the small Jockey Club courtyard, overlooking the High Street in Newmarket. And anyone in need of equine inspiration, and seeking to wonder at the perfect racehorse, should stop for a few minutes to feast their eyes. You will not be disappointed, I can assure you.

*

In a perverse sort of way, the most intriguing of my duties at Shalfleet was the comparison of our horses' handicap weights in the

Racing Calendar, which was delivered every Wednesday evening to the Jockey Club offices in Newmarket, by Weatherbys courier. There was a copy for every one of the 45 trainers in the town, at the time – some of which remained uncollected for weeks! HL insisted that I was down at the Jockey Club offices as soon as the Racing Calendar arrived – and that I had everything analysed for our horses by first lot the following morning. A tall order, but a labour of love for a young enthusiast, nonetheless.

In today's racing world, every horse that is qualified to run in handicaps has an official BHA handicap rating allotted to it, which is only altered after that horse runs its next race. But in the late Sixties, the system was entirely different. Racing was then administered and regulated by the Jockey Club, who employed a team of Handicappers to compile the weights for all horses entered in handicaps – based on their own individual assessment. Each Jockey Club Handicapper was allocated a group of four or five racecourses and was responsible for framing handicaps for all their race programmes. As a result, very often a horse could be four or five pounds better or worse off than another, depending on which Handicapper was in charge of the compilation. And sometimes there could be a differential of a stone, or more – which was very satisfactory and exciting! The secret was to do one's homework thoroughly – and only run when and where the horse was "best in". "You must always confirm the Handicapper's opinion" being HL's motto. It was no fluke that HL was such a brilliant handicap trainer.

*

No Mercy, a very good-looking grey colt by Fortino II, owned by Dr Carlo Vittadini, won the Free Handicap, a valuable and prestigious race for three-year-olds over seven furlongs at the Craven Meeting in Newmarket, and off a middling handicap mark – and was therefore very difficult to place from then onwards. He was seven or eight pounds below Classic standard – but, conversely, penalised in all future handicaps.

Luck was on our side, however, as the European Pattern Race programme had just been developed and produced – which gave top-class horses the opportunity to run in either Group 1, Group 2 or Group 3 races, dependent on their ability, in either UK, Ireland, France, Germany or Italy. I spent a lot of time studying the Pattern Race Book, and found what I considered to be the perfect race for No Mercy. The Group 3 Prix de Meautry at Deauville. But HL, for whom a visit to London was a three-day affair, was not like minded, and very dismissive. "I have no idea what you are talking about, Gavin. I love the wine and cheese in France, but I do not like the racing. Surely there must be something as suitable at Yarmouth," he says.

Fortunately, Keith Freeman, Racing Manager to Dr Vittadini, approved of my suggestion, and the entry was made. As HL did not want to travel to Deauville, I was sent as his representative – and No Mercy duly won the race on the day. It was all very exciting and satisfactory.

That evening, before celebrating in the hotel with Dr Vittadini, Keith Freeman and Brian Taylor, I rang HL to tell him the news. "Good evening, Mr Leader – everything went well here in Deauville this afternoon, and No Mercy won," I report.

"I am delighted to hear this, Gavin. I have had an equally successful day. I went to Brighton, where we won the two-year-old Seller. And there was no bid for the winner," replies HL.

Enough said!

*

Harry Lauder, a good-looking bay colt by Pinza ex Bonnie Flora, was another classy horse trained by HL for Dr Vittadini. He progressed through the handicap ranks to become a Group race contender – his end of season target being the Gran Premio de Roma. A race dear to Dr Vittadini, who lived, and was a very successful businessman in Italy. The journey from Newmarket to Rome by road would have been a marathon undertaking – so it was agreed that Harry Lauder should travel by plane on this occasion. The flying of racehorses was still very much in its infancy in the late Sixties – and a far cry from the professional and streamlined mode of equine air transport that we have come to expect today. As Harry Lauder was to be the only horse going from the UK to Rome, it was therefore decided that he would be transported aboard a cargo plane that carried newspapers from Heathrow to the major cities of Europe on a daily basis. In this case via Paris, Vichy, Nice and then on to Rome.

I was designated to be HL's representative on this mission to Rome, and travelled with Harry Lauder, plus lad and Travelling Head Lad, by horsebox from Newmarket to Heathrow Airport in plenty of time for a 11pm take-off. The newspapers were all stowed first into the body of the plane – Harry Lauder being the last to be loaded. Which later became a major problem – as, when we landed in Paris, Vichy and Nice, Harry Lauder had to be taken out of the plane, and walked around on the tarmac, in order that the newspapers could be brought forward and unloaded. Thank goodness, Harry Lauder was a very sensible, laid back and placid horse – and despite being woken three times from his slumbers, en route, took everything in his stride.

But things were to get worse. On our eventual arrival at Rome airport at 6am, because there had been an outbreak of equine flu in the area, we were informed that a vet had to check Harry Lauder, before he was allowed into the main confines of the airport. As it happened, the vets in Rome were all on strike and refused to come to examine Harry Lauder till 7am! It was a hairy experience, as one might imagine. Harry Lauder, now unloaded, standing in his pallet, on the tarmac, beside the main runway, as planes took off and landed, only a stone's throw from him, attended by three now-terrified humans. To his eternal credit, Harry Lauder remained totally unperturbed, oblivious to everything going on around him.

Our final destination was the Razza Dormello Olgiata, a beautiful stud farm, just outside Rome, given that we were not permitted to house Harry Lauder in the Racecourse stables, because of the equine flu outbreak. The following morning, Harry Lauder had to be exercised and cantered round a tiny stud paddock, which was littered with show jumps and cavaletti. But our hero was contented and relaxed, as always – and not in any way fazed by his new training quarters, which had absolutely nothing in common with Newmarket Heath.

The Gran Premio de Roma was run on the Sunday, and resulted in a comprehensive win for Chicago, trained by Harry Wragg, and owned by a charming man called Gerry Oldham. Harry Lauder performed with great credit, given his troublesome flight and preparation, finishing an honourable third.

After the race, a jubilant Mr Oldham invited Geoff Wragg, Harry's son and Assistant, and his lovely wife Trish, to dinner at the Grand Hotel in Rome, and very generously asked me to join them, booking me into a suite in the hotel as an added bonus. It gave me enormous pleasure to ring HL with a report on the race – and, when asked where I was ringing from, announcing that I was lying very comfortably in my bath at the Grand Hotel in Rome, with a large gin and tonic.

During dinner, by way of further gratitude and reward, Mr Oldham suggested that Geoff, Trish and I should go by train to Naples, the next day – and spend a couple of days in Pompeii, at his expense.

Harry Wragg and HL gave us their respective blessings – and we had the most blissful time.

The perfect finale to Harry Lauder's memorable excursion to Rome.

*

There were numerous equine celebrities at Shalfleet in the late Sixties – but the stable star was always Billy the Cob. Only 15 hands high, built like a Centurion tank, and with a mind of his own, Billy was the source of nonstop entertainment – and caused a great deal of consternation and grief, as well. For many years, he was HL's "hack", when he rode out with his string on the Heath – but, once HL had hung up his riding boots, his role changed to "schoolmaster" in charge of apprentice jockeys. He was highly intelligent and unbelievably devious in equal proportions. By all accounts, when HL was in the saddle, he was the perfect gentleman, never moved, and did exactly what was bidden. But, if an apprentice climbed aboard, who showed just one ounce of fear or trepidation, he assumed a pig-headed and frightening alter ego.

In those days, most aspiring young apprentice jockeys had never ridden a horse, or a pony before going to work in stables, which is surprising. The majority came from the poverty of inner cities, and because they were small, lightweight and ill fed were advised by the local labour exchange to write to a trainer and make a career in racing. Their initial riding tuition was undertaken by the Head Lad, Taffy Williams, in the paddock, after lunch every afternoon. For starters, this entailed riding Billy on a leading rein with Taffy by their side. Once the apprentice was considered to have made sufficient progress, he was then let loose on his own – and this is when the fun and games began. Billy usually took charge – going from walk, trot, canter to galloping round the paddock, doing his level best to dislodge his unfortunate novice rider. It was indeed a school of hard knocks, a baptism of fire, and many an apprentice packed his bags and went home. But those who had the courage, determination and natural ability did make the grade.

Billy's other important role was to accompany any difficult horses, who tended to misbehave on the Heath. One such was Palatch, a multi-talented but very fractious filly by Match III, owned by Dr Vittadini. She was being trained for the Yorkshire Oaks, but became mulish in the extreme – refusing ultimately to walk on to a canter, let alone a gallop. HL despaired – and, as a last resort, she was introduced to Billy, the two of them exercising in tandem, away from all the other horses. Palatch and Billy bonded, and became inseparable – and, as long as Billy was upsides her, Palatch consented to go onto the gallops and do the fast work which was necessary to bring her to peak race fitness. The tactic was successful, against all the odds – and there was a very happy result. Palatch won the Yorkshire Oaks – and Billy the Cob was the hero of the hour, earning praise and fame in the Racing Press the following morning, which he so rightly deserved.

*

Newmarket, in the late Sixties, was a thriving little market town, with a population of only 4,000 – the headquarters of Racing and Breeding, which was by far its biggest employer. The Jockey Club, which had its base in the High Street, were all-powerful, owning 2,500 acres of Heath land, two racecourses, and numerous properties, in and around the town. Wealthy Jockey Club members owned houses in the town or extensive stud farms in the vicinity. Established and successful trainers, such as Sir Cecil Boyd-Rochfort, Harry Wragg, Geoffrey Brooke, Jack Clayton, Ted Leader and Harvey Leader, had their stables on the Bury Road – while, amongst others, the stables of Sir Jack Jarvis, Teddy Lambton, Geoff Barling, John Oxley, Harry Thomson Jones, Sam Armstrong, Reg Day, Humphrey Cottrill, Jack Waugh, Tom Waugh, John Waugh, Paddy O'Gorman and Ryan Jarvis were dotted in and around the centre of town. Sir Noel Murless, Champion Trainer, held court at Warren Place, at the top of the Moulton Road – but there were no stables in the Hamilton Road, in those days.

The hub of the town was its attractive High Street, which was a continuous hive of activity and bustle, given that there were then no out-of-town supermarkets. Musk's, the butcher, Whipps, the fishmonger, and Goldings, outfitters, were established and flourishing retailers, whose reputations for excellence were acknowledged far and wide. Saturday was Market Day in Newmarket, when a range of different stalls were pitched on both sides of the High Street, attracting large numbers of loyal customers. The British Bloodstock Agency and the Curragh Bloodstock Agency had their offices in town, as did Crowhurst, Leader and Day, the veterinary surgeons – and Tattersalls, the auctioneers, was growing in stature, worldwide, year on year.

But there was one large blot on the landscape, one topic constantly on people's lips, which put the fear of God into practically everybody in the town, in particular those closely involved with the Racing and Breeding Industry. And that was "Overspill". The mechanism whereby Government was empowered to remove vast numbers of residents, living in poor accommodation in inner cities, and relocating them to unsuspecting little market towns, surrounding them with massive and sprawling conurbations in the process. Stevenage and Welwyn Garden City, north of London, and Crawley, to its south, being recent examples. We were reliably informed that Newmarket had been earmarked for extensive expansion, and that Newmarket Town Council was under severe pressure to accede. The Jockey Club, trainers and breeders were now up in arms, and terrified that Newmarket was in danger of losing its charm, its status and its heritage. Frantic meetings were held between these three groups, the conclusion being that the only solution was to put forward candidates from the Racing Industry at the upcoming council elections to regain control of the Newmarket Town Council, and reject the overspill proposals. John Oxley and his wife Serena, Geoff Wragg, Charles Rowe (a solicitor with Rustons and Lloyd) and Robert Fellowes (agent to the Jockey Club) agreed to stand as candidates. And my name was put forward by HL, who considered this to be in my future interest. I had to contest All Saints ward, just to the east of the High Street, which now encompasses the Racing Museum, canvassing and knocking on people's doors for their support every evening after Evening Stables for two months. The plan worked, we all won our seats, regained control of the Newmarket Town Council, and overspill was rejected.

Looking back, it was indeed a blessing – overspill would have ruined the whole infrastructure of Newmarket and its unique individuality. One only has to go to the town of Haverhill, only 15 miles southeast of Newmarket, to see what might have happened. The population of that dear little market town was increased fourfold.

*

Things do not always go to plan, however, and there were times when I was roundly cursed and reprimanded by HL for my mistakes and misdemeanours, and quite rightly, of course. One in particular comes to mind. HL loved his annual visit to the Goffs Yearling Sales in Dublin, where, over the years, he bought some very high-class, and inexpensive, horses, many of which were consigned by Jim Powell, a very successful breeder from Toomevara in County Limerick. He always stayed for the sales with Cyril Myerscough, the Chairman of Goffs, who lived in style in Dundrum, on the edge of Dublin overlooking the Wicklow Hills. The year in question, I was also invited to stay with Cyril Myerscough, whose son, Philip, later became a close friend – and it was agreed that I would meet HL at Denston Hall, at 8am on the Sunday morning to be driven by Dick Crapnell, HL's box driver and chauffeur, to Heathrow airport, to catch the plane to Dublin. As stated, HL was a demon for punctuality – and this is where it all went wrong.

On the Saturday, I was expected to go to the christening of my godson Alexander Meacock in Kent, driving down from Newmarket after Morning Stables at Shalfleet. But, after the christening, and a glass or two of champagne, being a little over adventurous then set sail for a dinner and dance ten miles north of Norwich – a journey from Kent of about 150 miles. Returning eventually to Newmarket at 4.30am on Sunday morning, I made the cardinal error of not packing my suitcase before falling into my bed, exhausted, after a long but very enjoyable day. Compounded by the fact that, having placed my alarm clock carefully by my bed – in a biscuit tin, the age old trick, to ensure that I woke in time, failed to press the set button! At 8.15am, the telephone rang downstairs in the passageway at Bury Hill – Scrivvy answering, and shouting to tell me that HL was on the line, and that he was "exceedingly angry".

"Where the hell are you, Gavin, we have been looking for you in every ditch in Denston", screamed HL in a state of hysteria. "We were meant to have left Denston at 8am, and we are already 15 minutes late. Be here in twenty minutes, otherwise we will leave without you."

I threw anything and everything into my suitcase – including my dinner jacket, thank goodness – and was at Denston in record time. Unshaven, dishevelled, and with a ferocious hangover. The drive to Heathrow was a horror story, HL telling me every five minutes that we would miss the plane – and Dick Crapnell, who did not like me, looking in his driver's mirror, smirking at my backseat torture.

But, Lady Luck was on my side. When we arrived at Heathrow, late by twenty minutes, HL, at the end of his tether, and beside himself with anger, despatched me to the Aer Lingus departure desk to make a booking on the next available flight to Dublin. To be told by a somewhat surprised stewardess that our flight had been delayed by two hours – and that everything was still in order! Overjoyed, and now mightily relieved, I rush back to the car to tell HL the wonderful news. He was happy, but not happy, if you see what I mean – unsure how to react. But Dick Crapnell was apoplectic, outraged that I had escaped further tirades and admonishment from HL – and that my bacon had been saved, miraculously.

*

My four formative years in Newmarket were very well spent. They were constructive, educational and fun. I learned so much about the Racing Industry, not just from HL, but also from his staff, from the vets, and from the time spent on the Newmarket gallops and at Beech House Stud. I also got to know HL's owners, all of whom were very friendly and supportive.

It was now time to move on – to further my knowledge of training, spending a season with two other trainers, who were based away from Newmarket. HL suggested that I should go to Ireland, and luck was again on my side. Colin Williams, younger brother of Head Lad, Taffy Williams, was apprenticed to HL, rode a lot of winners and became Champion Apprentice in the UK in 1969. He was subsequently approached to become stable jockey to Stuart Murless, Noel Murless's brother, who trained on the Curragh in County Kildare. It transpired that Stuart Murless was also looking for an Assistant Trainer – and, as a result of a conversation with HL, my name was put forward, and it was agreed that I would go to Ireland for the 1970 season.

11.
Joys of The Emerald Isle

I will never forget my first morning in Ireland in charge of a car – it soon led me to believe that the pace of life would be a little slower and more sedentary than it had been in Newmarket. The previous day, I had driven from home in Sussex to Holyhead, and put my car on the night ferry. I arrived at Dun Laoghaire, in Dublin Bay at 4am. On disembarking, the city of Dublin was fast asleep with no traffic. I followed the signposts to Naas and Kildare, and was soon on what I later gathered was known as "The Dual Carriageway", being the only one of its kind at the time in Ireland. It was still pitch dark, and there was nobody about, so I asked my little Mini to pick up pace – before spying, in its headlights, what appeared to be a large four-legged animal, standing stationary, in the middle of the road. I slammed on the brakes, and screeched to an abrupt halt, now aware that it was a solitary cow, which flatly refused to move, despite my continuous hooting – looking at me with disdain and an air of superiority. She was either very early or very late for her session in the milking parlour.

Whenever I return to Ireland and travel on the dual carriageway from Dublin to Naas, I always think back to that morning – it was indeed a desperate shock and a very rude awakening. For the record, there are still some ancient farm buildings by the side of the dual carriageway that mark the spot.

I loved Ireland with a passion, from the outset – and my affair still flourishes to this day. I am very happy to live in England, but my second choice of home would definitely be the Emerald Isle. Its people are warm hearted, fun-loving, positive and articulate – and possess an endearing and mischievous sense of humour. And the country has a natural beauty and its very own charm. If an Englishman has a bad day, he always thinks that the next day will be worse. An Irishman takes a contrary view – if his day is not going well, he thinks that things can only get better!

The Curragh, which is situated between the towns of Newbridge and Kildare, is an extensive expanse of heath and common land, interspersed with large random clumps of green and yellow furze, which closely resembles gorse. It is home to multitudes of sheep, which roam and mingle very happily with the many thoroughbred horses in the care of the 35 trainers that reside there. Being the headquarters of Irish Racing, it has much in common with Newmarket – the big difference being that, unlike Newmarket, where the trainers all have stables in the town, trainers are based the length and breadth of the Curragh.

Stuart and Beryl Murless made me very welcome from the start at Loughbrown Lodge Stables, which stood only a hundred yards from the Members Stand, and the Paddock, on the Curragh Racecourse. They found me digs in Newbridge, which were both comfortable and handy. I had an immediate rapport with the staff, all of whom were very capable and experienced horsemen, who had a close affinity with their horses.

In my first week, I was asked by Terry, the Head Lad, whether I would like to play rugby for Newbridge. I attended a couple of evening training sessions and was duly selected to play on the Saturday against Naas. After the match, I was then invited to join the two teams for the Saturday dance at Lawlor's Ballroom in Naas, a well-known and popular haunt in those days. Being one of the first to arrive in the large car park, I slot my mini into the front row, alongside the dozen or so cars that are already in position. It was one hell of a party but, come midnight, I thought it might be prudent to depart, given that I was scheduled to be on parade at Loughbrown Lodge stables for Sunday Morning Stables at 8am. However, there was a serious problem, which I soon realised was insurmountable. The car park was now crammed full with over a hundred cars, all bumper to bumper, with no room to manoeuvre between them. I was stuck, no way to escape. I returned to the ballroom office and found the concierge. "Very sorry to bother you, but I am in the front row of the car park and cannot get out. What time will everyone be leaving?" I ask politely. "Oh, for God's sake, you have no chance. You are here for the duration. They won't be gone till mid-morning tomorrow. They will either sleep with their heads on the bar – or where they fall over!" he replies resignedly.

This was my Irish initiation – a lesson soon learnt.

*

Stuart Murless (SM), known to his many friends as "Stu", had fifty horses in training in 1970 – and an impressive list of owners. Mostly prominent owner breeders in Ireland, amongst them Sir Edmund Loder – and some wealthy businessmen from across the Pond, including Richard Reynolds Jnr, and Garfield Weston.

SM was an able and successful trainer but did things very differently to HL, which was fascinating for me. His training schedules and routine were less regimented and structured, and he liked to delegate to his lads, giving them more freedom to develop individual programmes for their horses to keep them happy and interested. Evening Stables was an informal affair – the lads "doing" their horses, and letting them down, once the Head Lad had felt their legs.

SM was a private person – and, unlike HL, did not enjoy owners coming to see their horses, or entertaining them afterwards. He preferred to busy himself with his job, very conscientiously and without their interference. He was always very friendly and charming to his owners, when they visited – but delighted and relieved when they went! Beryl, on the other hand, was a gregarious and extroverted lady, who thrived on the company of others. So the combination worked well.

I was given a lot of responsibility by SM, which I enjoyed, and did my fair share of racing. In addition to the Curragh Racecourse, which was literally on his doorstep, SM liked to go to the metropolitan meetings at Phoenix Park, Leopardstown and Naas – leaving me to attend the smaller and more distant tracks, of which the Festival meetings at Killarney, Listowel and Tralee were my favourites.

My first assignment as SM's representative was a Bank Holiday meeting at Mallow, where we had runners on both Saturday and Monday. I was told to find digs in the town for the weekend, keep SM informed, make sure that the lads didn't misbehave, and see that they took particular care of the horses while away from the Curragh. I knew that would be a tall order – and was proven right on this occasion. On the Saturday afternoon, we had a winner, which the lads fancied, and backed heavily – and they had a massive celebration in the stable lads' canteen after racing. At 11pm, I tried my best to persuade them to go to bed, so that they would be on the ball for first lot, the following morning – but it was to no avail. They carried on partying till the early hours, and fell asleep slumped over the bar, where I found them at 8am!

We had another winner on the Monday afternoon, in the last race, after which I tried to find somebody returning by car to the Curragh – given that I had been given a lift from the Curragh to Mallow on the Saturday. Everyone was drinking and partying in the car park, and I soon realised that my intended journey back to the Curragh was going to be problematical. I searched in vain – most owners and trainers had left, during the afternoon after their respective races, while the remainder were based locally. By 10pm, I was panicking – until it was pointed out to me that one Aubrey Brabazon, whom I had not met, was still enjoying himself at the far end of the car park. Aubrey was one of the greatest National Hunt jockeys of his day and was now training at Rangers Lodge on the Curragh – and was the life and soul of every party. He very kindly said that I could have a lift, but that he and his fellow passengers, Lelia Harbord, and Peg Watt, were not in any hurry to depart. How right he was – we eventually left the car park at 11pm. And then stopped off nine times on the way back to the Curragh to have a drink with Aubrey's countless friends en route. Most of them were fast asleep in their beds – but, when Aubrey knocked on their doors, or shouted up to the bedroom window, were more than happy to put on their slippers and dressing gowns, come downstairs and open a couple more bottles.

We eventually arrived home to the Curragh at 5am, in broad daylight. At that stage, Aubrey was still in the driver's seat, heaven knows how, and feeling no pain. Announcing, as we disembarked "I never knew that the moon was pink".

As a result of that remarkable journey, I got to know Aubrey Brabazon and his charming family very well. They were very kind and hospitable to me, and we all had many a party together. Lelia Harbord, a wonderful lady, was Aubrey's sister, and had two lovely daughters – one of whom, Coral, I was to marry the following year!

*

Trainers on the Curragh were household names in those days, given the obsession with Racing, Hunting and all other horse related sports in Ireland. The likes of Charlie Weld, John Oxx Snr, Brud Featherstonhaugh, Stephen Quirke, Kevin Prendergast, Tim Rogers, Paddy Prendergast Jnr, and Mick O'Toole were masters of their craft and made regular incursions to the Winners' Enclosure. But the racing was dominated by Vincent O'Brien (no relation to Aiden, strangely), who trained at Ballydoyle in County Tipperary. He previously was a hugely successful National Hunt trainer, transferring his innate genius to the Flat – and, with Robert Sangster and John Magnier, built up a racing and breeding empire, the like of which had never been seen before, based upon the bloodlines of the magnificent Northern Dancer, whose reputation as a racehorse and stallion in the USA went before him.

Competition amongst trainers on the racecourse was fierce as a result – but SM did have one very high-class two-year-old in 1970 – Deep Run, a chestnut colt by Pampered King. After winning the Beresford Stakes, Trigo Stakes and Rathangan Stakes, he was legitimately looked upon as a future Classic contender – and was being aimed by Stu at the Dewhurst Stakes at Newmarket. Also the target of the brilliant Ribofilio, trained in England by Fulke Johnson Houghton. But it was not all plain sailing, sadly. Deep Run had always been a little wayward and not the easiest to train – but by August his attitude and behaviour started to deteriorate rapidly. To the point that he was refusing to go on the gallops and resented leaving Loughbrown Lodge for his daily exercise. SM had some painstaking and talented work riders, but even they could not master Deep Run's troubled mind, and coax him back to stability. SM was distraught, not surprisingly, and having put himself through purgatory for weeks on end, decided to go to Portugal for a week's break to settle his nerves and recharge his batteries, leaving the staff at Loughbrown Lodge, plus me, to conjure up a solution to the problem, if that was possible.

One evening, after Evening Stables, I went with some pals to the Hideout, a well-known pub in Kilcullen, nearby to the Curragh, which was a favourite haunt of the racing fraternity. As always, many a drink was taken, and many songs sung, and the party was soon in full flow, and still going strong at 3am! Amongst the revellers were former Flat jockey Paddy Powell, now Master of the Naas Harriers, and his close friend Francis Shortt, one of Ireland's most colourful and fearless National Hunt jockeys. In the course of conversation I regaled Francis about Deep Run, and the catastrophic problems that we were experiencing with his training. Always up for a challenge, and wanting to lend a hand, Francis, now pointing to his Land Rover and trailer in the pub car park, immediately volunteered to take Deep Run to the schooling ground and pop him over a few hurdles, to give him something else to think about. He would not be dissuaded, becoming more stubborn by the minute. Now jumping into his vehicle, pint pot in hand, driving to Loughbrown Lodge stables, and loading a very sleepy and surprised Deep Run into the back of his trailer – at 4am, when it was only just light!

Deep Run was a natural jumper – Francis, now in full cry, and feeling no pain, taking him over the three baby hurdles on the Curragh Schooling ground on his own, before reporting to me that he could now move on to the bigger hurdles, for his next session. Exclaiming, in a loud voice, as he and Deep Run turned away from us, "Gavin, he is the best novice four-year-old that I have ever sat on." And he proceeded to jump the three regulation hurdles, before I could remind him that Deep Run was only a two year old.

Deep Run's demeanour and behaviour improved appreciably, without fear of contradiction because of Francis's schooling, and he ran in the Dewhurst, finishing a very honourable second to his big rival Ribofilio.

Later in his career, Deep Run joined top National Hunt trainer Fred Rimell and won a race over hurdles at Doncaster, and later became one of Ireland's most prolific and renowned National Hunt stallions.

Francis Shortt will always be a legend, to my mind. And I can swear that I never told SM the true story!

*

I loved my time in Ireland, learnt a great deal about horses from the Irish, who are natural-born horsemen, and made countless friends, not just on the Curragh, but throughout the country, in the main as a result of introductions from the Harbord and Brabazon families, who were known and revered by everyone in the world of the horse. Lelia Harbord, and her lovely younger daughter Derna, were very good to me, from the outset – but it was only in the last two months of my Curragh stay that I met Coral, the older sister, who had been on a work experience mission to the USA. She was vivacious, warm-hearted, fun loving, and made people laugh – and I was smitten from the start. Our romance blossomed, the chemistry was right, and it was soon clear that our relationship was ongoing.

But it was now time to return to the UK, to spend a second season with another trainer who did not train in Newmarket. And luck was on my side, once more. Paddy Harbord, Lelia's late husband, had started the Curragh Bloodstock Agency, with Lelia and Aubrey Brabazon as directors in partnership with Major Victor McCalmont. It was now run by Peter McKeever and Johnny Harrington, as joint Managing Directors, whom I had come across on a number of occasions. They kindly suggested that I should contact Peter Walwyn (PTW) in Lambourn, a close friend, who it transpired was on the lookout for an Assistant Trainer. My letter was despatched forthwith, and PTW responded promptly, asking me to go down to Lambourn to spend a day with him, on my return to the UK.

Given that PTW was at the time Champion Trainer, and carrying all before him, this was a wonderful opportunity, and I was extremely grateful to Peter and Johnny for the introduction. But I knew that it was not a done deal – and that I would have to impress PTW in my interview before securing the position.

12.
With PTW at Seven Barrows

My excitement mounts as I drive down the hill into Lambourn, on an exceedingly cold and frosty morning in the middle of December, the road covered by four inches of snow. On through the delightful but still slumbering village to Seven Barrows Stables, home to PTW and his lovely wife, Virginia, known to everyone as "Bonk". I have allowed plenty of time, and arrive in the circular driveway in front of the house, at 6.45am, 15 minutes before the appointed hour of seven o'clock. It is still dark – and, on the dot of 7am, a light comes on over the front door, and out steps PTW, dressed immaculately in jodhpurs, boots, cap and shooting jacket. Striding meaningfully over to my little mini, opening the passenger door, putting his head inside and enquiring "Are you Gavin Pritchard-Gordon? I am Peter Walwyn. You are late, and I can't stand people who are not punctual." I nod, in the affirmative – but thinking that this was not the greatest start to my day.

"I ride out every morning with my string of horses," continues PTW "but, because you are here, we will have to go out in the car, which I hate. It's over there, jump in, and we will be off. The horses will be trotting on the roads this morning – we will meet them at the top of the drive and follow them on their exercise."

Kitted out in their smart winter rugs, knee boots and hoods, the string trot down to the end of the Seven Barrows Road and turn left up the long hill, past the gallops towards Wantage. It is still quite dark, and, in the distance, coming towards us, we spy a pair of headlights – the car appearing to be travelling at speed, despite the snow, and PTW's oncoming string.

"That sod is driving far too fast – I will sort him out!" screams PTW. Now putting his foot hard on the accelerator to head off our speeding villain. But, because of the ice and snow on the road, his car veers violently to the right, skids off the road, and its bonnet is buried unceremoniously into the opposite bank. And now at right angles to the road, blocking all oncoming traffic.

Our miscreant motorist is now heading towards us at pace – applying his brakes at the last minute and suffering a similar fate. His car careering off the prepared surface into the bank, left handed, in his case – and coming to a shuddering halt, only inches from us. Now wedged in parallel – two cars obstructing a still darkened highway.

PTW jumps out of our car, stumbling crazily on the snow and ice, lurching towards the passenger side of our assailant's vehicle, opening the front door, and shouting "What the hell do you think you are doing, you stupid idiot. You were going far too fast – you could have killed us, and my horses".

A monumental row ensues, PTW now flailing his fists at the other driver, who defends himself with his enormous left hand, and with his right hand winds down his driver's side window, while motioning to me to do likewise.

"Would you please tell your f......g grandfather to stop upsetting me – otherwise I am going to kill the bastard," pleads our new-found friend, a massive man, I note, in his mid twenties, who has the appearance of a gorilla, and is probably a professional boxer or wrestler, by trade.

I struggle from the passenger seat of PTW's Mercedes to the driver's side, jump out, and slip-slide my way to the passenger side of our assailant's car. Now terrified by what might happen to my would-be future employer. PTW continues to throw punches, with abandon, at the gorilla – and I try in vain to stop him. But to no avail. Concluding, in my confusion and panic, that my only option is to rugby tackle PTW to the ground, thus allowing our assailant to escape, and drive away, before someone is seriously injured.

The tactic works, but I am now the worst in the world. "What the hell do you think you are doing, you bloody fool!" shouts PTW, as he rises from the snow, incensed by my antics. "I was going to knock hell out of the wretched man."

Perhaps, or perhaps not, I think to myself, flabbergasted by what had taken place.

With difficulty we retrieve PTW's Mercedes from the bank, and continue on our way. Catching up with the string – the lads quite rightly very concerned about the safety of their Guv'nor – and returning to Seven Barrows for breakfast.

The remainder of my "interview" day unfolds without further incident, thank goodness and I have the pleasure and privilege of spending meaningful time with the Master of Seven Barrows, and Bonk, making myself acquainted with the modus operandi of his remarkable training business, and meeting key members of his staff. These include Head Lads Ray Laing, Matty McCormack and Tony Driscoll, all of whom were experienced and proficient horsemen. I am also introduced to Moira "Frisky" Briscoe, PTW's trusted and exceedingly capable Racing Secretary, who ran the office with great professionalism and efficiency.

Later in the day, I go round Evening Stables with PTW, which is a revelation in itself. We pass from box to box, at breakneck speed, PTW feeling the backs and front legs of 130 horses, while reciting the Sire, Dam and Dam's sire of every one of them, without a hint of hesitation. It is very, very impressive.

After Evening Stables, PTW returns to his office, makes some calls to owners and vets, and we have a large gin and tonic together, before he summarises our day. "I like you, Gavin, think we can work together, and would like you to start as my Assistant at Seven Barrows in three weeks' time. But there are three important points that I would like to make. First, when you return here, you must know the sire, dam, and form of every horse in the yard. And I will test you, on your first day, after Evening Stables. Secondly, you will muck out, and ride two racehorses, every morning, before you deal with your other Assistant's responsibilities. And, thirdly, 100 per cent effort is not good enough – 120 per cent should be your goal – like everyone here at Seven Barrows. Good luck."

It has been an incredible and mind-boggling day from so many perspectives, and I have so much to turn over in my mind, as I drive back to Sussex. I am over the moon to have landed the job – but in awe of the massive challenge that it presented.

*

For once in my life, I was right. Being Assistant to PTW was a colossal honour, but, conversely, a mammoth undertaking of gargantuan proportions. And, furthermore, it was a massive shock to my system, a sea change in circumstances, after the leisurely pace of life on the Curragh, and my former pupil role at Shalfleet.

In the spring of 1971, Seven Barrows was the Rolls-Royce of training establishments, and PTW was Champion Trainer, omnipotent. A genius in his métier, with 130 top-class horses in his care, an A-list of owners, and a wonderful staff. If he had not become a trainer, he could well have been Chairman of ICI. He took the training of racehorses to a new plane, and was way in front of the chasing pack. He pushed himself to the limits, with a stringent work ethic, and expected everyone who worked for him to do likewise. Which I did not find easy, given that I had very limited experience, was from a non-horsey background – and had never been to Pony Club, let alone ridden a racehorse.

To be fair, PTW always gave praise, when appropriate – but outbursts of admonishment still came thick and fast, in the ratio of three to one. I received my initial "bollocking" from PTW after Evening Stables, on my first day at Seven Barrows. To my shock and surprise, having handed me a very large gin and tonic, he suddenly announced that he was going to test me on the breeding of the horses in the yard. I had taken the precaution of going to spend a few days with Tattersalls, which was based in London in those days, to do some research – but still failed to make the grade, only answering 12 out of my 20 questions correctly.

"You have not done very well, Gavin. I will retest you in two weeks' time – and then, two months after that. I will expect you to be able to recite the names, sire and dam of every horse in the yard as they come up the canter or gallop towards you if I am ever away from Seven Barrows," exclaims PTW.

We now fast forward to the middle of March, when Mrs Dermot (June) McCalmont, who had twenty horses in training with PTW, comes to stay at Seven Barrows for the weekend. After first lot, as we are all sitting having breakfast, Mrs McCalmont, who had a runner that day at Catterick, unexpectedly proclaims that she wanted to go racing and that she would like PTW and Bonk to take her. This comes as a bolt from the blue to PTW, who had previously arranged for Lord Howard de Walden, Louis Freedman and David Oldrey to come and see their horses cantering on second lot. PTW is now in a quandary, and a kerfuffle, his well-laid plans thrown into confusion, and finding it difficult to come up with a solution. Eventually concluding that he would have to accede to Mrs McCalmont's wishes – and that GAPG would have to look after the owners.

Panic stations. Disaster. I am numbed with fright, my eggs and bacon now sitting untouched on my breakfast plate. Having given me numerous and complex instructions, PTW, with Bonk and Mrs

McCalmont, leave for Catterick – and I am left in charge of three frightfully important owners, none of whom I had previously met. I drive them in PTW's Land Rover to the gallops, alongside the Wantage Road, now shaking in my boots, and praying that I would not make a fool of myself.

There is an air of expectancy, as the first of 35 horses heads come into view, over the rise, a furlong from our little group. My binoculars are now shaking, my mouth is dry, and my nerves are in tatters – until I feel a gentle hand on my shoulder, and a mumbling voice whispering in my ear. "Don't worry, Gavin – I will never tell him". It was David Oldrey – a charming and very considerate man, whose kindness and forethought I will never forget. We still meet on occasions in Newmarket – and share a little chuckle.

*

For the first few months of my season with PTW, I shared a dear little cottage in Letcombe Bassett, eight miles from Lambourn, with a delightful man called Mark Smyly, then Assistant to Captain Tim Forster, who trained National Hunt horses in that village. Mark, who later became Assistant to PTW, was great fun, with a mischievous sense of humour, and we had many a laugh together. He must have been a passionate student of drama at school, as he was a master of mimicry and mime, always performed with a splendidly deadpan face. In those days, and still now, Mark had a striking resemblance to Prince Charles, now our King, in every respect. He could almost have been his clone and played the part to perfection. He was of the same height and build, and was remarkably adept at accentuating Charles's individual mannerisms and idiosyncrasies. Mark was known as Prince Charles by the locals in all the hostelries in the neighbourhood – and was introduced to any strangers, as such. Most of whom were convinced, hook, line and sinker.

The similarity could be more pertinent and advantageous when Mark and I visited pubs and restaurants further afield. If Mark was going to, say, Worcester, in his NH Assistant capacity, and I was representing PTW at a Flat meeting at Warwick, we would agree to meet for supper, after racing, at some hostelry that was mutually en route. On our arrival, I would make a point of introducing myself to the landlord, pointing at Mark, and requesting a nice table, which always worked a treat. Nine times out of ten, the landlord and his staff were totally taken in, and the service at our table was faultless and immaculate. On one occasion, when I asked for the bill after dinner, the headwaiter whispered confidentially in my ear that it was "on the house". Guilt possessed me, however, and we had to come clean – but did accept the two large glasses of port, on a complimentary basis.

*

Two weeks after my arrival at Seven Barrows, PTW and Bonk departed on their annual winter holiday, on this occasion to Barbados. I was asked to stay and look after the house, and the dogs, in their absence, which was very congenial and thoroughly enjoyed. My instructions were "to treat it like home", and send the occasional message to PTW and Bonk, while they were away.

As it happened, Coral, whom PTW and Bonk had previously met with Peter McKeever and Johnny Harrington, came for the weekend. And, in that duration, we got engaged, planning, in theory, and pending permission from our respective employers, that the wedding should take place in Ireland in July. Wishing to keep PTW and Bonk informed, I sent them a telegram immediately which read "Everything OK here at SB. Got engaged today to Coral Harbord. All the best Gavin." The postmaster in St. James's, Barbados, must have had a perverse sense of humour, as the telegram that PTW and Bonk received, had some minor but very ingenious amendments, which made everyone laugh out loud, by all accounts. It read "Everything OK here at SB. HOT engaged today to Coral HARDBOARD. All the best GAVEIN."

In April, Coral came to Lambourn for two months, to be Nanny for Stan and Elaine Mellor, and their two little girls, who lived at Linkslade, at the end of Seven Barrows Road. This could not have been more welcome or convenient, and gave us the opportunity to concentrate on our wedding plans. But there was going to be one very serious stumbling block – PTW laying down the law and saying that it could not take place on a Saturday, given my Assistant's responsibilities, at a busy time in the season. Lelia Harbord, Coral's mother, an equal of PTW, when it came to forthright strong-mindedness, fought our corner but PTW did not relent. Not to be denied, Lelia, Coral and I subsequently made an impassioned plea to the Protestant Bishop of Dublin for us to be married on the Sunday in Kildare Cathedral. Something that had never been thought of or considered previously. Luckily, the Bishop was a racing fan and the permission was granted.

Though I say it myself, it was one hell of a celebration – and Peter and Bonk, who flew over specially for the day, in a little plane, loved every minute, partying with their many Irish and English friends.

After the wedding, on our return to the UK, Mark very kindly agreed to vacate the little cottage in Letcombe Bassett, allowing Coral and me to start our married life together in peace and quiet.

But, a month later, he insisted upon returning – thus forming a "ménage à trois". Which, against all the odds, turned out to be the source of constant harmony, hilarity and entertainment.

*

Weekdays at Seven Barrows, during the season, were frantic and all systems go. But Sundays were always sacrosanct – when the manic pace of life dropped two or three notches, and the majority of the horses had a well-earned day of rest. The reason being that, in those days, there was no Sunday racing, which seems bizarre to us now. The routine was set in stone. Those horses that were to race in the early part of the week would go out for a shorter than usual exercise, and others approaching their first race would be put through the stalls.

Then, after breakfast, PTW's attention turned to the office. On one wall, there were three large white magnet boards, on which every horse in the yard had its own named metal disc – one for the two-year-olds, one for the three-year-olds, and another for those four year olds and above. Each board had three columns – the first for maidens (novices), second for handicappers, and the third for those considered to be Listed or Group class.

Our first Sunday ritual, conducted with ceremony and aplomb, and accompanied by loud shrieks of delight and glee from PTW, was to move any horse that had won its maiden, during the week, from the maiden column to that of handicappers. We then progressed to our second task – a painstaking and detailed examination of the weekly Weatherbys entry form, which included race programmes for every race meeting, with space allotted to each particular race. Every Monday morning, I was given my copy of the entry form, on which I had to write my suggested entries, if any, for each race. PTW did likewise – and we compared our separate forms on the Sunday morning. It was a very competitive, noisy and daunting experience. Taking each race at a time, I always had to make the opening remark – earning glowing praise from PTW if my suggested entry was valid and worthy – or, more often, a damning rebuke if it was not. Looking back, it was a very rewarding exercise, a rare opportunity to delve into the racing brain of a razor-sharp master trainer, which helped me enormously once I held my training licence.

Our office work finished at midday, on the dot, and it was time to greet owners and friends, have a large Bloody Mary or two, and settle down for a long and riotous lunch. PTW and Bonk were wonderful hosts, and Sunday sessions at Seven Barrows were legendary. An invitation not to be missed.

*

Mill House was one of the greatest and most popular steeplechasers of our time – and, with his regular partner Willie Robinson in the saddle, his epic battles with the equally prolific Arkle were an inspiration to all enthusiasts of National Hunt racing, whose admiration they captured.

When it was time for Mill House to be retired, in the late spring of 1971, he was given by his much-revered trainer Fulke Walwyn to PTW and Bonk Walwyn as a "hack". As one might imagine, this was the cause of frenzied excitement to the proud inhabitants of Seven Barrows, for whom this was very much a feather in their cap.

Mill House was subsequently transferred from his training base at Saxon House Stables in Lambourn, to the other side of the village, to begin his new career. But he was obviously not enamoured by this sudden change in role. The thought of standing at the top of a canter or gallop, looking down upon a succession of lesser and inferior thoroughbreds passing by did not appeal to him, being the great competitor that he was. "Bonk" Walwyn was a beautiful rider, and a very experienced horsewoman, but even she found it difficult to convey the message.

On the Saturday of Mill House's first week at Seven Barrows, PTW and Bonk Walwyn were scheduled to make an early departure, to go racing "Up North", and did not ride out first lot. And, at breakfast, realising that Mill House would need his exercise, PTW suggested that I should ride him second lot with the two-year-olds. My heart sank, my knees shook – the thought of riding Mill House filled me with horror. And, furthermore, I was more than aware that this could be unmissable cabaret for the lads and lasses at Seven Barrows on a cheery Saturday morning!

Having given myself the option of "hacking" up in front of the two-year-olds, or cantering alongside them, I decided upon the latter – which, in hindsight, was a major and very grave error. All went fairly well for the first hundred yards, but at that juncture, Mill House's stride quickened, getting longer and longer, and he changed quickly from third to top gear in seconds. From then on, I was the proverbial "passenger", now hundreds of yards in front of the string, failing spectacularly to pull up at the end of the canter, and continuing, at a flat out gallop across the rolling countryside of Berkshire, halfway to Wantage. It was a terrifying experience, but Mill House enjoyed it, needless to say. Until we came to a shuddering halt in front of a huge straw stack – for which, God bless the farmer!

Mill House and I proceeded to walk back very quietly to Seven Barrows, passing by the windows of the Staff Canteen, as the lads and lasses were finishing their lunch. I can still hear their whoops of glee and guffaws of laughter to this day.

*

The year 1971 was another hugely successful and record breaking year for PTW and Seven Barrows, who were almost unbeatable, on all fronts. Humble Duty won the 1000 Guineas at Newmarket – while Shoemaker was second in the Derby, and State Pension second in the Oaks. In addition to countless other major races, besides. It was a privilege to have been part of the team at Seven Barrows – and, on top of my four years as pupil to HL, and a season as Assistant to SM on the Curragh, was the final piece in the jigsaw of my learning about the training of racehorses.

Towards the end of the season, Jean Short wrote to tell me that HL was not well, and that he wanted me to go back to Shalfleet, as soon as possible. The timing was not good, but I was very concerned – and this was where my ultimate loyalties lay, of course.

I appraised PTW of the situation, made my sincerest apologies, and laid plans to return with Coral to Newmarket, post-haste.

13.
My Return to Newmarket

My respective sojourns in Ireland and Lambourn were fun, productive and rewarding – but it was good to be back in Newmarket. To see and catch up with HL, and his family, and to make detailed plans for our role reversal at Shalfleet. His health had deteriorated, but he was in cheerful form, nonetheless, and continuing to drive into Newmarket on most mornings.

Through the summer, HL, as promised, had written to all his owners informing them of his retirement, and that I would take over the licence at Shalfleet. There was 100 per cent agreement – which was very reassuring. By all accounts, Lord Cadogan sent a splendid response, stating that "I will have horses with Gavin, for as long as I live, and he is training." Which was so typical of that charming and wonderful man.

The staff at Shalfleet were made aware of the situation, and all happy to stay on under my employment. Taffy Williams would continue as Head Lad, Jean Short as Secretary – and Eddie Edwards, who had previously been with John Waugh, was to take over as Travelling Head Lad. While Jock Halsey opted for honourable retirement.

Shalfleet was professionally valued, and I agreed to purchase the whole property from HL – on favourable terms, I might add. Barclays Bank in Newmarket were very helpful and supportive as were my mother and father, who generously lent me part of the purchasing capital, but to be repaid over a period of ten years.

The bungalow, in front of the 45 stables at Shalfleet, was HL's Newmarket base. He used half of it for his office, study and sitting room – and his housekeeper, Mrs Finn, lived in the other half. When it was originally built, the bungalow had planning permission for a second storey – and HL very wisely suggested that we should go ahead with this conversion. So that Coral and I could live on the yard, close to the horses, and also have somewhere to entertain owners. This project was to take six months to complete – during which Coral and I moved temporarily into a cosy little cottage, South Lodge, at the bottom of Centre Drive in Newmarket. It was comfortable and convenient – and we were very happy there. And there was an added bonus. Mickey Greening, who had recently retired as lightweight jockey to HL, lived in North Lodge, on the other side of Centre Drive. We became firm friends, and he accepted the invitation to be my Assistant Trainer. He was a delightful man – supremely loyal, very knowledgeable about racing and horses, always immaculately dressed, and blessed with a dry and devilish Yorkshire sense of humour.

In November of 1971, I went to London to be interviewed by the Jockey Club at 42, Portman Square with regard to the granting of my Trainer's licence. My application was approved – and my father and I celebrated afterwards, in style, over lunch.

Through the winter, HL's health took a turn for the worse, and he was struck down by a chronic bout of pneumonia. He fought this very bravely, but very sadly lost the battle.

Looking back, I know that he died happy, in the knowledge that his legacy would remain, and that life at Shalfleet would carry on, as before, albeit, regrettably without our long-intended role reversal.

14.
The Start of My Training Career

We could not wait for the start of the 1972 Flat Season – anticipation and excitement mounted as the countdown began. Astrocan, ridden by a young and still-claiming Pat Eddery, was our first runner finishing a creditable third in the Roseberry Handicap at Kempton on Easter Saturday. And Trillium (by Psidium ex Grecian Palm), owned by Lord and Lady Willoughby de Broke was our first winner – at Warwick on Easter Monday. And thereby hangs a tale.

Only three weeks before the start of the season, which coincided with Easter, I received a letter from Lord Willoughby, written in his own fair hand. He preferred this mode of communication to the telephone. It read, "Dear Pritchard-Gordon – as you will be aware, little Trillium is on his winter holidays at Captain Andrew Johnstone's Brickfield Stud in Exning. You will make arrangements forthwith to bring him back to Shalfleet to resume his training. He is to be given one canter a day, as I would like him to run at Warwick, where I am the Senior Steward, on Easter Monday. He will have "a Joey" [an "easy" race in Lord Willoughby's vocabulary] – as I would like him to win at the York Spring Meeting, when Lady Willoughby and I will be staying with Lord and Lady Halifax, for the races. I look forward to seeing you at Warwick. Yours aye, Willoughby de Broke."

I did, as instructed, and Trillium duly returned to Shalfleet the following morning – looking like a little woolly bear and delighted to be back in training. At Brickfield Stud, he was turned out every day in the Stallion paddock, despite being a gelding – where he became extremely bored, hurtling round his very confined quarters at great speed to keep himself occupied and warm by all accounts. Consequently, being only 15 hands high, and lightly made, he was already half fit, on his return to Shalfleet – which Lord Willoughby might not have appreciated. Furthermore, Trillium only had two speeds – walking or flat-out gallop. And there was only one lad in the yard who could ride him, another important point, which may have escaped Lord Willoughby's scrutiny.

We now fast forward to Warwick on Easter Monday, where Trillium is entered and declared to run in the five-furlong Handicap. I am standing in the paddock, as Lord Willoughby enters and walks towards me. "Hello Pritchard-Gordon, have you wintered well – I have," he booms, his stentorian voice to be heard by all and sundry. "As instructed in my letter, you will give little Trillium a "Joey", as Lady Willoughby and I would like him to win at the York Spring Meeting, when we will be staying with Lord and Lady Halifax, for the races. I will give [Brian] Taylor his riding instructions." This he does – and as I leg Brian into the saddle, I whisper in his ear, "Trillium is a lot fitter than Lord Willoughby thinks – giving him an easy race might be exceedingly difficult."

There are 16 runners in the race. Trillium, always a bullet from the stalls, jumps out first, is never headed, and wins easily by four lengths. As he and Brian return to the Winners' Enclosure, beside the Weighing Room, my friends and fellow trainers gather round to congratulate me on my first winner, oblivious to the nuances of the situation. But there is no sign of Lord and Lady Willoughby de Broke. An hour later, we are now in the bar, into our second bottle of champagne, to celebrate this momentous occasion – when, from behind me, I feel a firm hand on my right shoulder. It is a very irate Lord Willoughby, who is beside himself with rage and fury.

"Pritchard-Gordon – if you thought that was wonderful, I did not," he bellows. "Come to my office in the Weighing Room, immediately." I follow obediently, like the naughty little schoolboy – and, as bidden, shut the office door, stand to attention and wait for Lord Willoughby to speak. "When I tell you to give one of my horses a "Joey", you do what you are told, young man. If you ever do that again, I will take all my horses away, and send them to another trainer. Do you understand?"

I am speechless, shell-shocked, terrified – quickly realising that attempting to make my defence, though entirely justified, was not going to help. The Jockey Club was all-powerful in those days. Lord Willoughby was a revered protagonist of the "old school" approach to racing, and I just had to take my reprimand on the chin.

Not only was Trillium my first winner – he was also my 100th winner as a trainer. And then, when he retired, was given to me by Lord Willoughby, as my "hack". But more of that later. In his long career, he won 14 races – and was one of the fastest sprinters in training. He was our little "pocket rocket" and a very popular horse – both at Shalfleet and with the wider racing public.

*

The following day, Lost Seal, a three-year-old gelding, owned by Lord Cadogan, to be ridden by the very likeable and experienced Tony Murray, is to run in the three-year-old maiden, over a mile at Wolverhampton.

Feeling a little frail and hungover, after celebrating Trillium's success at Warwick, Coral and I set off on our three-hour journey, looking forward to a positive performance. Lost Seal has shown ability in his previous races, as a two year old, is well-fancied by the pundits in the *Sporting Life* newspaper, and vying for favouritism, as the runners leave the paddock to canter down to the Mile Start on the other side of the racecourse.

In those days, there were no stalls, and races were all started from a "Starting Gate" or "Barrier", as it was known. This was a configuration of six thick reinforced elastic tapes, in parallel, which are strung across the course – and behind which the horses line up, once the starter signals that they are "under starter's orders", and the white flag has been raised. The Barrier is then released, when the starter presses his starting lever – and then rises vertically, at speed, allowing the horses, and their riders to proceed on their way. Lost Seal is a kind and willing horse, but a little headstrong – and, on this occasion, anticipates the start, charges the barrier, and dislodges poor Tony Murray, who is now caught and entangled in the strong elastic tapes. Much surprised and shaken by the experience, he escapes serious injury, thankfully.

Meanwhile, Lost Seal is galloping riderless round the track, completing the mile circuit, alone – and, mercifully, allows himself to be caught by Eddie Edwards, adjacent to the winning post in front of the stands. At this stage, the other horses in the race are still at the start, "under starter's orders" – the Stewards now awaiting a decision from me, the trainer, as to whether Lost Seal is to be withdrawn, or not. Having rushed down from the stands, Eddie and I are now in a quandary, which is particularly unnerving for a young, inexperienced trainer. Shall we allow Lost Seal to run, or not – a decision that is not made any easier by the bookmakers in the enclosures, who are all shouting and contributing their own penny's worth. Luckily Lost Seal is none the worse, despite his exertions, and we opt to take a chance – Eddie leading Lost Seal, at a trot, back to the Mile start, to the accompaniment of constant barracking from the crowd.

Thank heaven, all is well, from here on. Tony Murray, who has been passed fit to ride by the doctor, is reunited with Lost Seal, and rejoins the other runners at the start. This time, the Barrier is safely negotiated, the partnership remains intact, and Lost Seal and Tony Murray are triumphant, despite the preceding furore.

There is nothing straightforward about the training of racehorses – that cannot be denied.

*

Lord (Bill) Cadogan (LBC) was one of the HL's closest friends – and became a very loyal and supportive owner of mine, when I took over the licence. He was a kind, considerate and very generous man, who commanded instant and universal respect. You would never have guessed that he owned swathes of Chelsea, and a very large estate in Perthshire – he was reserved, self-effacing and down-to-earth – and loved the company of other people from all walks of life.

In fairness LBC never really liked Flat Racing – his passion in life being National Hunt. He had his NH horses with his great friend Neville Crump in Yorkshire, who trained many high-class horses for him, including Kerstin and Snaigow.

As promised, LBC had a horse in training with me till he died and, every year, allowed me to buy him a yearling, if a replacement was needed. But there was one proviso – which, being LBC, came very much tongue in cheek. The yearling to be purchased had to have the potential to run on the flat, over hurdles, and also over fences – which, needless to say, was nigh impossible. But it did happen once – which was very satisfactory.

At Doncaster Yearling Sales, I bought a horse for LBC for 1000 guineas, Killer Shark – a raw-boned, rangy but very likeable individual, who appeared to me to be "dual purpose". As a two-year-old, he showed a little bit of promise in his first two races, and LBC tentatively suggested that I might send him to Ayr for the Western Meeting, where he was Senior Steward, so that he could see him run. I was not in favour, being of the opinion that he would be outclassed – but LBC was gently persuasive and prevailed. He won in a canter, by ten lengths, loving the almost bottomless ground, which pleased LBC enormously. It cast a slur on my judgement as a trainer, which was never forgotten!

As a three-year-old, Killer Shark won again on the flat – and then went jumping, going on to win races over hurdles – and over fences, in a long and distinguished career. One of my finest training feats, probably!

One day, Killer Shark ran over fences at Cheltenham – it was an evening meeting in April, and Steve Smith-Eccles was in the saddle. After the race, there was an enquiry, and I was one of those called before the Stewards. As I entered the room, the Senior Steward of the day, Sir Piers Bengough looked me up and down and announced in a very loud voice, "Pritchard-Gordon, before we start this enquiry, I have something to tell you. When you come to Cheltenham, you must wear a country suit. Do you understand."

As it happened, I had been Flat Racing at Warwick earlier in the afternoon, and reckoned that I was very smartly dressed in my dark blue suit. I opened my mouth to give my explanation – but was silenced before uttering! Those were the days!

Killer Shark was one of my favourite horses, and much loved by LBC, and everyone at Shalfleet. But his career ended in very sad circumstances, when he broke a leg on the Limekilns Gallop. We were all devastated. After breakfast, I summoned up the courage to ring LBC with the horrible news. "Why are you ringing me at 9am, Gavin? Is there something wrong with the family? Are you, Coral and the children alright?" enquires LBC.

"Yes, we are all fine, Lord Cadogan, thank you," I stutter. "But poor Killer Shark is not. We had to put him down this morning." I reply, adding a brief summary. There is a pause before LBC continues. "This is most unfortunate, and I am desperately sorry for you and your wonderful staff at Shalfleet. Please go to your Petty Cash box in the office, take out £50 and give it to Theresa, the lovely girl who looks after Killer Shark. I will put a cheque in the post this morning to recompense you. And please buy me a suitable replacement at the next Doncaster Sales."

I will always have the fondest memories of LBC – a very special person, and one of nature's gentlemen.

*

In the Sixties and Seventies, Geoffrey Barling (GB) was one of Newmarket's most respected and gifted trainers. He never had many horses in training, but had some wealthy aristocratic owners, who kept him constantly stocked with well-bred horses, which he always trained to perfection. His yard, at Primrose Cottage stables, was just behind the High Street – and, later demolished, to make way for what is now the town's main shoppers' car park, a sheltered housing complex, Barling's Court, and Newmarket Day Centre. GB was a very popular man in Newmarket and had been a close friend of HL – so I got to know him quite well.

At the beginning of March, 1972, GB rang me out of the blue. "Gavin, I would like to do you a favour, as a young trainer in his first season. I am going to employ a very promising young apprentice rider, Pat Eddery, who still claims three pounds, as my stable jockey. And, because I don't have that many horses for him to ride, would suggest that you might like to use him, too. I will have first claim on Pat – and you could have a second retainer. We both gallop our horses on a Tuesday and Friday mornings, so this should work out well. He is apprenticed to Frenchie Nicholson, as you will know – a trainer who is renowned for producing young, aspiring, talented jockeys, who are well taught and looked after. Have a think about it and let me know."

I had already marked Pat down as a future star – and, in the knowledge that I was not going to be able to retain a top jockey on my own, decided to sound out my owners, to gauge their reaction.

They were in total agreement, so I rang GB to tell him that I wanted to proceed on the basis that he had proposed.

I liked and admired Pat, from the start, and was immediately struck by his natural riding ability, and his innate empathy with, and understanding of the horses he rode. He came from a large family in Kildare, which was steeped in horses and racing – and had a twinkle in his eye which portrayed his wonderfully Irish charm and personality.

My arrangement with GB flourished, and Pat came to Newmarket every Monday and Thursday evening, ready to ride work respectively on Tuesday and Friday mornings. GB's first lot pulled out three quarters of an hour before ours – so we were able to coincide our schedules very satisfactorily.

When the season began, I spoke regularly to Frenchie Nicholson, who booked all Pat's rides for him, on a Sunday morning. We also met after at the races, when he was always present, if his apprentices were riding that day for outside trainers. Advising them and keeping a wary eye on their progress. One day, Frenchie asked me whether I could find digs for Pat on Monday and Thursday nights in Newmarket – and I immediately suggested that he could come and stay with Coral and me at South Lodge in Centre Drive.

Coral, being Irish, knew the Eddery family well, given that her family had always lived close by to Kildare, home to the Edderys, on the Curragh – and our friendship with Pat blossomed. He had perfect manners, was very polite and blessed with an impish and infectious sense of fun and humour. After supper, he would go to bed early – and was always up bright and breezy, on time, the next morning. The perfect house guest, to Coral and my eyes.

However, one day in June, I saw Frenchie Nicholson at the races – and, in the course of our conversation, he told me of his concerns that Pat, when staying with us at South Lodge, was going AWOL. He had heard, on good authority, that Pat had been seen, on a regular basis, in nightclubs in Lowestoft, Yarmouth and Norwich. An assertion that I refuted, very strongly – given that, to the best of my knowledge, Pat was always in bed and asleep by 10pm.

The rumour still persisted, and I was again confronted by Frenchie – who by then had done his own homework and made further investigation. The verdict being that Pat had definitely been spotted in nocturnal dives all round East Anglia – and was guilty, beyond all doubt.

Coral and I were perplexed and stunned by this bombshell. But it was in fact true. It transpired that, after supper, when we thought that he had retired to bed, Pat was actually climbing out of his bedroom window at South Lodge, scaling the garden wall, and being picked up by Terry, his brother-in-law, in his Jaguar, at the bottom of Centre Drive. To be taken, chauffeured, on a jamboree – on a biweekly night of illicit entertainment.

It came as no surprise that Pat became one of our greatest Champion Jockeys – a brilliant horseman, with a razor sharp and resourceful brain, who was never afraid to take chances. In or out of the saddle.

*

I was on good terms with all my owners, but had a closer rapport with some, understandably. One of these was Leslie Cohen (LSC), a small, dapper but rather portly man, whose family had a major shareholding in Tesco, and who lived stylishly in a large flat in London's Grosvenor Square. He was ebullient, forthright and somewhat demanding – but we had a sound owner–trainer relationship, chatted regularly, and enjoyed the banter between us. He had strongly held views about his horses, and liked them to run at Grade 1 race courses, preferably in the environs of London.

Smaller race courses were not on his agenda – so, in my first season, when I suggested that his two-year-old Aberlour, who had run promisingly in his first start at Newmarket, should go for his maiden race to Newcastle, he was not best pleased but was prepared to listen to my reasoning, thankfully. However, there was a further problem. The race was on a Saturday, the first on the card at 2pm – the same day that my best friend Tim Preston was to marry his lovely wife Rossie, and when I was to be an usher.

LSC gave his blessing – but on one condition. I had to watch the race live on ITV – and ring him from a BT telephone box, en route to the 3pm wedding. The traffic around London that day was horrendous, and we were getting very late – so, as we were travelling, at the time, through a very rural part of Hampshire, our only option was to stop, and knock on the door of a little cottage in an isolated village, eight miles from our church destination. As was to be expected, the two elderly inhabitants were a little taken aback, when I asked politely whether we could watch a race from Newcastle on their television – but happy to oblige and to have a small wager on my advice. Aberlour won, and all was well. LSC was thrilled – as were our two new-found elderly friends – and Tim and Rossie's wedding was a very happy and jovial occasion.

The following year, LSC's two-year-old Ascendant, made an impressive winning debut at Yarmouth, after which I earmarked him for a valuable nursery handicap at Ayr's Western Meeting. He had top weight, but I still considered that the Handicapper had been lenient to him. Brian Taylor was booked to ride – but rang me from the Weighing Room at Ayr, two days before, to tell me that he had been "claimed" by Ryan Price to ride for him at Newbury. And he had booked Lester Piggott (LP), who was also riding at Ayr that day, as his replacement. I took this on the chin, knowing that this was a fait accompli – and alerted LSC to the change of jockey.

On the day in question, I drove from Newmarket to Heathrow, to travel by air with LSC to Glasgow, from where we would take a taxi to Ayr races. The weather was appalling, and it never stopped raining all day. Ascendant was a warm favourite, and my riding instructions to LP were brief, and to the point: "Jump out well, make the running, and make the best use of his stamina." The Mile start at Ayr is immediately opposite the stands, on the far side of the course, so we had a clear sideways view of the start. As the stalls opened, to my horror, Ascendant started exceedingly slowly and was well to the rear from the outset. Remaining there, as the runners came round the bend into the straight – until making very late headway, in the final two furlongs, to finish fourth. If I was furious – LSC was beside himself with rage. Rushing off the stand to meet Ascendant and LP, as they returned to the Paddock – given that only the first three placed horses unsaddle in the Winners' Enclosure at Ayr. By chance, the rain actually stopped for our race, so LSC confronted Lester by shouting, at the top of his voice, while attempting to hit him with his now furled umbrella. Sensing danger, quite rightly, LP ripped off his saddle and weight cloth, and sprinted back to the Weighing Room – closely followed by a puff-panting LSC, who continued to flail his furled umbrella, unmercifully. LP got there first and slammed the Weighing Room door behind him – leaving an out-of-breath LSC stamping his feet, hurling abuse, battering at the Weighing Room window, but unable to inflict injury and pain on his prey.

My return journey to Newmarket was long, frosty and very testing and the conversation with LSC animated and repetitive. And I was mightily relieved that LP was not on board our flight back from Glasgow to Heathrow.

*

Commander Kenneth Grant (RN retd) was a longtime owner of HL's, and a great personal friend of Lord Willoughby de Broke.

He was a charming, delightful man, of a certain age – but a little forgetful and absent-minded, on occasions.

La Linea, a strong, brown four-year-old filly by Linacre was bred, owned and loved by Commander Grant, and the apple of his eye. She won three consecutive races, in the early part of 1972, and was favourite for the valuable and prestigious Zetland Gold Cup at Redcar. Two weeks before the race, Commander Grant came to see and admire his filly at Shalfleet, much looking forward to her upcoming race and delighted that Brian Taylor had been booked to ride. But at this stage, the tale took a strange turn – when, during lunch, Commander Grant suddenly announced to Coral that he wanted to give La Linea to her as a present and that she was to run in her name and colours at Redcar. At first, in shock, we thought that this was his idea of a joke, but it was not – he was deadly serious, adamant and insistent that his wishes be granted. Needless to say, this was extremely embarrassing for both Coral and me – and we were left in confusion and quandary not knowing what to do for the best. La Linea was now a valuable filly, with a rating of 102 in Timeform, the racing man's bible.

By chance, I saw Lord Willoughby, two days later, and, in confidence, told him about Commander Grant's intended bequest. He too was perplexed and surprised, but candid and to the point with his advice. "If that is what the old boy wants to do, so be it. I hope she wins for Coral at Redcar."

My conscience was now clear, the transfer of ownership forms were completed and lodged at Weatherbys, and the Harbord family racing colours were despatched post-haste from the Curragh to Newmarket. All was now set for La Linea's participation at Redcar – now in Coral's name.

As you might well imagine, we were beside ourselves with excitement, on the day – but things did not go to plan, regrettably.

The mile and a quarter start at Redcar is immediately opposite the winning post, on the far side of the course – so, from the stands, we had a clear and uninterrupted view of the action. As the stalls opened, all the other runners departed, but La Linea failed to come out, planting herself in defiance and refusing to race. It was a disaster – we were mystified, incredulous, and absolutely gutted. Prior to Redcar, La Linea had never put a foot wrong – and her antics were totally out of character. But now earning herself "a squiggle" beside her 102 Timeform rating – denoting a tendency to mulish temperament.

Brian, Coral and I deliberated for twenty-four hours, not knowing how best to proceed. Eventually agreeing that we should give La Linea one more chance to redeem her reputation – in the hope that her behaviour at Redcar was just an isolated blot on her copybook. Another valuable handicap at Doncaster, three weeks hence, was considered suitable – but, to our ongoing horror and disappointment, she repeated her misdemeanours, and refused to leave the stalls, once more. Thus bringing her racing career to an abrupt and very sad end.

I can only assume that dear Commander Grant had a premonition – a message from the Almighty. The whole saga was bizarre, beyond belief – and very upsetting. For the record, post Doncaster, La Linea's Timeform rating remained at 102 – but now adorned with two "squiggles", which in reality, reduced her value by more than half when she was sold at Tattersalls December Sales!

15.
My Training Days at Shalfleet

Our trusted Newmarket builders came up trumps, and the "bungalow" at Shalfleet was cleverly remorphed into a striking medium-sized house, its second storey now decked in a mid-tanned timber cladding. We moved from South Lodge to Shalfleet in midsummer – thrilled to be amongst and in touching distance of our horses, who were our best friends, our business and our life. The new Shalfleet boasted four bedrooms, plus a modern kitchen, an attractive sitting room, and small dining room, which were ideal for the entertaining of family, friends and owners.

We created a little garden, around the house, more postage stamp than Versailles – which, despite its meagre square footage, became a feature of, and enhanced the overall look and landscape of Shalfleet stables.

We shared a short drive, from the Bury Road, with Johnny and Philippa Winter, who trained next door at Highfield. They became close friends – Johnny later becoming a godfather to my eldest son Rupert. While I returned the compliment for his youngest child, Johnny Jnr.

Two of our first houseguests at Shalfleet were Great Uncle John Pritchard-Gordon and Great Aunt Gwen. The former wrote to me, weeks before we moved in, longing to see the new house, asking the two of them to stay and suggesting a late Sunday afternoon arrival on the date that we both agreed. But, silly me, I forgot to pass this message to Coral.

On the afternoon in question, which was tropically hot and steamy, we are sprawled out on towels in the garden, recovering from a lengthy alcoholic lunch – when Great Uncle John and Great Aunt

Gwen appear round the corner of the house, dressed immaculately, and in a state of animated anticipation. I awake from my slumbers, in a jolt, covered in confusion, initially – but then riven by panic and consternation, recalling, in my haze, the conversation that I had previously with Great Uncle John.

I quickly determine that I have two options – the first to come clean, and apologise profusely – the second being to "bullshit" my way through this "unexpected" and fast-moving nightmare. I choose the latter, very bravely. Having jumped up and greeted my elderly relatives in my tatty shorts and T- shirt, I offer them a cup of tea, and rush into the house, where Coral is still removing the dirty plates, glasses and debris from the dining room table. Explaining my predicament, and apologising, unreservedly – the more so, given that it suddenly dawns upon me that I had invited them for dinner, and to stay the night. Coral is amazing, unfussed – quick as a flash clearing the dining room, and relaying the table, as if this was always intended.

I now realise that time is of the essence, if my recovery mission is to succeed, and I am not to be found out. And this is when Lady Luck comes to my rescue. While Great Aunt Gwen, now comfortably ensconced in an armchair, in the sitting room, is sipping her tea, she slips into a trance, statue-like, seemingly unable to move or speak. Poor Great Uncle John is very embarrassed and concerned, explaining that this was a regular occurrence – and assuring me that she would make a full recovery and be back to normal "in a while".

He was right. Half an hour later, Great Aunt Gwen returns to a state of compos mentis, and "rejoins" the conversation, as if nothing has happened.

This heaven-sent and timely interlude gives Coral the time and opportunity to cook dinner, make beds, and give my Great Uncle and Aunt the impression that they really had been expected. It is a miracle. My bacon is saved – against all the odds.

*

In the 1970s, Japanese owners were very supportive of racing in the UK, and some had horses in training in Newmarket. In consequence, the British Bloodstock Agency (BBA), who were based in the High Street, had a close working relationship with the Japan Racing Association – and, every year, invited two aspiring Japanese horsemen to spend a season with a licensed trainer in Newmarket. I think because HL and Colonel Robin Hastings, Chairman of the BBA, had been close friends – I was asked whether I would take a young man called Kazuo Fujisawa as a pupil. I was delighted to oblige, given that I considered this to be a compliment to a fledgeling trainer – and that, in the future, I might curry further favour with the BBA! Kazuo was polite and charming, a very hard and conscientious worker in the yard, a capable rider, and extremely popular with my staff at Shalfleet.

One very cold and frosty early March morning, Kazuo was riding Rose White, a two-year-old half sister to Trillium, owned by Lord Willoughby de Broke, who had come to see his filly out exercise first lot. As the horses were trotting round the asphalt circular ring, in front of the "house" at Shalfleet, Rose White stumbled, slipped and fell over on the grass, inside the trotting ring – dislodging Kazuo, who quickly got back to his feet in the process. Rose White did her best to get up, not aided by the frosty ground – but, instead of helping her, Kazuo jumped on her head, and pinned her down. To the horror of Lord Willoughby, Taffy Williams, Coral and myself, who were standing together, in amazement, on the other side of the post and rails.

"Get that young fellow off my lovely filly, immediately", shouts Lord Willoughby – as he, Taffy, Coral and I leap over the fence in unison.

Pulling Kazuo away from Rose White's head, with difficulty – and reuniting him with a now very startled filly.

All was well, thankfully – and both Rose White and Kazuo were none the worse for their mishap, and able to rejoin the string, as they made their way across the Bury Road to the Heath. Needless to say, we were all dumbfounded, and at a loss to understand why Kazuo had reacted in such a way – knowing that this was totally out of character. It later transpired that Kazuo was mortified and embarrassed that he had made such a fool of himself, in his eyes, in front of Lord Willoughby. And, for some reason, he assigned the blame to, and took his revenge on, the hapless and innocent Rose White.

I would now like to put the clock forward about 15 years – to a lunch party in August at Fairway, our home next to the yard, when we moved from Shalfleet to Stanley House Stables. It is about four o'clock, and the port is circulating, when the telephone rings in the kitchen. It is Brough Scott, who is in Deauville, writing his report on the day's racing.

"Hello Gavin, it is Brough Scott here – sorry to bother you on a Sunday, and no doubt interrupt your lunch, but I need some background information. I have been doing some research on the Group 1 race at Deauville next Sunday, in which there is a much-fancied horse, with excellent form in Japan. It is trained by a man called Kazuo Fujisawa, who has been Champion Trainer in Japan for a number of years. If successful, he would be the first Japanese trainer to saddle a Group 1 winner in Europe. I am told that he spent two years with you as a pupil – it would be very helpful if you could tell me a little bit about him and any stories that you might recall."

I give Kazuo a glowing reference, as you might expect – and then, having enjoyed a lengthy Sunday lunch, furnish Brough with a brief resumé of Kazuo's infamous interlude with Rose White at Shalfleet. Before exchanging au revoirs, putting Deauville and Kazuo out of my mind, and returning to the dining room for another glass of port.

The following Sunday, at precisely the same time, there is another telephone call from Brough, who is still in Deauville. "Just to tell you, Gavin, that the Japanese horse won the Group 1 today – and can I print the story that you recounted to me last weekend?"

"I think not, Brough," I suggest, trying to be diplomatic. "Please keep this one to yourself, on this occasion. And give Kazuo the credit he deserves – this is a magnificent achievement and a proud moment for Japanese racing."

*

As a young trainer, in his first season, I was looking forward to August Bank Holiday Monday – in the knowledge that horses of varying ability have winning opportunities, on that particular day, not usually available to them. There were ten meetings, the length and breadth of the country – the majority at smaller racecourses, keen to maximise their profits, by entertaining large crowds of holidaymakers, on a hot summer afternoon. The main meeting was at Epsom, which put on the most valuable card, and included the Moet and Chandon Trophy for Amateur Riders, over the full Derby distance.

I targeted the two-year-old fillies maiden at Wolverhampton, the first race of the day, for a very attractive chestnut filly called Harbrook, owned by Cheshire-based Joe and Kevin Wilcox, whose daughter Paula was a very talented and much-admired actress. I booked Brian Taylor to ride her – a coup, in reality, given that he would have been offered a number of fancied rides at various race meetings on the day.

I was at Wolverhampton in good time, excitement mounting – but Brian was not, regrettably. Failing to arrive by the stated time permitted to weigh out – this necessitating a late replacement rider if the filly was to be allowed to run. Panic reigned, given that there were no other jockeys available – and I will be eternally grateful to Frenchie Nicholson, who noting my predicament, kindly suggested that I should engage Terry McKeown, one of his former apprentices, who just happened to walk in to the Weighing Room at the very last moment.

However, there was a happy end to this saga, thank goodness – Harbrook winning the race in style. It later transpired that Brian Taylor had driven trainer Harry Wragg to the wrong racecourse – Doncaster, one of the few tracks where there was actually no racing that day! Brian was a fine jockey – but a touch vague and disorganised in his day to day life out of the saddle!

My owners were not pleased with Brian, and nor was I – but there was a positive addendum to the story, for which I must thank Brian, in hindsight. While celebrating in the bar, after the race, with Kevin and Joe, Frenchie Nicholson pointed me towards a tall, good-looking young man, standing in the corner. "That is my son, David Nicholson, the National Hunt jockey. I think you should have some jumpers, young man – I will introduce you to him," he says.

"That sounds very interesting, but I know nothing about the training of National Hunt horses," I reply, sheepishly.

"This will not be a problem – I will ask David to go to Newmarket, to do some schooling for you," continues Frenchie. And that is exactly what happened. David came to stay the night at Shalfleet, three days later, and schooled four horses that I selected, over some sleepers in the paddock the following morning. All three-year-old novices, who had never left the ground before. Amongst them King Pele, who went on to win the Gloucester Hurdle at the Cheltenham

Festival – and Do Justice, who became another top-class hurdler and afterwards a chaser.

But more of that later!

*

One Sunday in late August of my first season, I am deadheading roses in the garden, when down the drive from the Bury Road comes a smallish, long-haired, scruffy looking man – dressed only in tatty bright green shorts and t-shirt. Sorry, correction – he is actually stumbling, weaving his way from side to side, and obviously the worse for wear from drink. Reaching me, with difficulty, and propping himself precariously on the post and rail fence. "Hello Guv'nor", he starts, in a broad Irish accent. "You's having a great first season. Would there be any chance of a job?"

I look at him with incredulity, before replying tersely "I am sorry but we have no vacancies. And, if we did, I would never be employing you. You are a disgrace – unbelievably untidy, unshaven for weeks, and, stinking of drink, having obviously had a long liquid lunch in the pub. Please go away and annoy somebody else."

At the end of Evening Stables, I chat to Taffy, my Head Lad, and, in the course of conversation, he asks tentatively "Did an Irish lad come for a job this afternoon?"

"He did," I reply, "and there is no way that I would ever employ him. He is not the sort of lad we need at Shalfleet."

"Oh, that's a shame, Guv'nor," continues Taffy, "Billy Cahill does like his drink, I grant you. But he is recognised by everyone as the best horseman in town, and would be a great asset to our team."

Taffy goes home, and I resume my chores in the garden, other things on my mind. An hour later, spying out of the corner of my eye, a man dressed in a smart blue suit, shirt and tie, clean shaven, Brylcreemed hair, striding meaningfully down the drive towards me. He leans over the fence, and exclaims joyfully "Hello again, Guv'nor. I have smartened myself up a little – would you have me now?"

To my amazement, it is Billy Cahill, on a retrieval mission. I am won over by his charm, his perseverance, and his delightfully Irish impertinence. And very conscious of the glowing recommendations given to me by Taffy, earlier in the afternoon.

"You win, Billy," I reply, with a laugh, and a shrug of the shoulders. "Be here at 6.30 tomorrow morning."

In terms of my training career, this was one of the best quick decisions that I ever made. Billy was an exceptional lad, and stayed with me for the twenty-three years that I trained. Yes, he did like his drink – but there was no better stableman in Newmarket, and he had the most incredible empathy for, and understanding, of horses. He was a very capable and sympathetic rider – and simply the best, when it came to the breaking and early preparation of a young horse.

I adored Billy, from the very start – he was one of the world's most loveable and talented rascals.

And there will be more stories about him, later in these pages.

*

Dermot "Boggy" Whelan was a much-liked trainer in Epsom – an exceptional horseman, and a larger-than-life character, despite being small, but also very tough in stature. He was very popular, not only in Epsom, but throughout the racing world – renowned as a serial prankster – causing mischief with his great friend, Geoff Lewis, when not on official racing business. Boggy often used to stay with HL at Denston, if attending the sales at Tattersalls, so I got to know him well.

When I started training, Boggy took a keen interest in my budding career, and made a point of coming to chat to me at the races – regaling me with Irish jokes and stories, and sharing his love and knowledge of racing. At the end of my first season, he rang me, out of the blue, after Evening Stables. "Gavin, I have been thinking. We are good friends, you have had a successful first season, and I would like to send you a horse to train – a two-year-old called Woodcote. The owner is a very likeable man, and in total agreement. Woodcote is a handsome brown colt – I think a lot of him and rate him very highly. I will make arrangements for him to come to Newmarket early in January," says Boggy.

I thanked Boggy profusely, considering this to have been a major compliment, and then reached for my Formbook, to look up Woodcote's racing record. Noting that he had run four times, as a two-year-old – and, to my astonishment, had never been closer than seventh, in any of his races. I knew that Boggy was a shrewd judge of horses, and racing – but this did not make any sense.

From the moment we started to give the horses some faster work in early March, I soon realised that Woodcote was a great deal better than his form figures might suggest. He was able to gallop with some of my better three-year-olds, so I had the perfect yardstick. It therefore came as no surprise to me that, off what I considered to be a very lenient mark, Woodcote won his first race of the season, a competitive three-year-old Handicap at Sandown, with plenty in hand. He went on to complete a hat-trick of races afterwards.

Boggy knew exactly what he was doing, the old rascal! And the bookmakers took a hammering, as well!

Like all Irish horsemen, Boggy Whelan had a gift for and an understanding of horses and took infinite care of their wellbeing. He was an excellent stableman, a canny feeder, and performed any dentistry on his horses that was required, himself. A skill in itself, I might add.

In the summer of 1982, I am saddling a two-year-old called All Systems Go, owned by Arno Rudolf, before the Lanson Champagne Stakes at Goodwood – a Group 3 race, for which he is greatly fancied. To my surprise, the door of the saddling box swings open and in walks Boggy, all smiles as always, to wish us luck. Eddie Edwards and I carry on with our saddling procedures, tightening and adjusting the girth and surcingle – while Boggy stands at All Systems Go's head, beside the lad who looks after the horse, appearing to be playing with and stroking his muzzle. How wrong could I have been – he has actually removed one of All System Go's front teeth, handing it to me surreptitiously, and whispering in my ear "He will run even better without that!"

I am taken aback, and not best pleased, at the time – but, knowing full well that Boggy was a very competent and professional horseman, who would never have done anything to prejudice All Systems Go's health and chances on such an important day.

All Systems Go, ridden to perfection by George Duffield, wins the race in a photo finish, returning to the Winners' Enclosure to whoops of delight from our now-ecstatic entourage, over the moon to have won a Group race at Goodwood's prestigious summer meeting.

As the horse is led away, Boggy beckons me over to the rails of the Winners' Enclosure, on which he is leaning, and gives me his verdict. "For your ears only, Gavin, the removal of that tooth made the difference between winning and finishing second! I look forward to receiving my bottle of champagne in due course!"

16.
Ardoon, Record Run and King Pele – Happy Days

When writing this book, I have veered towards the random anecdote, and away from repetitive chronology on the basis that a constant flurry of dates, though pertinent to me, might be considered irrelevant to the reader. However, there will always be the odd exception – 1975 proving a case in point. A vintage year for Shalfleet and GAPG, in which, amongst other notable successes, we notched up a dream double on the first day of Royal Ascot, courtesy of Record Run (Pat Eddery) in the Prince of Wales stakes, and Ardoon (David Maitland) in the Royal Hunt Cup.

Record Run (by Track Spare ex Bench Game) was a remarkable bay colt, bought for only 6000 guineas as a yearling at Tattersalls for Sidney Grey. He won his maiden race as a three-year-old at Newmarket, worth a paltry £1,483 to the winner, before progressing meteorically through the handicap ranks to win the Zetland Gold Cup at Redcar, on his way to victory in the Group 1 Prince of Wales Stakes. He was later sold privately to Stanhope Joel, and went on to victory in the Prix Gontaut Biron at Deauville, where he was ridden by Brian Taylor. He was tough, classy and consistent, winning 14 races in a wonderful career.

Ardoon (also by Track Spare) was a top-class handicapper in Ireland, who was sent to me by his owner Frank Feeney, at the end of his four-year-old season, with the Royal Hunt Cup, as his target. In those days, there was no direct correlation between handicaps in UK and Ireland, so he had to run three times in Condition races, at the back end of 1974, to qualify, before being allotted an official handicap mark – which, as it turned out, proved to be particularly lenient, in hindsight! After winning the Liverpool Spring Cup, the last ever on Grand National day, he went on to win the Royal Hunt Cup with 7 stone 10 lbs – and then the Queen Anne Stakes at Royal Ascot, and the Hungerford Stakes at Newbury, the following year! He was another outstanding colt.

Before the start of the 1975 season, Lady Tavistock (now Henrietta, Duchess of Bedford) came to look round Evening Stables with me at Shalfleet. Over a drink afterwards, Henrietta, who has a remarkable knowledge of racing and thoroughbred pedigrees, complimented me on the presentation and well being of my horses – but remarking, in passing, that she knew nothing about the stallion Track Spare. As Ardoon was led away from the Winners' Enclosure at Royal Ascot, after the Royal Hunt Cup, Henrietta came out of the crowd, dressed immaculately, and looking stunning, kissed me on the cheek, and said quietly to me "That was a wonderful Royal Ascot double, Gavin – I will know a lot more about Track Spare, for the future!"

It was a red letter day for Shalfleet, Sidney Grey and Frank Feeney, and, as a postscript, Henrietta later had horses in training with me, shared in partnership with her longtime friends Sir David Sieff and Lord (David) Wolfson. We celebrated big time in the car park afterwards – and were very late for an important drinks party in Camberley, with our kind hosts, Tommy and Viv Wallis. Arriving somewhat the worse for wear at "twenty to eight".

*

Looking back over my life, dear Brian Taylor did me an enormous favour when he went to the wrong racecourse on that very hot August Bank Holiday Monday – absentmindedly driving to Doncaster, where there was no racing, and not to Wolverhampton. He would have ridden Harbrook, not Terry McKeown – and I would never have been introduced by Frenchie Nicholson to his son David (known to everyone as the Duke), trained jumpers, nor had the fun we have shared with the Nicholson family over the last 45 years.

It all basically started with King Pele, who was one of the four horses that David schooled in the paddock, on the first occasion he came to Shalfleet. At the time, he was owned in partnership by HL's lovely daughter Gay, her delightful husband "Mac" MacRae, and his splendid mother-in-law Miry Leader. Very well named, by Nice Guy ex Brasilia, he was a rangy but very likeable three-year-old gelding, who had limited ability on the flat, winning a small maiden at Warwick. In a deal brokered by David Minton (Minty), he was then sold, for very reasonable money, to a syndicate which included John Richardson (then Minty's boss), Peter Gorvin and comedian George Roper.

It is incredible the difference that eight flights of hurdles can make – especially when the horse in question is such a natural and spectacular jumper. King Pele won his first ever race at Windsor at the end of February – this mightily impressive performance prompting a confident Duke to advise connections that the Gloucester Hurdle at the Cheltenham Festival should be his next race. I could not believe how easily he won that day – and was awestruck at the thought of having a fancied runner at the Cheltenham Festival, in my first twelve months with a trainer's licence.

Coral, Minty and I stayed with David and Dinah, the night before – and could not wait for the Gloucester Hurdle, which was the last race on the card the following day. King Pele jumped like a buck, and battled his way to a tremendous victory, which was beyond our wildest dreams. Ridden by a very determined and delighted Duke – who, for the record, was still riding as a professional jockey, while also holding a trainer's licence.

The celebrations in the car park afterwards went on till we were kicked out by Racecourse staff at 10pm – and continued with a riotous dinner at the Unicorn in Stow-on-the-Wold. By all accounts, the chef at the Unicorn had already left for home, when the Duke rang to book our table – but was persuaded by the owner of the hostelry to return, on the basis, quite rightly, that it would be well worth his while!

We then returned to the village of Condicote, just outside Stow, where David and Dinah lived and trained, in the early hours of the morning – and were still partying when the lads arrived to muck out at 6.30am!

We have all stayed with the Nicholson family for the Cheltenham Festival every year until our reunions were brought to an end by the wretched Covid.

*

Thanks to the camaraderie and togetherness of our wonderful team of lads and lasses, we very soon became one big happy family in those four years at Shalfleet – whose numbers were to be increased by two, with the arrival of our sons Rupert and Paddy. The sound of two pairs of little pattering feet – a joy, and a new dimension on life. Surrounded on all sides by horses and immersed in constant racing chit-chat from an early age, it was inevitable that they would want to ride horses – and Rocky, the rocking horse, soon became their best friend. Rupert rode countless finishes on Rocky, pulling his "Jerks" up to the top hole, putting his little "Bum" in the air, flailing his whip skywards, and alternating his jockey loyalties between his two great heroes, Lester Piggott and Brian Taylor. To this day, I am convinced that Rocky considered himself to be a racehorse – and for one evening only, he was!

While staying with David and Dinah Nicholson for the Cheltenham Festival, we were introduced to Lord (Sam) Vestey, who was one of David's first and leading patrons, as a trainer. He and Sam were firm friends, sharing a passion for National Hunt racing, and young potential steeplechasers – and also a birthday, for good measure! As a result of our meeting, Sam very kindly sent me a Flat horse to train, called Ibn el Harem – in partnership with the Hon. Mrs W. Eykyn, referred to religiously by Sam, as "Great Aunt Dorty". To Sam's surprise, and delight, Ibn el Harem developed into a fairly useful handicapper, winning three races over the course of his two years at Shalfleet – but Sam was never present when he won, nor came to see him in Newmarket, despite numerous invitations to do so.

However, this failing was put to rights one cold January late afternoon, when I received a telephone call from Sam, out of the blue. "Hello Gavin," he said. "I have been shooting today in Norfolk and would very much like to call in to Shalfleet, to see Ibn el Harem on my way back to Gloucestershire, if that is ok with you?"

"That would be brilliant," I reply. "We would love to see you. If you can be here by 5.30pm, we could look round Evening Stables together, and see some of my other horses, as well."

I was thrilled and immediately formulated a strategy – which, in retrospect, was particularly cheeky and disrespectful to my noble new owner, given that I did not know him very well.

I went into the yard, and very quietly asked Taffy, the Head Lad, to move Ibn el Harem from his stable, and put him in the box next door – and then sought permission from Coral to replace Ibn el Harem with a very startled Rocky! Standing him with precision, head to his manger, sideways to any admirers, beneath the black rectangular metal nameplate, on the far wall – "IBN EL HAREM" inscribed in bold capitals, with white marker pen, for all to see.

And perching Rupert's favourite teddy bear, now adorned in Sam's blue and white racing silks, on Rocky's back.

Sam arrived on time for my tour of Evening Stables, when every horse in the stable is presented formally by its lad or lass for the trainer to inspect. Everything went to plan, as we admired the first six horses, in the line, all looking healthy and immaculate – before entering Ibn el Harem's box – the bold Rocky now in prime position, his lad in revered attendance.

At first glance, Sam was a little perplexed, needless to say – and there was a moment when our normally jovial Jockey Club Member might have had a sense of humour failure. But all was well – he quickly regained his composure, saw the funny side, cursed me roundly, and then went to meet the real Ibn el Harem, a few minutes later!

*

I was sitting at the desk in my office at Shalfleet, late one morning, towards the end of my first season, when there was a knock on the door – and in walked one of my best work riders, a lovely girl, very popular in the yard, and an exceptional horseman.

"I am sorry to bother you, Guv'nor, but I need to speak to you urgently," says the girl, plainly in an emotional state, and close to tears.

"You are not your normal cheerful self – is there something wrong?" I reply sympathetically.

"No Guv'nor, I am alright – but am sorry to tell you that I will be leaving Shalfleet, in a month's time, to take another job, which I cannot refuse. I love working for you, but have been offered a responsible position with a man called Nat Sherwood, who farms a large arable estate in Essex, but also has a hunting lodge in Northamptonshire, where he wants me to look after and be in charge of his horses," she says.

I was taken by surprise and upset, naturally, knowing that this was a fait accompli – but anxious to reassure the girl that she was making the right decision.

"I fully understand, we will miss you – and wish you the very best of luck in the future. But please keep in touch – and if Mr Sherwood has a horse you consider to be worth putting into training, please let me know," I reply, at the end of our conversation.

A year later, I was sitting at the same desk, when the telephone rang. It was my former work rider, touching base, to tell me that she was loving her job – and that her employer had a good-looking three-year-old colt, who showed speed, which he wanted me to see. I thanked her profusely – and then spoke to Nat to make arrangements to meet the following week.

On the day in question, I am running late, after dealing with second lot in Newmarket, but arrive almost on time at Nat's Northamptonshire cottage – dressed in jacket and random tie, which I had grabbed fleetingly before my hurried departure.

Nat greets me at the door, dapperly attired, looking long and hard at my tie and then at his own – before exclaiming in a loud voice "We are both old Radleians – that is marvellous. Come on in." Before shouting down a dark passage to his two teenage sons, still at Radley, who are making their way sheepishly from the kitchen.

"Oliver, my boy, this is Mr Pritchard-Gordon – you are going to be a Pupil Trainer with him in Newmarket when you leave school." And then, turning to his younger son Simon, adding "And Simon, you will go to Mr Pritchard-Gordon when Oliver finishes. Everything has been agreed."

I am taken aback, speechless, unable to keep up – but that is exactly what happened. Both Oliver and Simon spent time with me as Assistants, the horse duly came into training at Shalfleet – and thus started my long and happy association with the Sherwood family.

Nat was a larger than life character, with a long foxlike nose, and ruddy complexion, who oozed charm, goodwill and bonhomie. He loved horses, pretty girls and partying. As did his two rascally sons – who both went on to be hugely successful in the racing world. Oliver, as a much respected trainer in Lambourn, who saddled a Grand National winner in Many Clouds – and Simon, as a very talented professional jockey, who rode numerous winners, including the magnificent Desert Orchid in the Cheltenham Gold Cup.

As a postscript, I must confess that I very rarely wear my Old Radleian tie – but that it did me an enormous favour, on this occasion!

*

In the four years that we were based at Shalfleet, Coral, Rupert, Paddy and I became firm friends with Johnny and Philippa Winter, and their three children, Nicky, Emma and Johnny Jnr – despite what was affectionately referred to as "the Berlin Wall", a tall and imposing edifice, which separated our two closely adjacent properties!

Johnny and I were rivals, and competitive, as trainers, but very supportive of each other's careers – and many were the parties that we indulged in at our respective venues if one or other had a notable racecourse success.

One particularly hot July evening, as families, we were celebrating a Winter winner in the garden at Highfield. The children were having fun in the tree house, a popular pastime, while the grown-ups were partying raucously, partaking of quantities of booze, of course. Towards the end of the evening, the children formed up and suggested that one of the 'Oldies' should climb the vertical wooden ladder and join them in the tree house. GAPG, surprise, surprise, was chosen as the Mug, and duly began what was, in the circumstances, a very precarious and hazardous eight-foot ascent. Safely negotiating the first nine wooden rungs of the rope ladder, before proving too weighty and cumbersome for the tenth and last, which snapped, disastrously. Falling rearwards very heavily upon the bottom of my back onto rock hard ground which had not seen rain in months. At first, the children, being young and naïve, thought that I was play-acting the fool – but very soon realised that this was for real. The last thing I remembered was the terrified looks on their little faces as I passed into unconsciousness.

I must have been 'out' for a while, as my first recollection of this mishap was being put on to a stretcher by two kind medics and loaded on to the waiting ambulance, now fortified by a much-needed painkilling injection. Having been informed that I was to be taken to Bury St. Edmunds Hospital – as Newmarket Hospital, which was still in existence in those days, closed punctually at 10pm.

As the ambulance progresses along the Bury Road, lights flashing, siren blazing, there is a call on the intercom from Suffolk Ambulance Headquarters. "Urgent. Heart attack case – a Mr Lambton, at Mesnil Warren on the Bury Road in Newmarket. Please proceed there immediately," says the voice, with authority. "I cannot, I am afraid, as I am already taking an emergency casualty to Bury St. Edmunds Hospital. Please make alternative arrangements," replies the medic, at the wheel of our ambulance.

At this stage, now feeling more comfortable and relaxed, and quickly gauging the significance of this call, I shout to our medic driver, "Please go straight to Mesnil Warren immediately, we are almost opposite the front gate – Mr Lambton is a good friend of mine, and time is obviously of the essence."

We have a brief altercation, which I win, and turn right handed down the drive to Mesnil Warren, where the unfortunate Manuel, Teddy Lambton's long serving and trusted Italian butler, is standing at the front door, shouting and gesticulating, in a state of intense panic. The two medics rush into the house, retrieve Teddy, a much-loved former trainer, on a second stretcher, and deposit him in the back of the ambulance, parallel to, and alongside me. I fear the worse, the noise is excruciating, as Teddy is connected to the life-support machine – and I am very relieved when our driver calls Newmarket Hospital, albeit closed, requesting that it should reopen immediately to take a 'Red Alert' emergency. Teddy is admitted, five minutes later – but I am now informed that the ambulance will continue to Bury St Edmunds, as per the original plan! I am not happy – and, furthermore, terrified that I would never see Teddy again.

The following day, late afternoon, I undergo an operation to remove a chip from the wing of my vertebrae – and am just returning from the operating theatre, and being wheeled into my hospital bedroom, when the telephone rings at the side of my bed.

"I know that you have just returned from your operation, but there are two visitors here, who are adamant that they must see you, very briefly. Would that be alright?" says a very polite hospital receptionist.

"That is fine with me, send them up." I reply.

Two minutes later, there is a knock on the door – and, to my utter amazement, in walks Teddy Lambton, with his wife Pauline. I am stunned, thinking it must be a ghost.

"Hello Gavin, Pauline and I just had to come ASAP – you saved my life, and I am so, so grateful," says Teddy, bending down and giving me an enormous man hug. And placing a magnum of vintage champagne on my bedside table.

It was indeed a miracle. By all accounts, Teddy had dismissed himself from Newmarket Hospital that morning – after being refused a Gin and Tonic at breakfast!

Against all the odds, Teddy made a fairly speedy recovery, and lived, thank goodness, for two more years.

They were born survivors in that era – and life was very much for living.

*

While we were at Shalfleet, I was fortunate and privileged to have the Saudi Arabian Ambassador to London, Mr A. S. Helaissi, as one of my leading owners. I trained some useful horses for him, amongst them Whistling Glory, Kings Equity and Corraggio – the last named pair, winners both on the flat and over hurdles. He loved his horses and made frequent visits to Newmarket to see them. Before his arrival, I was obliged to inform Newmarket Police Station, and let them know timings. The High Street was then closed to all traffic, on those occasions, to enable his motorcade to pass through, without stopping – a contingent of police outriders on motorcycles, lights flashing, in attendance, front and rear. Which always tickled me and excited the children, I might add.

Corraggio was a fast and smart two-year-old, who won his first race, before going to Kempton Park for his "Maiden At Closing".

Carrying a penalty for his initial success, but starting as red-hot favourite, nonetheless. He was ridden that day by Lester Piggott (LP) and drawn 19 of 19, on the far side of the straight five-furlong track, in those days, at this popular West London race course. Before racing, I had walked the five-furlong course, being concerned about Corraggio's poor draw – and spoken to jockeys who rode in previous races – and concluded that it would be best to come over to the nearside rail, with the other runners, despite the ground that might be lost, in the process. And made the point, very forcibly to LP, in the paddock, before the race, in front of Mr Helaissi. But, to my horror, as the stalls opened, LP went on his own up the far rails – and was beaten a head in a photo finish by a horse racing on the nearside, needless to say! My important owner was extremely angry, and so was I – and this incident caused a diplomatic furore, which did not enhance our owner–trainer relationship.

The trials and tribulations of raining racehorses.

Which reminds me of another story involving LP – but this time relating to another trainer; Ben Leigh, or to give him his proper title, the Honourable Benjamin Leigh, who had a small stable in Lambourn, and was one of Racing's many and much-loved characters.

Ben had booked LP, then many times Champion Jockey, and in constant demand from trainers throughout UK, France and Ireland, to ride a very useful two-year-old filly, again at Kempton Park, where she had the best form in the race and was greatly fancied. After leaving the paddock and passing the stands on the way to the five-furlong start, the filly jinks, drops her shoulder and deposits LP – before galloping off, now riderless, around the track, and being subsequently withdrawn by order of the Stewards.

After the race, the filly is being led back up the course by her lad past the stands – LP walking, carrying his saddle, to her nearside, accompanied by whistling, shouting and catcalls from the crowd. Ben, who is small in stature, but big on frank and forthright opinion, rushes down from the paddock to meet them – beside himself with anger and indignation to be steered specifically at LP.

"I just cannot believe it, Lester", he exclaims. "The girls in my yard ride this filly every morning – and you fell off her on the way to the start. You will never ever ride for me again".

As was his wont, LP took this rollocking in his stride, expressionless – replying, quick as a flash, in his customary tongue in cheek way, "Well, Ben, if that is the case, I will have to retire immediately."

Ben, who, in his youth, coxed a very successful Eton First Eight, somehow managed to ram the boat into the bank in a race at the International Rowing Regatta in Lucerne – but counted this as a mere triviality, when compared to his infamous contretemps with LP at Kempton Park!

*

I have been infatuated by Newmarket, ever since I first arrived there in 1966, and always will be – despite the fact that it is no longer the town it once was. It has its very own charm, allure and way of life, devoted to the horse – which distinguishes it from any other market town in the country. Steeped in Racing history, it is also Racing's "Headquarters", where the thoroughbred is still king.

Where else does traffic stop, without hesitation, for strings of horses, as they cross its myriad of little roads and streets, every morning – or can local townspeople walk their dogs after 1pm on the two thousand acres of manicured gallops and heathland, owned for two centuries by a caring Jockey Club. Other businesses have grown substantially, over the years, but the town is still dominated by the

Racing Industry, and the people closely involved with its day-to-day activities and organisation.

Bearing all this in mind, it was therefore a tragedy for the town of Newmarket, when the stable lads strike was initiated – in the spring of 1975. It should never have happened and did untold damage. Focused upon wages and hours and terms of employment, it should have been negotiated peacefully through the proper channels without resorting to strike action. It caused venomous and high profile confrontation between the Newmarket Trainers Federation and the Stable Lads Association, the flames of which were fuelled, ignited and fanned by the all-powerful Transport and General Workers Union (TGWU).

At Shalfleet, we were badly affected because of our shared access from the Bury Road with Highfield, given that Johnny Winter, poor man, was Chairman of the Newmarket Trainers Federation at the time. Only one of my staff of 21 went on strike – but almost all of Johnny's participated. Our respective young families and members of staff were terrified and intimidated by large numbers of pickets, who congregated at the top of our drive every morning – mostly big burly strikers, not even employed in the Racing Industry. It was almost impossible, and extremely dangerous, for our horses to exit Shalfleet, cross the Bury Road onto the Heath. Injuries to both horses and riders were frequent, and Oliver Sherwood, who was an Assistant at the time, broke his leg, when the horse he was riding reared over, having been scared by vociferous and unruly pickets.

The strike reached a crescendo at the Guineas Meeting in Newmarket, when strikers dug a ditch across the Rowley Mile Racecourse, and sat in line, defiantly, at the start, in their unsuccessful attempt to stop the 2000 Guineas from taking place.

Very fortunately, and thank goodness, the strike was resolved, and brought to a close before the start of Royal Ascot. But, by that stage, a great deal of damage had been done – and the close relationship between trainers and staff, which hitherto had always been so cordial was seriously tested and tainted.

*

The playing and watching of sport, featured prominently in my training career – especially when an afternoon of relaxation and distraction, away from the day job, was needed! Many were the happy days spent on a cricket pitch, the golf course, or out shooting (at which I did not excel!) – or lapping up the atmosphere and excitement at Lords or Twickenham. I was often roped in by my lads to make up numbers for the Shalfleet football team – or to represent the yard at darts in one of the many local pubs.

After racing on the July Course, one summer's evening, some of us young trainers, who had been amongst the winners that day, are celebrating at one end of the Members Bar. And somewhat surprised when endless bottles of wine keep appearing, paid for by a group of cheery Norfolk farmers, drinking copiously at the other end, having backed all of our horses, it transpired! As one does, we introduce ourselves, join up – and continue partying until thrown out of the bar by Racecourse management at 9pm! As we are having fun, Minty and I invite our new found friends, Tim Finch, David Mason and Colin Bothway, to call in at Shalfleet for another bottle of wine, and a light supper, on their way back up the Bury Road to Norfolk. The celebrations continue till past midnight – by which time, Tim, David and Colin have bought a two-year-old colt of mine, to be named Pistol Pukka – after an unexpected and alcoholic late night inspection.

In order to consecrate the deal, my new owners challenge us to a game of cricket – having heard that I had just started a Newmarket trainers team. Our first match was played near Newmarket against a team brought from Sussex by my father, and younger brothers

Giles and Grant. It is suggested, and agreed, that an evening match should be staged at Old Buckenham Stud, near Thetford, following afternoon racing at Yarmouth, on our way home.

It is a beautiful evening, and a very attractive ground – and my team are all in excellent form, having enjoyed a successful afternoon at Yarmouth – which has also benefited our Norfolk farmer friends, I might add. Prior to the match, Pimms is being poured for us, very liberally, by the pint, behind the Pavilion, from the biggest cask I have ever seen. But I just happen to notice that the opposition are drinking their Pimms from a different cask! On closer inspection and a brief sampling the penny drops. There is no alcohol in this one! But the fiver that I smuggle surreptitiously into the hand of the nice Stud groom, in charge of Pimms, does the trick – and the two large white rectangular cards, denoting the two teams, are swapped over!

The Norfolk Farmers win the toss and bat first, and make heavy weather of their task, not surprisingly – putting together a total which, to our minds, looks very gettable. The more so, given that most of our opposition are now very much the worse for wear, when it is their turn to field. Their bowling is innocuous – and Tim 'Noisy' Mason, their wicket keeper, passes out, in an alcoholic stupor, midover, and is abandoned, where he falls, on the flat of his back, by his teammates, prostrate and motionless, still padded and gloved – a striped cricket cap thrown over his face.

The result is a glorious victory for the Newmarket trainers – which heralded the beginning of a series of annual cricket matches between the two teams – and a lasting friendship between all its participants.

As for the bold Pistol Pukka   he was a very sound, amenable and lovable horse, but devoid of speed and ability, sadly. However, at the behest of his very sporting owners, he was obliged to run at every smart racecourse in the country, where he was always outclassed – Newmarket, York and Royal Ascot included. And there was always a huge party if he did not finish last!

Those were the days!

*

The stable lads strike provided a sad, torrid and very regrettable chapter in the history of Newmarket – but, beneath its exceedingly dark cloud there was a silver lining, from my perspective, which came from an unexpected source, and out of the blue.

When my horses and riders were being prevented from crossing the Bury Road from Shalfleet to the Heath, by striking and militant strikers, Bernard Van Cutsem, who trained next door to Shalfleet at Lord Derby's Stanley House Stables, very kindly suggested and gave permission for me to exercise my horses on Lord Derby's Private Ground – which formed part of this magnificent training establishment only two-thirds of a mile from the centre of town. It was a godsend and a lifeline to me, and I could not have been more grateful.

Not long after the end of the strike, Bernard Van Cutsem's health deteriorated very rapidly and he died in the December of that year, leaving the stables, which he had leased from Lord Derby, unoccupied.

One afternoon, I am walking my two dogs along the back drive at Stanley House, past the rear of the stables, without permission, as it happened – and very cheekily make a detour in order to have a brief and sneaky glimpse of the Main Yard, about which I had heard so much but never seen. Thinking that there would be nobody about, to my horror I am caught out red handed, on this occasion – by Lord Derby's land agent, whom I knew, and who, by chance, was surveying the property at the time. I apologise profusely – to be told by the Agent, very confidentially, that Stanley House Stables – but not Stanley House itself – is now on the market, that he could show me round, and that I should seriously consider a purchase.

On my return to Shalfleet, and having discussed this with Coral, we decide to make further investigation at once, despite being aware that the whole scenario was "pie in the sky", and way beyond us financially. On the basis that this information is not in the public domain – and would present the opportunity of a lifetime – I ring a trusted local estate agent, an expert valuer of racing properties in Newmarket, and beseech him to make a swift appraisal of the property that evening at dusk, under cover, and report back ASAP. He is overcome by the sheer magnificence of what he sees, and suggests that I should write to Lord Derby immediately requesting an asking price for sale. My letter is despatched first post next day – and I receive an answer from Lord Derby by return of post suggesting that I make him an offer. This I do – following a careful, detailed and strategic conversation with my now excited estate agent friend. A one line response from Lord Derby arriving the next morning. "It's yours. Good luck. Sincerely, Derby."

We were stunned – as was the town of Newmarket, and indeed the world of Racing, when the news hit the Press. It was beyond our wildest dreams, and beggared belief.

Against all the odds, we had acquired one of the finest and most historic training establishments in the country.

17.
The Move to Stanley House Stables and Fairway

To my mind, the best book ever published about the Racing and Breeding of the thoroughbred was "Men and Horses I Have Known" – written by the Honourable George Lambton, who was one of the finest trainers in the history of our great sport. A unique commentary, not only about the best horses of that era, but also the many celebrated individuals closely involved with the administration of the sport, most of whom were his personal friends.

He was based at Stanley House Stables for most of his training career, where he trained numerous Classic winners, amongst them Sansovino, Swynford, Colorado – and probably the most famous of all, Hyperion. A brilliant racehorse, and later a magnificent stallion. Hyperion, amongst other notable races, won the Derby very easily, and the Prince of Wales Stakes at Royal Ascot. And headed the list of winning sires in 1940, 1941, 1942, 1945, 1946 and 1954. Dying at the ripe old age of 30 in 1960.

As you might imagine, the thought of taking possession of these legendary stables at Stanley House was exciting beyond all belief. Built in the first decade of the 20th century, by the 17th Lord Derby, Stanley House Stables boasted 25 superb boxes in the Main Yard – forming three sides of a large and spectacular rectangle, with immaculate lawns in its midst, looking out over Stanley House itself, a magnificent and hugely impressive Victorian mansion only a stone's throw away. Behind the Main Yard, there were 20 more boxes, two paddocks, and a circular covered ride – and two hundred yards beyond, a Bottom Yard with 16 more boxes, adjacent to Stanley House Stud. In addition to this splendour, there was also a private five-furlong circular grass canter, with a sand track on its inside – situated, amazingly, between the stables and the Snailwell Road. The property, as a whole, comprises a staggering 25 acres, right in the middle of Newmarket.

Don't get me wrong – Shalfleet was a lovely little yard, and a very lucky one, for all its incumbents over the years, for which I will always have the greatest regard and affection, but Stanley House Stables were without doubt in another stratosphere. It was like comparing a 3-star to a 5-star hotel – or football clubs from Division Two to those in the Premier League. The ambience and scale of the property, and its outstanding facilities, were majestic in comparison and included three staff cottages, a hostel for staff (which we never had at Shalfleet), and Fairway House, a very attractive six-bedroomed house, fifty yards from the stables built specially for the trainer. A joy.

Needless to say, there was an enormous amount to do, before we could make the move – but, fortunately, everything went without a hitch. A sale of Shalfleet to Paul Kelleway was swiftly completed – and we made plans to have the horses, staff and the family safely in situ at Stanley House Stables before the start of the 1977 season. The equine relocation went very smoothly – three lots of ridden horses left their boxes at Shalfleet for a final time, to do their regular exercise on Newmarket Heath. And then returned, a little lost and bemused, to their new and palatial quarters at Stanley House Stables. It was an emotional but very exhilarating experience.

However, over the next few days, it was not all plain sailing, for horses or humans – and, as one might have expected, there was just the occasional blip.

On the top side of the Main Yard, there were eight large boxes, built specifically for big, well-grown colts, of three years and above. Between each of these boxes there was an interconnecting door, for humans only, supposedly – an old fashioned concept, and not seen in modern boxes today. I have a feeling that the intention was to make "toing and froing" easier for stable staff, at Morning and Evening Stables, and to keep the Trainer and Head Lad warm and dry when the horses were undergoing their evening inspection in inclement weather!

As Taffy was giving the horses their early morning feed, on the first morning, he was astonished to find two of our older colts in the same box – perfectly happy, and not having injured themselves, thankfully. One or other had obviously leant his backside on the "human" door, unintentionally – and made an unexpected transfer. A lesson learnt, early on, for everyone – to make sure that the bolts on the "human" doors were properly bolted at night times.

Later that first morning, as the first lot horses were collecting round the Main Yard, Caporello – a very handsome three-year-old colt, belonging to Dr Juan Hernandez, a charming man from Venezuela – whipped round, dislodged his rider, ploughed through the beech hedge, which separated the Main Yard and Stanley House, and galloped riderless at full throttle up the front drive. Taking a sharp right turn, at the top of the drive, down the horse walk, which borders one side of the Bury Road. Whether he was homesick or not, we will never know – but, as it happened, he continued his gallop past the entrance to Shalfleet, towards Newmarket High Street, four hundred yards away. By the grace of God, he screeched to a halt, by all accounts, at the roundabout, by the Clock Tower – where, by the greatest of good fortune, one of my lads, who was on a week's holiday, was on the zebra crossing on his way to breakfast at the cafe. He immediately recognised Caporello – and then proceeded to catch and ride him back to Stanley House Stables. None the worse and without a scratch amazingly!

There will be more about Caporello, anon.

*

Fairway was a lovely house and home with a large lawned area in front of it – and a good-sized kitchen garden behind. At the bottom of the kitchen garden was a sizeable belt of silver birch trees – which swayed precariously in the strong wind that blew for the first three nights we were in residence. Being a little scared of the dark, in a new environment – and having a vivid Irish imagination – Coral was convinced that there were people, with torches in the trees about to invade and burgle us. I tried to persuade her, to the contrary, but on the third night, as we were going to bed, she demanded that I should ring Newmarket Police Station. Officers came down our drive at the rate of knots ten minutes later, lights flashing, sirens blaring – a Sergeant with seven constables in two separate police vans.

It is akin to a whodunnit thriller on TV, as the eight policemen, having been apprised of the situation and divided into two groups of four, creep very stealthily around the exterior of the house and kitchen garden. Meeting, head on, ten minutes later round one corner of the rose garden, emitting howls of surprise, astonishment and fright.

"Mrs Pritchard-Gordon," explains the Sergeant, having pulled himself together, "We have had a thorough look around, and there is absolutely nothing to find or report. Just one question – do you realise that the new A14 Dual Carriageway has recently opened, and is only 200 yards away? It could just be the headlights of cars, shining through the wood that you have mistaken for torches.

"Oh, Jesus, Mary and Joseph," replies Coral, covered in confusion and embarrassment. "I am so sorry to have wasted your time. Please come into the house for a cup of coffee."

I quickly suggest that a large alcoholic drink might be more appropriate. And, having discarded their helmets by the back door, and been pronounced "Off Duty" by the Sergeant, the PCs tuck into beer, whisky and a large slice of currant cake.

*

Flying in little planes from Newmarket was, without doubt, the fastest and preferred means of transport, but there was always an element of danger, which tended to be exacerbated by poor weather and mechanical failure. I was party to a number of "hairy and scary" moments in the air – which, for some strange reason, neither frightened me at the time, nor left a lasting phobia of flying. Three particular flights come to mind – all of which could have had life-threatening implications.

Coming back from afternoon racing at Beverley in the late Seventies, we were subjected to the most terrifying electric storm. Ear-piercing thunder, sheet lightning and torrential rain – which soon prompted Ground Control to instruct our pilot to make an immediate and emergency landing in the environs of Doncaster. By chance, we identified a grass landing strip, just outside the town – the only problem being that it had been taken over by a large herd of Friesian cows, who were oblivious to our immediate arrival. We were dangerously close to six or seven unsuspecting milk-producing ladies – but landed safely, nonetheless!

My second flying horror story occurred when we were aboard a six seater from Cambridge to Dublin for the Goffs Sales. It was a lovely early September day, no wind, perfect flying conditions. For the first half hour of our journey, all was well – we chatted merrily, looking forward to a few fun days in Ireland. When, suddenly, the plane went into a violent nosedive, while still locked into cruise control mode. For what seemed like an age, the pilot fought with his instruments in a vain attempt to regain command of his plane

– but, to no avail. The ground came closer and closer – and, it was only hundreds of feet from crash landing that he was able to release the cruise control mechanism and avert certain disaster.

To make matters worse, I was in the co-pilot's seat that day, headphones clasped to my ears – so privy to the fraught conversation that our unfortunate pilot was having with Ground Control, somewhere in the vicinity of Bristol. The third of my near disasters was probably the most horrific – as the agony lasted for fifty terrifying minutes. I had been racing at Epsom, and, afterwards joined Julian Wilson and Willie Carson for a flight from nearby Redhill for evening racing at Haydock Park, between Liverpool and Manchester. Again it was a beautiful afternoon – Trillium had finished a gallant second in the big five-furlong sprint, Willie Carson had ridden a winner, and Julian Wilson was on his way, in his capacity as BBC TV Racing Correspondent, to present a live outside broadcast of the popular Nationwide programme from the racecourse. Flying conditions were perfect, we were in good time, and everything was going to plan until literally minutes from landing in the middle of the racecourse. As we circled round, prior to our final descent, our pilot became very anxious and apprehensive, very concerned that the undercarriage – the assembly of wheels, shock absorbers and struts beneath the plane – might not have locked into position for landing. We continued to circle the racecourse for another ten minutes, while the pilot consulted earnestly with Ground Control, before being told to divert to Ringway Airport, near Manchester.

By this stage, Julian Wilson, who was in the front seat with the pilot was in a state of flux and consternation – distraught that he was going to be late for his Nationwide presentation. Willie Carson, who was in the second row of the plane, was equally agitated, as he thought that he was riding "a certainty" in the first race. For my part, perched comfortably in the back of the plane, time was not critical – I was just concerned about our present and ultimate safety.

The pilot's instructions were to fly as close to the Central Tower as possible so that the Chief Controller could establish whether or not the undercarriage of the plane was down. Three times we passed over the tower – but still the Chief Controller could not be sure, despite his high-powered binoculars. Soon concluding that we would have to fly around the airport for half an hour, while foam was poured on the arrivals runway, and the airport was put on emergency status prior to our landing.

It was a very, very frightening experience for Julian, Willie and me – and our pilot, who was now sweating profusely and in a state of nervous shock, as well! He talked, at length, about the landing process on foam, and the taking of "brace" positions – and we made a couple of dummy runs, before our final and crucial attempt. If the undercarriage locked into the correct position, we would be saved – but, if it did not, landing on the belly of the plane could have been disastrous. The likelihood was that the plane would burst into flames immediately.

Those last moments, before touchdown, seemed like hours – heads bowed, not a word was spoken, we just "braced", hoped and prayed.

By the grace of God, our supplications were answered, and all was well. Willie missed his winning ride; Julian had to leave the Nationwide programme to his understudy; and I was mightily pleased to make the Ringway terminal, unscathed. And to return to Newmarket, by car!

*

Driving by car to race meetings from Newmarket in the late Seventies was a nightmare, particularly on a Saturday. The more so, given that the nearest Flat racecourse to Newmarket (apart from the Rowley Mile and July Course) was Yarmouth, 65 miles away, believe it or believe it not. Very little of the A1 had been dualled, the

A14 had not even been dreamt about, and ring roads around large towns were still a rarity.

To drive from Newmarket to Wolverhampton, for instance, was a veritable "carathon"! Negotiating the High Street in Newmarket, on Market Day (before the A14) took ten minutes, for a start, and one then had to drive through the centres of Cambridge, Huntingdon, Kettering, Market Harborough and Lutterworth, before hitting the A5, which eventually took you to Wolverhampton, via Hinckley, Tamworth and Brownhills! It was, therefore, a great deal easier to fly in a little six-seater plane, which was not that expensive in those days – taking off very conveniently on the July Course in Newmarket, and landing, in most cases, in the centre of the racecourse in question.

I had horses running one Saturday at Redcar, by the sea, not far from Middlesbrough and travelled by small plane, which took just over an hour, landing on the course. That was three hours less than the car and not as stressful! The big race of the day, the Zetland Gold Cup, was won by a horse called Pee Mai, trained by a lovely little Yorkshireman called Arthur Goodwill. He was nicknamed "Fiddler" as, when he first arrived as a young lad in Newmarket to start his apprenticeship with Harvey Leader, he brought with him his faithful fiddle on which he played a mean tune. He only used to have a handful of horses – but was a very canny and knowledgeable trainer, and a wonderful character, brimming with wit and charm, and extremely popular. And a dab hand at training greyhounds as well. After the race, Fiddler's fellow Newmarket trainers, delighted that he had won such a valuable and prestigious prize, took him to the bar for a bottle or two of champagne to celebrate. Fiddler, who always drove his horses to the races in his own horsebox, was quickly into top form, enjoying the party – and it soon became clear that he should not be driving Pee Mai back to Newmarket.

A volunteer replacement driver was found – and, as there was one spare seat on the plane, Fiddler was eventually persuaded to come with us.

He had never been in a little plane before, so this was to be a new experience, which had its problems in this case. Half an hour after take off, there was a pained request from the back of the plane "Is there toilet on plane. Must have pee!" exclaims Fiddler.

"No," we all reply in unison. "There is not. You will have to wait till we land in Newmarket."

Twenty minutes later, Fiddler repeats his impassioned plea, now in dire straits – adding the word "desperate". But to no avail. Five minutes from landing on the July Course, Fiddler can be denied no longer. Thankfully, thinking very quickly, one of our fellow passengers has a brainwave. "You will have to pee into the plastic champagne cups, which are behind your seat, Fiddler. Hand them to us, one by one, when you have filled them – and we will have to hope that the pilot makes a perfect landing!"

All was well. Looking back in racing's history, Pee Mai was very well named. The owner must have had a premonition.

A day that I will never forget.

18.
Happy Humans Make Happy Horses

As a trainer, Harvey Leader was a great believer in "stable spirit" at Shalfleet – on the basis that, "Happy humans make happy horses". And he was absolutely right. When the mantle of Elijah passed to Elisha, I did my best to conserve and continue that mantra.

There was no staff accommodation at Shalfleet, but this all changed, when we moved to Stanley House Stables. Head Lad, Taffy Williams lived in a house on the yard – and his number two, David (Ginger) Tyers, was based next door.

At Shalfleet, my apprentices used to live in digs in the town, and were looked after by landladies, all hand chosen, but now there was a hostel where they could all be together on the spot. To be honest, it was a little antiquated and spartan – George Formby was an apprentice at Stanley House Stables in his youth – but we made sure that they were warm, comfortable and well fed.

Yvonne Conway, married to one of my senior lads, Chris, did all the cooking – and Coral made twice weekly visits to the Cash and Carry to buy their food and provisions.

In those days, there was a binding written agreement between trainers and their apprentices, usually for a period of three years. The trainers were obliged to pay their keep and lodgings, and all working clothes, like jodhpurs, riding jackets and jodhpur boots, related to their apprentice status. In return, the trainer was entitled to a percentage of their riding fees, and winnings, when they rode in races – that was the incentive. The system worked well, friendships were made, camaraderie developed – and there was a great deal of friendly rivalry between our apprentices. Football, darts and boxing were their preferred sports, and we produced several champions at the annual Stable Lads Boxing Championships at the Hilton Hotel in London's Park Lane, organised very professionally by the Stable Lads Welfare Trust. Henry Cooper was a regular and always maintained that it was his favourite night out of the year.

In many ways, racing stables were run by the trainer very much on military lines. Leadership, respect, discipline and morale were all paramount, and part and parcel of the ethos and organisation of the stable on a daily basis. The trainer played the part of the Platoon Commander; the Head Lads were the Sergeant Majors; the "squaddies" were the lads and lasses; and young apprentice jockeys, the new recruits. Everything was done to time – first, second and third lots in the morning and later at Evening Stables.

One of the highlights of the year was the Staff Christmas Party – which took place in the cellar function room of the Coronation Hotel, opposite Newmarket station. Attendance was deemed by my staff to be obligatory, in deference to the Guv'nor. Beer and wine flowed, noise levels were seismic – and being on time for first lot the next morning was considered to be an absolute must. Only once did someone fail to turn up – and the rollocking he received from the other lads was much more potent than mine!

One of my best lads, known to us all as "Manch" was a party animal, with a wonderful Mancunian sense of humour. As he was leaving the party, on that particular night, he bet me a fiver – a lot of money to him in those days – that he would ride out stark naked first lot the next morning. We shook on the bet and sure enough, he did! I lost my wager but still had the last laugh. Being late December, very cold and frosty, Manch persuaded himself that we would be confined to trotting round the Indoor Ride, for the duration.

He was mistaken! I thought it would be much more entertaining if my string of horses and riders filed down the Bury Road, across the

Severals, and Fordham Road, through the town to the Racecourse Side on the horse track.

Early morning shoppers in St. Mary's Square were aghast and agog – the male version of Lady Godiva had come to town!

19.
Noalcoholic

It was a joy and a privilege to train horses at Stanley House Stables – and I sometimes had to pinch myself to be sure that it was really happening. Our horses were housed in magnificent and palatial stables, steeped in history – and the facilities were second to none.

But I had the feeling from time to time that I was housing Marks & Spencer products in the hallowed confines of Harrods or Fortnum's. Over the years, before our arrival, every horse that went into training at Stanley House Stables, was bred in the purple and had the potential on paper to be a Group/Classic winner. Whereas, the majority of my horses were mostly middle of the road performers, with less distinguished pedigrees, more suited to Handicaps and Listed races.

However, there were some notable exceptions to this rule, in fairness. All Systems Go won two Group races as a two-year-old. The Lanson Champagne Stakes at Goodwood, and the Seaton Delaval stakes at Newcastle – and Caporello triumphed in the Lingfield Derby Trial and Goodwood Stakes. While Buffavento, and Baz Bombati were both Group winners. But the best of them all came to me by chance, and out of the blue, in the late spring of 1982.

Noalcoholic, by Nonoalco out of Alea, began his racing career in France, proving himself to be a useful Listed race contender, before his owner, Bill du Pont III, who owned Pillar Stud in Kentucky, decided that he should be sent to Australia to stand at stud. As a result of a meeting with Tim Preston of the Curragh Bloodstock Agency and John Sparkman, Stud Manager at Pillar Stud, it was agreed he would spend his quarantine in England, prior to his Southern Hemisphere departure – and arrived at Stanley House Stables, to be kept active and on the move, before shipment. It soon became apparent to me and my very experienced work riders that Noalcoholic, now five years old, was better than Listed Class, and most definitely Group race material. I consulted Bill du Pont, and, as there were no other suitable alternatives at the time, suggested that he might take his chance in the Queen Anne Stakes at Royal Ascot. He finished a gallant second to Mr Fluorocarbon, and it was then agreed that he should spend the rest of the season with me in Newmarket. He went on to win the Prix Messidor at Maisons-Laffitte, and the Bisquit Cognac Challenge Stakes at Newmarket, thereby earning himself a reprieve, and the right to remain in training at Stanley House Stables the following season.

The following year of 1983 proved to be a vintage year for Noalcoholic, now six years of age. He won the Lockinge Stakes at Newbury – before triumphing in the Sussex Stakes at Goodwood, winning by a clear margin and lowering the track record, which had stood for 12 years. He was also recognised as the Champion Miler in Europe. On that glorious day at Goodwood, I flew in a small plane from Newmarket to Goodwood and was back home again by 6:15pm. Coral and I were inundated with messages of congratulations – but one in particular will always stand out. As I set foot on the front door step at Fairway, I am surprised to find an envelope – and immediately recognised the handwriting on its front. Mark Prescott had penned two sides of writing paper, stating that Noalcoholic's Sussex Stakes victory was a triumph for the trainer, for George Duffield the jockey, and for Newmarket – and delivered it in person to Fairway. What a kind and very thoughtful gesture, which says a lot for the man.

Noalcoholic was a revelation and gave me, and everyone at Stanley House Stables, an enormous sense of pleasure. He was ridden in all his races by George Duffield, who found the key to Noalcoholic's remarkable improvement. In France he was ridden for speed at the end of his races – whereas George always allowed him to lead, making full use of his blistering pace and stamina.

20.
Wis

In hindsight, it was a blessing that I did not land the job with the BBC, as Television Racing Correspondent. I was far too young and inexperienced at the time – and would have floundered and been out of my depth from the outset. Julian Wilson was by far the best qualified and most knowledgeable candidate – and proved to be a consummate professional in his role, respected by everyone in Racing.

The bonus for me was that I then became a close friend of Julian (known to us as Wis), and he was very supportive of my training career. He introduced me to several new owners, for whom he acted as Racing Manager. He was an avid follower of form and helped me enormously with the placing of horses, with which he was associated. By and large, betting on horses is a mug's game to my mind – but, in Wis's case it was not. He landed some sizeable gambles, all of which had been meticulously researched and planned.

Wis introduced me to a lovely man named Walter Mariti, who owned Pontevecchios, a smart and very popular restaurant in Knightsbridge. His best horse was Pontevecchio Notte, who was a top-class handicapper. Walter was very warm-hearted and generous, and gave me free rein to dine at his restaurant whenever I was in London. Which in fairness was not very often! One evening, I did partake of his hospitality with a couple of friends after a rare night out at the theatre. In the bar, before dinner, I spy Wis in the dining room, a deux, with a particularly glamorous young lady. Seizing my opportunity, I ask the barman for a pencil and paper, on which I write, "Swindon Town 0 – Brighton and Hove Albion 5". I ask the barman to takes it to Wis's table in the knowledge that he would immediately sense danger, given that he was passionate about Swindon, and I was a long-standing Brighton fan. But, as always, he has the last laugh. Without raising his head, writing his reply very swiftly, and handing it back to the barman. "Thank you for that, Gavin – I'm actually having a lovely dinner with my god-daughter. Now piss off!"

Sir Clement Freud also became an owner of mine, courtesy of his friendship with Wis. At the time he was looking for a horse that he could name "Weareagrandmother", subsequent to Mrs Thatcher's much-quoted remark. It just happened that I had a two-year-old filly for sale.

Sir Clement loved his racing, and became a proficient amateur rider, participating in a number of sponsored match races, but he was not the most straightforward of owners and took pleasure from keeping his trainers on their toes. Only two days after buying Weareagrandmother, my telephone rings at 5:30am. It is Sir Clement. "How is my filly Gavin – and is this a convenient time to call you?" he asks in his dry and sardonic way. "Good morning, Sir Clement," I reply, a little drowsily and somewhat surprised. "I normally get up at 6am – so it might be more beneficial for the two of us, if we chat about the filly at 5:30pm in future!" I am delighted to report that Weareagrandmother went on to win a nursery handicap at York – pleasing Sir Clement immensely and earning copious coverage in the newspapers, the next day.

I spent several hilarious holidays with Wis, mostly in Barbados in winter and thrived on his company. He tended to take himself a little seriously, and considered himself to be a ladies' man, but that was part of his charm. He became an easy and obvious target for playful pranks from his friends – but always saw the funny side afterwards.

Wis was passionate about racing, football and cricket – and was the slowest and most infuriating left-arm spin bowler I have ever seen or faced. But his abiding love was Harrow School. At his funeral at St Mary's Church in Newmarket, William Haggas, appropriately an Old Harrovian, gave a touching and memorable tribute to Wis – and the last hymn on the Order of Service was entitled "Harrow Songs". Very few of us in the church knew the words, but the mayhem and chaos caused would have made Wis exceedingly happy!

21.
Spanker

My younger brother Giles loved his school days at Radley College – despite a loathing for everything to do with authority, discipline and school rules. He excelled at sport, in particular cricket, rugby and boxing – and spent the rest of his time, whenever possible, frequenting pubs and betting shops in Oxford and Abingdon.

He was the unofficial leader of a gang of rascally reprobates in C Social (house) which also included Philip Beck, Quentin Wallace, Chris Thin and John Garnsey. And they were the bane of my life, when I was appointed Head of Social. One Saturday evening, Giles and "Garnsey" were absent from Evensong in Chapel without permission, thereby flouting school rules for the umpteenth time, which constituted a beating from our Social Tutor, James "Tonk" Thompson. Tonk, as it happened, had planned to be away from College for the rest of that weekend, so instructed me to beat "Garnsey", and the Second Head of Social to cane Giles in his absence.

Garnsey was a bespectacled, studious and scruffy youth, at first sight. But intelligent, artful and scheming, with a wicked sense of humour, beneath the surface. And always at the epicentre of any mischief or skulduggery. I had never beaten anyone before and was in a state of confusion and dread when Garnsey entered Social Hall. I tell him to bend over the table to receive six strokes of the cane. Now shaking with fright, my first lash hardly touches Garnsey – who proceeds to jump up, run round and round the table, shouting obscenities at his tormented assailant. It takes me ten minutes to complete my task and I am horrified and shaken to the core.

Three weeks later, Philip Beck, Quentin Wallace and Garnsey come to stay with my parents in Turners Hill. And as I shuffle down the stairs for breakfast, I hear guffaws of laughter emanating from Giles's bedroom. The drawled monotone from Garnsey is unmistakable, and I stop to listen, "Giles, do you remember that evening your stupid brother gave me that beating in Social Hall? He hardly touched me," booms Garnsey. I burst into the room, fuming and defiant – but soon realising that I am on a loser. Garnsey had triumphed – game, set and match.

About 15 years later, Charles Benson then "The Scout" tipster and Racing Correspondent on the *Daily Express*, retired to be replaced by a budding young journalist called John Garnsey. As he was not known to readers of the *Daily Express* racing page, the Editor wisely publishes a photograph of Garnsey, appended to a Question and Answer tabulation, to introduce him on his first day in his office. The Editor's first question to Garnsey is "What was your first introduction to the world of racing?" Garnsey's answer: "When I was beaten very hard by "Spanker" Pritchard-Gordon at school."

At the time, my training career is in the ascendancy, my name is getting known, and I am not best pleased with his uncalled-for outburst and the adverse publicity. But I'm nonetheless amused by Garnsey's audacity, cussedness and ready wit!

We have remained firm friends ever since – and, to this day, whenever he sees me chatting to a group of people on the racecourse, he chooses his moment to greet me with a loud rendition of "Hello Spanker", which never ceases to make people laugh!

22.
A Far-Eastern Odyssey

When Ryan Jarvis retired as a trainer in Newmarket, Mr S. Liem, a wealthy and influential businessman based in Singapore, sent me some of his horses to train. They were to be ridden in their races by Eric Eldin, who had been stable jockey to Ryan Jarvis.

We had some luck on the racecourse for Mr Liem, and as a token of his thanks, he very generously invited Coral, Eric and me to be his guest for a week – staying at luxury hotels in Singapore and Bali. Singapore is a vibrant and beautiful city, and we were in awe of its infrastructure, cleanliness and sights, and were very well fed and entertained for the first three days of our trip. We saw very little of Mr Liem in that duration, as he was permanently preoccupied with his business commitments. But on the rare occasions that we did meet, he was always at pains to stress that we should be very punctual for our flight from Singapore to Bali, which puzzled us.

As bidden, and on arrival at the tiny little airport in Bali – not much more than a large wooden hut with a straw roof in those days – we are fascinated to see two white stretch limousines parked outside the arrivals hall. Assuming that unbeknown to us there must have been some VIPs on our flight, we were taken totally by surprise when two smart liveried chauffeurs approach us, enquiring whether we are guests of Mr Liem. Eric, Coral and I are ushered into the first of these white limousines, and our luggage is stowed in the second. We drive for about five miles past rice fields on a deserted local track until we come to a little Balinese village, where the locals are all lining the route, waving their flags and chanting their welcome. We then turn right in the centre of the village through the two large iron gates of a vast cigarette factory – which it transpired belonged to Mr Liem!

All the factory workers are gathered to greet us, more flags raised and a band plays as we are escorted to our seats on a flower-strewn raised dais, reserved only for visiting dignitaries. Garlands are placed round our heads, and we are honoured with a traditional Balinese play, music and dancing known as a Legong, characterised by intricate finger movements, complicated footwork, and expansive gestures. Men are wearing Udeng head coverings, collared jackets, Kamen and Saput. Women are in Bun, Kebaya, Kamen and Shawl.

It is a mind-boggling experience, and totally unexpected. The highlight of our wonderful Far-Eastern Odyssey.

No wonder that Mr Liem insisted that we were on time for our flight from Singapore to Bali.

23.
The Derby Dinner

When Coral and I moved to Stanley House Stables and Fairway, Lord Derby retained Stanley House, the large and impressive mansion, with an extensive garden, that adjoined them. Lord Derby's main residence was at Knowsley, on the outskirts of Liverpool – but Lady Derby liked to spend quite a lot of her time in Newmarket, where she had many friends and enjoyed the local gossip. Quite understandably, whenever we met, Lady Derby was not overly friendly – given that she did not know us, and that Stanley House Stables were very close to her heart. However, everything changed one evening when I bumped into Lady Derby and Colonel Dick Warden, who was staying with her at Stanley House, as I was returning from the Bottom Yard. Noting her frostiness, Dick tactfully suggested that she should invite me for a drink at Stanley House, after Evening Stables. Under duress, and after some persuasion, she agreed – and, from then on, we never looked back and became firm friends.

On the rare occasions that he was in Newmarket, Lord Derby would sometimes ask Coral and me to dinner at Stanley House – and, not long afterwards, sent me some of his horses to train. We developed a very cordial owner–trainer relationship, enjoyed a number of winners, and had some fun times together, despite the large difference in our ages. Wiveton, High Tension and Asia Minor were not superstars, but decent Handicappers, nonetheless.

One early June evening, Lord and Lady Derby, Coral and I were having dinner in the dining room at Stanley House, just the four of us, the butler in attendance as always. The wine flows and we are in full swing – but it soon becomes apparent that the butler wants to tell me something, confidentially. He fills up my glass and whispers in my ear that Lord Derby has to ring Ronnie Corbett. Plucking up courage, and choosing my moment carefully, I relay this message to his Lordship, who is, to say the least, most displeased. Given that it is now 11pm, and he is much enjoying himself, he gets up grudgingly, leaves the dining room and goes to the telephone in the hallway – returning to the dining room, three minutes later, in a fearful rage. Announcing, with disgust, "that F……G shit Ronnie Corbett is an absolute disgrace. He agreed to be the speaker at my Derby Dinner in two days' time, and has let me down, at the last moment. What can I possibly do to find a replacement, at such short notice?" He hurtles round and round the table, raging bulls coming to mind, stopping periodically behind my chair and booming "Do you know anyone who is funny, Gavin?" Recognising the urgency of the matter, and that I am going to have to say something, I stutter "Mark Prescott is an excellent speaker and very amusing."

"Who is Mark Prescott?" replies Lord Derby impatiently. "Sir Mark Prescott, who trains here in Newmarket," I explain. "I don't care whether he is Sir Mark Prescott, Lord Prescott or Jesus Christ – ring him immediately and ask him whether he can speak at my dinner," is his answer. "That might be difficult, Lord Derby – he goes to bed at 9:30pm every night and gets up at 4am," I reply, now at the end of my tether. "I insist – go to the hallway at once and ring Prescott," demands Lord Derby.

I stumble to the telephone in a darkened hall, Lord Derby now standing almost over me, ring Mark's number (which I know fortunately as we both have riding retainers on George Duffield) and await the tirade that I will be receiving. "Who the hell is that, ringing me at this time of night?" shouts Mark. "It's Gavin, Mark, really sorry. A request from Lord Derby – can you speak at the Derby Dinner in two days' time?" I reply. "Of course I can, no problem. But please do not ring me in the middle of the night ever again," bawls Mark as he slams down the receiver. Lord Derby is initially ecstatic, the best port is brought up from the cellar, and peace returns to the party. But, before long, his delight turns to remorse, the tables are turned, and recrimination rears its ugly head. "Are you quite sure that Prescott is amusing and will entertain my distinguished guests, Gavin?" he fires at me again and again. Proclaiming, as Coral and I leave, in the early hours of the morning to walk back to Fairway, "Be it on your head, Gavin, it will all be your fault if he is not."

As a long-time Member of the Derby Club, I look forward avidly to the Derby Dinner every year, which precedes the Epsom Derby two days later. But this year I am in dread. After dinner, Lord Derby steps up to the microphone and announces to his guests, "Ronnie Corbett agreed to be the speaker this evening but the little sod has let me down at the last minute. However, one of my trainers, Pritchard-Gordon, assures me that Sir Mark Prescott, his replacement, is very amusing. Over to you, Prescott."

Mark rises to his feet, with confidence, tells three hilarious stories, against himself, without a note and receives a five-minute standing ovation. He is brilliant, as he always is. Later in the evening, Lord Derby crosses to my table, imparts his thanks, and informs me that he has invited Mark as his guest to Epsom on Derby Day.

I can't wait to ring Mark on his return from Epsom, and ask him how his day went. "I really enjoyed myself, Gavin, thank you. It was a pleasant change from Catterick."

"And who did you sit next to at lunch," I enquire "Lord Derby, of course, Gavin," he answers quickly. "And who was sitting on your other side?" I add. "Her Majesty, The Queen, if you really want to know," which ends our conversation.

As a footnote, three months later, Lord Derby sends three yearlings into training with Mark and with justification. Very much deserved – and justice was done.

24.
Ladbrokes Lunch

Bookmakers rely on the Racing and Breeding Industry for their product – and the sport of Racing derives a sizeable annual income from Bookmakers' turnover, so the two entities are inextricably linked, in effect. In order to promote their businesses, bookmakers used to host lunches and dinners at upmarket London venues, to which a cross section of Racing's participants were invited. I made the cut sometimes – one such lunch was at the Hilton Hotel in Park Lane, sponsored by Ladbrokes.

It was a jolly and genial affair, and an opportunity for a young Newmarket trainer to do some networking, to find some new potential owners. Having thanked my kind host and said my goodbyes, I leave at 3:30pm, as I have a fancied runner in the 3:45pm race at Carlisle, and walk swiftly to the Ladbrokes betting shop, only 100 yards away.

I enter the premises, as the runners and riders are cantering to the start – and am intrigued by the conversation of two rough-looking Cockney characters, standing beside me. They are both dressed in scruffy shorts and t-shirts, and have no doubt been downing several pints of beer in the pub beforehand. The older one is a very large man, with a pudgy face and a bulging tummy, who thinks he knows everything about racing and makes up what he does not. His younger and much smaller mate is a novice to racing by all accounts and is listening intently to the expert.

Now in full swing, the larger man continues his spiel, and I am spellbound and agog. "I was talking to my close friend Gavin Pritchard-Gordon in Newmarket, the other day," he says "And he tells me that this horse at Carlisle has been laid out for the race, and is a f…g certainty." They both take wads of dirty notes from their pockets and have their wagers.

My horse wins and their wild celebrations begin. I am thrilled too but lost for words. Eventually being brave enough to tap the larger man on the shoulder and congratulate him on his success. He turns round abruptly, looks down on me with disdain and says "Yes, I did have a good few quid on the nose, but it is none of your f…g business. And, what is more, who the f…g hell are you – we have never met, I don't think." Very quietly and politely, I introduce myself – and he looks me up and down, dumbstruck, before rushing for the door of the betting shop, never to be seen again. His poor little pal, who is mightily perplexed, apologises on his behalf.

Memories of that day in the London betting shop are still very vivid and never cease to make me giggle. Betting shops attract all sorts – that is for sure!

25.

Princess Genista

Ian and Jane Stewart-Brown were long-standing owners of mine, passionate about their horses, and huge supporters of my stable. Ian was a very popular stockjobber in the City, and, when he was not at his desk, enjoyed a lively party. He had a wry and unusual sense of humour and we gelled well together.

Ian and Jane were very lucky owners and thrived on the social side of racing as well. One of their best horses was Princess Genista, a top-class filly, picked out and bought for them by Jane's father, John Fenwick, who had a small stud farm in Kennett just outside Newmarket. Princess Genista won four races and ran creditably in the Oaks at Epsom.

One Sunday morning, I had a telephone call from Ian, informing me that he had found me a new owner, who wanted to buy a half share in Princess Genista. A wealthy and distinguished Arab by all accounts. I was over the moon with excitement, as no Arab owners had patronised my stables thus far. He asked me whether he could bring the Sheikh to Newmarket to see Princess Genista the following Sunday – emphasising the importance of the visit.

Stanley House Stables looked at their very best as a long wheelbase Mercedes came down the drive and parked by my office. Princess Genista was looking immaculate, as were my staff, and the scene was set. On entering her box, Ian then gave a brief resume of the filly's form and pedigree – and the Sheikh stood in admiration, nodding his approval when asked to confirm that he would take a half share in the filly.

As we returned from the stables to the white Mercedes, Ian asks whether we could have a quick glass of champagne to celebrate the forming of this new partnership. This surprises me somewhat, as I was under the impression that this was not Arab custom. As we walk back to Fairway, I look across to the Sheikh, who grins, albeit briefly, before regaining his composure. Rudely, in retrospect, I fix my gaze, and the Sheikh begins to smile visibly and then laugh out loud. It is in fact my first cousin Michael Meacock (always pronounced Mee-ko), now the longest serving underwriting Member of Lloyds, dressed head to toe in flowing light-brown Arab regalia. I had been conclusively hoodwinked, and Ian and Michael, who had become firm friends, are greatly amused. Ian remarking – "Gavin, old boy – I didn't think that you knew "Sheikh MeCock"!

Michael went on to take a half share in the filly – his first venture into racing – and this was the start of a very happy and rewarding partnership in horses. Princess Genista continued to excel – and later became a prolific broodmare, going on to produce 14 foals, 13 of which won races. For me initially and then with John and Ed Dunlop when I retired from training.

Very sadly, Michael died in 2023.

26.
Ayr Races

When asked what was my favourite racecourse in the British Isles, people were very surprised to hear that it was, most definitely, Ayr. One of the most distant in mileage from Newmarket!

There were three good reasons, in fairness. First, I fell in love with the town, the racecourse, and its ambience – where the people associated with it, from Stewards to gatemen, were so warm and friendly. Secondly, I had a lot of winners there – recording my biggest percentage of winners to runners on a course to course basis. And, thirdly, because I met a load of new friends who were very kind and hospitable to me when I was racing at Ayr. Two in particular stand out – Tony Collins and Nigel Angus, both of whom I stayed with on many an occasion.

Tony was a loveable rogue, who enjoyed himself and the company of others. A stockbroker by trade, he loved his golf, trained a handful of jumpers, and was closely embroiled in the infamous Gay Future betting scandal at Cartmel. He was a very generous host – and, if he liked you, a very loyal friend. The life and soul of any party, who became a close confidant of, and court jester, to Robert Sangster. He had a number of horses in training with me – the best of which was Easy Prep, who landed a massive gamble for Tony at York's Spring Meeting.

Nigel Angus was a fellow trainer, whose stables were right beside the racecourse at Ayr. He trained plenty of winners, the best of which was probably Roman Warrior, who won the Ayr Gold Cup, and was a top-class sprinter. He was also an exceptional golfer – and one time Amateur Champion of Scotland.

Nigel lived a few miles from Ayr, with his mother Lady More, in the lap of luxury – and it was a joy to stay with them. Lady More did absolutely everything for Nigel, as if he was still a teenager – and when I was there, I was treated likewise. Breakfast, for starters, was a veritable feast – and the porridge was to die for.

One evening, as Nigel and I were about to depart for dinner in Ayr, I impress upon and plead with Lady More, very painstakingly, to wake me by 9am the following morning. On the basis that, "I hated to disturb you when you were sleeping so soundly", it was 11:15am when Lady More actually knocked on and opened my bedroom door! In those days, being a very long journey, our stable runners from Newmarket were transported by box to Ayr two days before races. So, on this occasion, I had three horses, destined to run the next day, safely ensconced in the Racecourse stables but now unable to run, as I had failed to ring Weatherbys by the 9:30am 24-hour declaration stage. Disaster – an unmitigated disaster – and so, so embarrassing. With no further recourse, I contact my owners, apologise profusely, admit that it is totally my error, and assure them that the trainer will be standing all the transport charges. Owners would not be so tolerant in today's world!

A very expensive exercise, the memory of which still haunts me. I don't think that Lady More ever found out – and because my digs were so comfortable, I was never going to tell her!

27.
Doncaster Bloodstock Sales

Now known as Goffs UK, the Doncaster Bloodstock Sales (DBS) September Yearling Sales week was always one of the highlights of my racing year. I bought some useful horses there over the years, for very reasonable money – and had loads of fun besides. Harry Beeby, Ken Oliver, Michael White, Michael Dale, Henry Beeby and their fellow directors were very professional in their compilations of the catalogue and their presentation of the sales – and made vendors and buyers very welcome. Trade was always buoyant through the various sessions – and it was then time to party at hotels and restaurants in and around Doncaster, afterwards.

My Doncaster quarters, for many years, were at The Crown Hotel in Bawtry, which attracted a regular clientele of like-minded souls, for the sales and St. Leger week racing. Partying after the sales was almost mandatory, and sleep at a premium.

One night we had a particularly late session, well into the early hours of the following morning, after dinner with Hamish Alexander, Willie Macauley, Minty, Geoff and Noelene Lewis, and other reprobates. Geoff was due to ride the favourite, Attica Meli, for Sir Noel Murless, in the Park Hill Stakes the following day – but it did not stop him enjoying himself hugely. Four times he was taken to bed by Noelene – only to reappear 15 minutes later, stuttering profusely, very adversarial as always, and intent on yet more to drink. The fifth time, Noelene locked the bedroom door, hid the key, and went to sleep. But our hero was not to be denied, too sharp by half – escaping through the bedroom window, and returning to the bar once more. Noelene was peacefully oblivious to what had happened.

At 5:45am, there was a loud knock on the door to the street. Standing there, looking immaculate, was a very polite man in chauffeurs uniform, who announced that he had been instructed to pick up one Mr Geoffrey Lewis and take him to the racecourse to ride Attica Meli a blowing canter, in readiness for the Park Hill Stakes later in the day. Sensing danger, and ultimate calamity, we grab Geoff, take him back to his bedroom, throw him into a cold shower, pile him into his jodhpurs, and launch him into the car. He is returned to the hotel by the chauffeur at 9am – now a little more compos mentis but suffering from a ferocious hangover.

That afternoon, Attica Meli and Geoff combine to win the Park Hill Stakes very decisively. As a footnote, the next day's paper had a photograph of Geoff, passing the post, left hand on the reins, standing bolt upright in his stirrups, turning his whole body to the crowds and giving them a flamboyant victory salute. However, on closer inspection, it is actually a two-fingered V-sign – intended no doubt for his fellow revellers in The Crown Hotel.

God bless Geoff – he was a superb jockey with an incredible constitution. And God bless Noelene, too – she possessed the patience of Job and was equally long suffering!

*

In their mind's eye, I suspect that most people have a phobia, or a nightmare scenario, which they dread. Be it spiders, rats, crocodiles or the unexpected arrival of the bailiff or taxman. Mine played out, for real, one night in The Hilton Hotel in Doncaster.

After dinner, and a few digestifs, I returned to my bedroom, which I had already discovered was very small and cramped, containing more doors per square foot than most others that I had frequented. At about 4:15am, I wake up, desperate for a pee. Stumbling in the dark into what I thought was the bathroom. How wrong I was – on opening the door, which shuts automatically behind me, and very swiftly, I find myself in the ground floor corridor of the hotel, stark naked. Thank God, the corridor is dimly lit and there is no one about – although I could still hear voices and laughter from the bar. I conclude very quickly that there is only one course of action. I must hasten to the swimming pool area, 35 yards away, and take a towel from the pile outside. Arriving there, hands now clasped to my private parts – but, alas, no bloody towels!

In panic and desperation, knowing that I had to confront the Night Porter, at his desk, and request a spare bedroom key – I spy some cheap curtains, on flimsy curtain rails down the swimming pool passage, rip them down, and wrap them round my torso.

The Night Porter surveys me with surprise and suspicion and hands over the spare bedroom key – and I promise to reward him later with a crisp £5 note as long as he promises to keep his mouth shut.

Surprise, surprise everyone knew about my nocturnal antics at breakfast – and word had reached the Sales Paddocks by lunchtime!

*

Hamish Alexander was a very successful vendor of yearlings, and his consignment at DBS September Yearlings Sales was always eagerly awaited. He was charismatic, capable and hospitable, and I used to stay with him sometimes at his stud farm near Darlington in County Durham.

On one occasion, I took Eric Eldin, then my stable jockey, with me, as we had horses running at Newcastle the following day. Hamish had been invited to dinner with friends, some distance away – and his kind host very generously extended their invitation to Eric and me.

It was one hell of a party, and we did not get back to Hamish's stud until the early hours as the Sun is rising. I thought it was bedtime, but Hamish had other ideas. He wanted to show us his Doncaster yearlings, still fast asleep in their respective boxes.

Everything is going to plan until we come to a particularly likeable and impressive bay colt by Jukebox. Eric, who at this stage is in fine fettle, alcohol fuelled – and naturally very agile – suddenly takes a flying leap onto the back of the unfortunate yearling (unbroken of course), grabs it by the ears, and starts to ride a finish. Hamish, who is standing at the yearling's head, is totally taken by surprise, dumbstruck, and exceedingly angry, quite rightly. He drags Eric off the yearling's back, and a fierce fight ensues, before I manage, with difficulty, to separate the two combatants, whilst the yearling looks on with disdain and disinterest, as if this is a regular occurrence. Eric and Hamish, dust themselves off, shake hands, make peace, apologies are made and accepted, and we retire to bed at long last.

Two weeks later, I am at DBS Yearling Sales with Minty, inspecting Hamish's yearlings – and again, very taken by the Jukebox colt, whose obvious good looks had previously caused commotion. I'm now determined to buy him, for a number of reasons, and if selling for sensible money. We ring Charlie Pick, a good and mutual friend of ours, who farmed in Lincolnshire, and tell him the story. He is amused and intrigued, backs our judgement and instructs us to bid for the horse on his behalf the following day. We buy him for 4000 Guineas, which we consider good value, and everyone is happy.

Eight months later, now named Another Nickel, our Jukebox colt wins his maiden race at Newcastle. Ridden of course by Eric Eldin! And greeted into the Winners' Enclosure by a very proud Hamish Alexander!

In addition to Another Nickel, I trained a number of winners for Charlie and Sandy Pick, including Matou, Great Optimist, Cleat, Ipo and Two Minutes. They were very loyal and lucky owners, and we had a lot of fun together.

28.
Quick Review

Bloodstock agents are now part and parcel of the Racing and Breeding Industry – bringing in sizeable annual investment, thereby supporting and promoting our sport and business. They come in all shapes and sizes – but few are as rotund, cuddly and genial, as David (Minty) Minton, who has been a close friend of mine for many years. Minty is Shropshire born and bred, and I first met him and his father, when as a small boy I used to go with my younger brother Giles to stay with our Grandmother Helen (known to us as Doodie), who was then married, second time around, to Tom Corrie. "Uncle Tom" lived at Leighton Hall, near Shrewsbury, an imposing house overlooking the River Severn, with a large estate, which he farmed very professionally. He also trained a small stable of racehorses, and was a very shrewd judge. Uncle Tom later married, second time round, Sarah Taylor, much younger than him. Sarah thus became my "Step-Grandmother". She is great fun, loves a party, and I am very fond of her.

Minty was always passionate about racing and breeding, and first came to Newmarket as Secretary to Ryan Jarvis, a colourful and very capable trainer, based on the Fordham Road. He then moved on to work for the Curragh Bloodstock Agency (CBA) at Crossways – their Newmarket office in the Avenue – and then The British Bloodstock Agency.

Minty's first purchase for the CBA was Quick Review at the Ascot Sales. Selected by him as a potential Point-to-Pointer for Pam Sly, then an aspiring and decorative young lady rider, who went on to train racehorses, with great credit in Lincolnshire, winning the 1000 Guineas at Newmarket with Speciosa in 2006.

Quick Review showed promise, from the outset, and excitement mounted, when he was to make his Saturday debut for Pam in a maiden race at Cottenham Point-to-Point – a popular little track only eight miles west of Cambridge. Pam's "support team", large in number, gathered for drinks and lunch before racing – but it later transpired that, as there were numerous divisions of the maiden race, Quick Review's race had to be rescheduled for 6pm. Pam's and Minty's worthy band of well-wishers included Hamish Alexander, Willie Macauley, Jim and Robin Wilson, Macer Gifford, Derek Sly and Sandy Pick – and GAPG was able to attend, as he had no runners that day on the Flat.

Not surprisingly, a great deal of liquid refreshment was consumed in the course of a long afternoon of expectation – and Jim Wilson and GAPG were visibly rocked with shock and apprehension when asked by Minty to saddle the bold Quick Review before his participation.

As the 16 runners make their way from the Paddock to the 3 Mile start, Minty and I pass the long line of Bookmakers' boards. Minty is indignant and insulted to see that Quick Review is a 100 – 1 chance. "That is an outrage!" exclaims a ruffled Minty. "You and I will have a £5 each-way bet to teach them a lesson, Gavin!"

Passing the stands for the second time, before going out on the final circuit, Pam and Quick Review are in fourth place, jumping with fluency, and travelling easily. Going to the final fence, Quick Review jumps to the front and wins by four lengths. Euphoria erupts, until Macer Gifford, a Steward of the Meeting, and wearing his black bowler hat, points out discreetly that Pam's weight cloth has parted company with her saddle, falling to the ground, only spitting distance from the line. Leaving the stand in very orderly fashion and trying our best not to attract attention to our actions, we proceed to kick the weight cloth gently over the line – now in dread of the Stewards Enquiry that will be announced, once Pam weighs in, a stone light.

Panic stations as GAPG is instructed by Minty to represent connections. Robert Fellowes, Agent to the Jockey Club, and Clerk of the Course at Cottenham, gives a detailed appraisal of the situation to the three Stewards. The Senior Steward, Nat Sherwood, having obviously enjoyed himself greatly during the afternoon, requested the evidence to be repeated a second, and then a third time, to assist his befuddled comprehension. Before concluding, given the complexities of the case, that he was going to be late for his dinner engagement and that the result should stand. Uttering the infamous words, "first past the post".

As GAPG exits the Weighing Room, albeit 35 minutes after the last race, giving the thumbs up, there is a roar of delight, sprinkled with chunks of relief and of disbelief. As the celebrations begin, Minty and GAPG rush to collect their winnings from those insolent Bookmakers. But, horror of all horrors, they have scarpered with their ill-gotten gains, never to be seen again!

29.
Moments in Sport

People and sport, preferably in tandem, were part and parcel of my life when I was training – and because of Racing's high media profile, I met and became friends with several top sportsmen, mostly from the worlds of Cricket, Rugby and Football. Trainers, by and large, were fond of most sports – and conversely, a number of leading lights in sport were keen followers of Racing, some becoming owners.

In the early years of my training career, there was no racing on a Sunday – so this was the perfect opportunity to entertain owners and play sport. In particular, cricket during the summer. When at Shalfleet, my father, who had by then become pals with a lot of my Newmarket friends, issued us a challenge. A game of cricket between a side of his friends in Sussex and the Newmarket trainers. Game on – and the start of the Newmarket Trainers Cricket Eleven, which continues to this day. It was a needle match, great fun – we soon realised there was some latent cricketing talent amongst our Newmarket Trainers fraternity.

Our opening batsmen were Jeremy Hindley, a master stroke-maker, who played cricket for Winchester College, and the bold Minty, more Boycott than Stokes, who was a solid and staunch defender of his wicket. Quick singles between them were not considered, and forbidden, but runs still amassed, and their pairing soon became legend.

Michael Stoute, who had represented Junior Barbados in his late teens, and counted Gary Sobers and Michael Holding amongst his friends, was stylish and effective – and three more of our "Racing Ringers", Tony Jakobson (Jak, "Warren Hill", the Newmarket Correspondent on the *Sporting Life*), plus leading Newmarket veterinary surgeons Nick Wingfield Digby (Digby) and David Ellis, were competent middle-order batsmen.

James Toller and Mark Tompkins were useful contenders on their day – and Ben Hanbury, when concentrating, and John Oxley, another non-runner, and static first slip fielder, plus GAPG, were waggers of the tail.

Our dark horse was Jeremy Richardson, then a prominent solicitor in Newmarket, who went on to do sterling work as Chief Executive of the Injured Jockeys Fund. A 3rd Eleven cricketer at school, he proved to be a late developer – a hard-hitting batsman and an exceptionally competent wicket keeper.

Jak and Digby were a daunting opening bowling partnership – both quick, accurate and aggressive. Ably supported by Mark Tompkins and James Toller, who always understated his cricketing ability. And in later years by William Haggas (who captained Harrow School and had a county trial for Yorkshire), Julian Wilson (who considered himself to be one of the finest left-arm spinners on this planet) and William Jarvis (a close friend of William Haggas at Harrow), who was a much better player after lunch.

Arthur Boyd-Rochfort (who once introduced himself, at a very smart ennobled London wedding, as "Sir Arthur Fart", and the name has stuck ever since) made the occasional appearance. As did his illustrious half-brother, Henry Cecil, a genius amongst trainers, who starred at Exning on one memorable occasion. Henry was signing autographs on the square-leg boundary, with his back to the wicket ,when David Nicholson, captain of the National Hunt Jockeys Eleven, skied a huge catch in his direction. Henry swung round, at the very last moment, and caught it! He was, quite rightly, elated, as were his astounded fellow Newmarket trainers – but David Nicholson was not amused.

John Oxley, a former Army Boxing Champion in his time, enjoyed his cricket – and had a distinguished training career at Hurworth House on the Fordham Road. He had some very influential owners, who included Major General Sir Randle Feilden, Lord Halifax and Dick Hollingsworth – and trained some top-class horses, amongst them Hermes, Homeward Bound and Frankincense. Barry Hills, who later became one of our leading trainers, based in Lambourn, was his Travelling Head Lad, landing some hefty gambles, I might add.

John had a little brush with the law, which he won, surprisingly. He was driving home, one cold, foggy night after dinner, when he was flagged down by a police car. Suspecting that John might just have been over the limit, the Constable, who had unwisely parked his police car behind John's, asked him to walk down the white line in the middle of the road, there being no breathalyser tests in those days. But John was one jump ahead of the Police Constable. As he stumbled past the police car, he twigged that the driver's side front window was wound down and wide open, removed the car key from the ignition, jumped smartly back into his own, and took off at speed. Leaving the unfortunate Police Constable aghast and stranded, and now obliged to ring his Sergeant at Newmarket Police Station, come clean, and request a colleague to come and collect him. By all accounts, the Constable was severely reprimanded for his professional stupidity. No charges were made and John escaped scot-free.

Our Newmarket Trainers Eleven went from strength to strength. More fixtures were added to the list and other home venues chosen. Exning, Chippenham, Poslingford, Newmarket, Mildenhall and some Cambridge College grounds. My father's match became an annual event – as did games against the National Hunt Jockeys, Norfolk Farmers, Dana Brudenell-Bruce's Eleven, Lambourn, an Irish Eleven, and Burrough Green, courtesy of Julian Wilson.

Highlights, there were many – two in particular: Thanks to the generosity of Stanhope Joel, son of diamond magnate Solly Joel, Middlesex County Cricket Club were invited to play an all-day Sunday Charity Match against the Newmarket Trainers at Exning. On the Saturday, Middlesex were beaten by Sussex in the final of the Gillette Cup at Lords – but, very sportingly, honoured their agreement to play us. Their spirits raised, perhaps, by the thought of a cheery pre-match Saturday night party in Newmarket. Middlesex sported their full first team – amongst them England Captain Mike Brearley, Fred Titmus, John Emburey and Clive Radley. After the toss, and as this was a charity match to entertain the 4,000 spectators who had gathered in Exning, Fred Titmus elected to put us into bat – remarking generously, "We will let you score 150, and then, after tea, we will knock off the runs, and everybody will go home happy." But this did not happen. The Newmarket Trainers performed better than Middlesex might have expected, and reached their target, as planned. And when Middlesex batted, after only a handful of overs, they were 32 for 5 – the outgoing batsman at this juncture, was heard to confide to his incoming teammate, "These buggers can bowl a bit – we better pull our fingers out and do a damn sight better". But it was too late. They proceeded to pile on the runs, but it was not enough. Middlesex were very gracious in defeat – but it must have hurt them and been very exasperating, having been defeated by Sussex the previous day as well.

Our second high-profile encounter was a Charity Match against an Old England Eleven at Cheveley, five miles east of Newmarket. It was the Tuesday evening of the July Meeting in Newmarket, which the England players had attended, supported by a vast gathering of spectators, despite a very wet and dreary evening. Bob Willis, Andy Lloyd, David Gower and David Brown all played – but Ian Botham was the undoubted star of the evening. He thrilled the crowd with a scintillating big-hitting performance – at one moment lofting one of GAPG's slow leg-breaks into the third row of the cars, parked behind the boundary line. And – what were the odds against this? – smashing the windscreen of GAPG's car in the process.

A personal view, I hasten to add – but, when Sunday racing was introduced, it was not universally popular amongst trainers or their staff. We all missed those magical Sunday sporting moments – but regrettably, we cannot rewind the clock.

30.
Rugby

I've always been a rugby enthusiast – a "rugger bugger" as we used to call them. From the age of 8 to 18, rugger was a major part of my school curriculum and taken very seriously. I played to a reasonable standard on the wing, being small and light – relying on my speed, dare I say, to outwit and evade those giantlike and terrifying scrummagers.

In my Pupil Assistant days with Harvey Leader, I used to play for the Newmarket All Blacks – the 1st Fifteen was far too much like hard work, so Jeremy Richardson, Willie Hastings-Bass (now Lord Huntingdon) and I turned out for the 2nd Fifteen, which was less arduous and more fun.

One Saturday afternoon, we had an away fixture against local rivals Sudbury. On arrival, we were informed by the opposition that they were a man short – and, would it be possible to "borrow" our reserve? A very small but exceedingly thick set 17-year-old jumped at the opportunity, and started the game as their hooker. Five minutes from full time, the scores level, our little reserve, but now our opponent, picked up the ball and ran towards our scrum. He was stopped in his tracks and upended by Robin Ratcliffe son of the Senior Partner at Rustons and Lloyd Solicitors in Newmarket, one of our two mammoth second-row forwards – 6 feet 4 inches tall and built like a Centurion tank. He proceeded to put the little lad on his left shoulder, plus the ball, and march toward the oppositions try line with intent. He dumped him over the try line, falling on top of him and claiming a try. Confusion reigned, tempers flared, the poor referee eventually ruling no score. The game ended in a draw, which was a just result in the circumstances.

My stint with Newmarket All Blacks should have been my last

hurrah, but I did play two more games before finally hanging up my boots, both of which were a disaster. I was invited by a group of old school friends to have lunch at the Honourable Artillery Company Headquarters (HAC) and afterwards to watch the Old Radleians Fifteen play rugby against the HAC on their little gem of a ground in the heart of the City of London. Lunch was particularly heavy and alcoholic, and, as the Old Radleians are warming up on the pitch before the match, one of their enormous second-row forwards pulls a muscle in his groin and is declared unfit to play. As there is no reserve, Leo Cooper, captain of the Old Radleians team, and married to famous author Jilly, comes over to the touchline and asks his supporters for a volunteer replacement. My name is put forward, and within minutes I am standing on the wing now changed into the second row's kit, wearing shorts three sizes too big and size ten-and-a-half boots. Not exactly practical, more hindrance than help, especially when you are a size eight! The pitch is saturated, almost underwater, after two days of torrential rain – and every time I am passed the ball, I fall over. It is so, so embarrassing. The final irony comes at the end of the game, when Leo strides over to me and says, "Many thanks for helping us out at the last minute, Gavin – that was very much appreciated. Just one query – have you ever played rugby before?"

My final game of rugby was for the Newmarket Trainers side against Lambourn Trainers in Newmarket. Despite being in my mid 30's, I was persuaded to play on the wing, alongside William Haggas, William Jarvis, John Ferguson and David Batten, a doyen of Tattersalls. It was sheer purgatory. Rivalry between Newmarket and Lambourn had always been fierce – but this was a rare opportunity for physical confrontation. It was a pitched battle, from start to finish, a free for all – and, if you were only 11 stone, unfit, and too old, it was pure hell. At one stage, the referee threatened to abandon the game, but regrettably it did go to full time. I have no recollection of the final score – but as I left the pitch I vowed this would definitely be my last appearance.

Playing days now firmly behind me, my passion for rugby as a spectator continued to grow – and was further enhanced when I was introduced to Ian Robertson by former Newmarket trainer Ryan Jarvis, who was then President of Cambridge University Rugby Club. Ian, a superb fly-half in his day, who won his Blue for Cambridge and was then capped eight times for Scotland, was coaching the University Fifteen at the time, and had just become BBC Radio Rugby Correspondent. We hit it off immediately and soon became firm friends. He was infatuated by racing – and had syndicate horses with Ryan Jarvis and Ian Balding – and I was equally obsessed with International Rugby. So it was a friendship made to last. He came to stay regularly at Fairway, given that he lived in London, and only came to Cambridge on a part-time basis. And when Ryan Jarvis retired from racing, it was suggested that Ian's syndicate horses should be transferred to Stanley House Stables.

I became a frequent visitor to Grange Road to watch Cambridge University play, and befriended many of the team. And I will never forget the day that Ian brought his Cambridge backs to Newmarket to go racing, and then round Evening Stables at Stanley House Stables. As it transpired, every one of those Cambridge backs went on to play International Rugby for their respective countries – Rob Andrew, Gavin Hastings and his brother Scott all becoming worldwide rugby legends. At the request of my two older sons, Rupert and Paddy, Ian very kindly set up a three-quarter passing movement on the lawn – how lucky we were.

In return for my hospitality, (and inside information!) at Fairway, Ian invited me, on a regular basis to Twickenham, where if room permitted I would join him in the Commentary Box for the match. Lunch in the BBC Marquee always preceded this and I was privileged to sit next to Terry Wogan, my hero, a couple of times.

On one of them, when instructed by Ian to follow him to the Commentary Box, only 50 yards away, Terry declined the offer, very firmly, stating he would much prefer to watch the match on TV – from the comfort of the BBC dining room, with a large glass, or three, of wine and no interruptions.

On the Monday morning, two days afterward, my horses were trotting around the Covered Indoor Ride at Stanley House Stables, given that severe frost and snow had prevented their exercise on the Heath. To keep my lads, lasses and horses happy during the winter months, we fitted four loudspeakers into the eaves of the Covered Ride – and, to my amazement, I hear Terry Wogan, on his daily morning program, make a very unexpected announcement. "I would like to dedicate the next record to Newmarket Trainer Gavin Prichard-Gordon's lads and lasses, who are now riding their horses round the Covered Indoor Ride at Stanley House Stables. Please be especially nice and polite to the Guv'nor this morning – he is probably still suffering from the hangover he inflicted upon himself at the England vs Ireland match at Twickenham on Saturday."

During the racing season, Ian would ring me every Sunday Morning for an update on his syndicate horses, and being very partial to a flutter, hear what horses of mine were fancied that week. But on one occasion there was a major deviation from the norm. "Where are you going racing on Saturday, Gavin?" asked Ian. "To Kempton, as I have already told you," I replied. "And what will you be doing after racing?" he continued. "Going home to Newmarket, of course, you silly arse." I replied wearily. "Oh no you are not," interjects Ian. "You are going to Heathrow, where I have arranged for you to be given a First Class return ticket to Harare."

I was dumbfounded, lost for words, thinking that Ian had lost his marbles – but over the moon with excitement when he informed me that I was to be the Tour Manager of an unofficial "Wanderers" rugby team on a four-day visit to Zimbabwe. The original British and Irish Lions games there were cancelled by Robert Mugabe's new government – but Ian had organised a team of full international players to honour the fixture, only under a different name. Ian was to have managed the team but was later advised not to do so by the BBC for political reasons.

It was a mega and magical experience – some of the best days of my rugby life. Ireland Rugby legend Fergus Slattery captained the side – and amongst the many other stars on tour were Ian McLaughlan, Moss Keane, and Les Cusworth. My only designated responsibilities, as Tour Manager, were to shake the hands of all of the Zimbabwean dignitaries before the match in Harare in front of 35,000 people – and to stand up and thank our very kind hosts after the official dinner!

I have a lot to thank Ian for, but one of his biggest favours was to introduce me to the England Rugby Team, and then persuade them to have a horse in training with me at Stanley House Stables. I could not believe my good fortune. After due consideration, I advised Ian that they should lease a horse rather than buy one. And, having made a few calls to potential lessors, agreed a deal with Peter Player, a good friend and owner of Whatton Manor Stud in Nottinghamshire, who leased them a likeable bay colt to be called Big Trouble. The legendary Billy Beaumont was captain of England at the time – and, amongst other notables, Peter Wheeler and Clive Woodward were prominent members of his team. From the outset, the England players were very enthusiastic and regular racecourse attendees when Big Trouble ran. But, very sadly, none of them could go racing when he won his only race at Yarmouth.

I was very spoilt, on reflection.

31.
Footnotes on Football

Trainers appeared on the Football field less frequently – but, in my case, I was happy to make up the numbers for our stable side whenever they were short. Inter-stable football was ultra-competitive and rivalry was fierce so this was not my favourite pastime. My footballing skills were limited and my fitness debatable – so I was a prime target for the opposition, always finishing the game with bruises and a pair of sore shins.

As I was President of Newmarket Town Football Club at the time, I was determined to raise funds for the club, and also for various Racing Charities. Charity matches on the Town Ground were popular. England star Terry Paine was their captain and a passionate follower of racing, so I was able to organise a match between Premier Division, Ipswich Town, and a Newmarket Racing Eleven, at the ground. This was played under lights, after a day's racing on the Rowley Mile, which attracted a large crowd.

But, there was one Charity Football match, which will remain long in the memory. Tim Finch, a former amateur rider, owner of Old Buckenham Stud, and an owner of mine was an ardent Norwich City fan and became a close friend of Norwich captain, Colin Suggett, a devotee of racing. In order to raise money for Racing Charities, and to give Norwich supporters something to keep them enthused, in their off season, Tim and Colin asked me to put together a Racing Eleven to play a pre-season game against a Norwich Eleven, at Carrow Road. I am sometimes prone to exaggeration, allegedly – but the Norwich fans came in their thousands to support their Premier Division team, which included Mick Channon, amongst others – and to see some Racing celebrities in footballing action. Willie Carson, Joe Mercer and Brian Taylor all played – as did, amongst other notables, David Nicholson and Julian Wilson. But, without a shadow of doubt, the star turn of the evening was Minty – who, despite his Billy Bunter frame and physique, defended his goal line heroically. Making a series of acrobatic saves and dives, which stunned the Norwich strikers and demoralised their faithful and vociferous band of supporters. The result, not surprisingly, was a 9-0 win for Norwich – but this could have been 20-0 had it not been for the skill and bravery of our genial hero!

After the match, the two teams gathered for dinner in a leading Italian restaurant on Norwich High Street. It was a riotous party, which continued into the early hours of the following morning. As Coral and I were about to leave – in broad daylight – anxious and aware that it was a "work morning" for our horses in Newmarket, an hour's drive away – John Wales, a renowned prankster, appears to take the car keys from the pocket of my jacket which is slumped over the back of my chair. He then runs out of the restaurant, up the High Street, and "throws" the keys over the awning of an old hardware shop, before driving off, at speed. Now in a state of frenzy and panic, we enlist the help of an unsuspecting beat Constable, who just happens to be passing by. Being 6 foot 3 inches tall and very public spirited, he very kindly volunteers to give Coral a leg up to make the retrieval from the awning – when, driving very slowly down the High Street comes John Wales, hooting his horn, and looking very smug. Winds down his window, waves my car keys very flamboyantly, and throws them onto the pavement – adding, with provocation, "I hope that you get back to Newmarket in time for first lot, Gavin."

Traffic was light at that time of the morning, and we made first lot, with minutes to spare, albeit a little jaded. Looking back it was all part of Racing's rich tapestry. Training racehorses was our passion – but we had to enjoy all aspects of it as well.

32.
Newmarket Trainers Federation

In the Seventies and early Eighties, the Racing Industry was the biggest employer in Newmarket, and there was a moral obligation to reciprocate with the town, its Council and its inhabitants. Supermarkets were in their infancy, and local retailers, hotels and pubs, relied on owners, trainers and their staff, for their custom.

The National Trainers Federation was the trade body for trainers across the country – but the Newmarket Trainers Federation looked after the interests of the trainers in the town and represented them in all matters and negotiations relating to the Jockey Club, Newmarket Urban District Council and Newmarket Heath. Sir Mark Prescott has only recently stood down as Chairman of the Heath Committee, after 45 years in post, devoting his time, energies and experience to the task. A remarkable achievement.

Humphrey Cottrill and Johnny Winter both did their stints as Chairmen of the Newmarket Trainers Federation, but Harry Thomson Jones (known to one and all as Tom Jones) held this position for most of my time with a licence, and I was his Vice Chairman. Tom was a very accomplished trainer – first under "National Hunt Rules" before switching his allegiance to the Flat, where he was equally successful. He ran and oversaw an immaculate racing stable on the Severals, where stable management was at a premium and everything ran like clockwork. His staff were always impeccably turned out in the yard, on the Heath, and on the racecourse – and it was an eye-opener to go round Evening Stables with the Guv'nor, when standards were so high.

Tom was a very intelligent and charismatic man. A wonderful raconteur who wrote ribald poetry and was the heart and soul of any party. He was strict with his staff but they respected him. He had a steady stream of Pupil Assistant Trainers, who could not have been better taught – and produced a number of top jockeys, who included Steve Smith-Eccles and Ian Watkinson.

Supporting all Stable Staff-related clubs, institutions and charities was our main concern – and we were always well represented on the Committees of the Astley Club, the British Racing School, the Stable Lads Welfare Trust and the Newmarket Town Council. We gave our support and encouragement to Stable Lads Football, Cricket, Boxing and Darts – and took a keen interest in welfare issues flagged up relating to the three churches in Newmarket – namely St Marys, All Saints and St. Agnes.

One January day, Tom very kindly invited me to go shooting with friends near Newmarket. It was a fun day, the post shooting lunch was particularly alcoholic and lengthy, and we did not return to the Severals until 5:15pm. As Tom, now in flying form and a little unsteady on his feet was pouring himself another large whisky and settling himself into his favourite armchair, the telephone went on the little table beside him. "Hello, Tom Jones here – who would that be?" he enquires, a little incoherently. "It is Sheikh Hamdan. I spent the day at Shadwell and am on the way back to London and would like to call in at Newmarket to see my horses," comes the reply. Tom, who then trained 25 horses for the Sheikh, was taken aback and thrust into a state of panic by this totally unexpected chain of events. Insisting that I should help him, which I soon worked out to be impossible. "I think that I should be going, Tom," I tell him, heading for the door, "but, before I leave, I promise that I will go and tell your lovely Head Lad what is happening. I am sure that everything will be alright."

The next day, I see Tom's Head Lad, about to enter The Horseshoe Pub, by the Clock Tower – and cannot wait to hear his report. By all accounts, Tom duly took Sheikh Hamdan round Evening Stables, bending down to feel the horses' front legs, as per normal.

Everything went well to begin with but there was a little hiccup towards the end of his round. No doubt instructed by the Head Lad, every Lad gave Tom a helping hand to stand upright – until one particularly truculent little fellow decided not to play the game and be of assistance to the Guv'nor. Now wobbling precariously, Tom toppled over backwards, landing on his bottom onto a bed of neatly raked shavings – and was unable to move.

Fortunately, Sheikh Hamdan, who had a wonderful sense of humour, and adored Tom, thought it was very funny. Also doubtless aware that he had not given sufficient prior warning of his visit to Tom – which he would normally have done.

*

Throughout my training career in Newmarket, the Newmarket Trainers Federation had a very cordial rapport with the Newmarket Police, which was concreted every Christmas Eve, after Morning Stables, with a party hosted by the Chief Superintendent in the Police Station on Vicarage Road. Police staff and trainers were invited to congregate in a relaxed atmosphere, get to know each other better, and have a few beers as well. In those days, there were twenty-five Bobbies on the beat, and, as each one finished his shift, the Chief Superintendent would instruct them to throw their helmets on the table, consider themselves off-duty and enjoy themselves.

His advice to trainers being to make merry – but not to drive home, if over the drink drive limit. Conscious of our responsibilities, we trainers took note – but one in particular did overstep the mark, for the records. Ron Boss was a hardworking and affable trainer – but strong of character, forthright, and not averse to a bit of gentle disruption. On leaving the party, a little the worse for drink, he clambered into his car parked in the Police Station car park and proceeded to ram the main gates, which were then firmly shut. The Chief Superintendent was very diplomatic, played everything down, and instructed Ron to ask his wife to collect him from the Police Station and take him home. Advising him, very firmly, not to repeat his sins the next time.

Twelve months later, Ron again attended the Christmas Party – but did not travel by car. He dressed up as Father Christmas and rode his impressive grey "hack" up the High Street and turned right along Rous Road to the Police Station. Throwing the reins over the rails of the Police Station, and announcing to the Superintendent, on arrival, "I would just like to tell you that I will not be breaking any drink-drive regulations this year, Superintendent."

Newmarket was a happy little town in those days. People helped and looked after each other – and life was a lot less stressful.

33.
Manager and Boom Patrol

My mother and father, Bill and Lesley (known to us as Manager and Secretary) Pritchard-Gordon, founded a dynasty of P-Gs, of which they were very proud. They were loving and very responsible parents and grandparents, who gave us all the best possible start to our lives. They were very supportive of my training career and loved to come to Newmarket to see the horses, and, of course, their grandchildren, Rupert and Paddy.

I was the eldest of their five offspring – my younger siblings, Giles, Grant (nicknamed Badger), Tessa and Amanda (known to us as Panda) completing the family line-up. At this juncture, I must add that Badger, after a youthful stint with Savills in Norfolk, joined his elder brother in Racing, and was a very much-liked and respected Racing Manager to Prince Khalid Abdullah for 16 years. Between us we begat no less than 17 children – who have since gone on to produce another 33 of their own. The number is rising all the time!

Giles, Badger and I began our lives in Princes Square, Hove, Sussex – but moved when I was seven, to Hill House, Turners Hill, in Mid Sussex, between Horsham and East Grinstead, where Tessa and Panda were born. When I left home for Newmarket, aged 19, Hill House was sold, and my father and mother relocated to Burleigh Farm on the other side of the village, before moving finally to Bosworths, a little cottage in Slaugham, twelve miles away – where my brother Giles, and his wife Lou, had already set up home at Slaugham Park, only half a mile from Bosworths.

Manager was very ill with Hodgkin's Disease at that stage of his life, and used to walk his dogs from Bosworths every morning to see Giles's foals – one of which he fell in love with – a strong, plain and rather ugly bay, with a Roman nose, who had cost 1500 guineas as a foal, but failed to reach his reserve price of 600 guineas at the sales as a yearling. Manager was distraught and heartbroken, bid Giles the reserve price, and the deal was agreed to go into training with me at Stanley House Stables.

Manager's pride and joy was by Bold Owl out of Night Duty, and he named him Boom Patrol – very aptly, given that Manager was in joint charge of Royal Marine Boom Patrol Detachment during the war. They were training at the time for their daring raid on Bordeaux Harbour, which earned the name "Cockleshell Heroes". Their unlikely task was to patrol in canoes the boom – four miles of fixed and floating obstruction, painstakingly pieced together in defence of Portsmouth Harbour from Southsea to Seaview on the Isle of Wight.

Prior to Boom Patrol, Manager had three horses in training with me over the years – Panda's Gambol, who won a small race at Pontefract; Atrobes, a winner of a little contest at Wolverhampton; and Passing Glory, a good-looking but very disappointing filly who failed to feature. Boom Patrol proved conclusively to be the best of them – and far and away Manager's favourite.

He won on the Flat at Leicester, ridden by George Duffield, beating a horse of Sheikh Mohammed's – before winning over hurdles at Fakenham with Steve Smith-Eccles aboard, where he sustained a strained tendon. This necessitated a long rest and treatment – and it was a miracle that he reappeared two years later on the racecourse to triumph in his last race at Plumpton in 1987. Again, Steve Smith-Eccles was in the saddle.

This was Boom Patrol's final hurrah, as he incurred a further and much more serious tendon injury in the process. But it gave Manager enormous pleasure, as he had always wanted to have a winner at what was his local track, trained by his eldest son, and ridden by the Ecc of whom he was very fond.

Manager died very shortly afterwards – and there wasn't room for his many friends who came to his funeral in the large village church at Turners Hill.

My father was a very brave and determined man, who reached the rank of Major in the Royal Marines at the tender age of twenty-two. At the end of the war, he embarked on a career in the City of London, starting in Lloyds as an Insurance Broker, before going on to H. Clarkson and Company, where he became Managing Director of their Shipbroking Department. He was a hugely charismatic man, who was greatly admired and respected, throughout his life and – especially in the world of shipping, more latterly.

My dear mother was equally talented for her own part. She qualified at the Bar in 1939 – one of the first Lady Barristers to do so. She then served as a Wren for the duration of the war, before marriage to my father, and motherhood.

"Sec" wrote two superb books – one, a perfectly researched biography of my father entitled "Befriend the Ebbing Tide." And the second about herself, titled "War and Before". They were beautifully produced and bound in leather, but for members of the P-G family only – but not published to the general public, sadly.

A great shame in hindsight, as they recounted and portrayed the life and times of two remarkable and special people – which would have been of interest to a much wider audience.

34.
Staff at Stanley House Stables

"A Trainer is only as good as his Head Lad," someone once remarked to me, and there was a lot of truth in his comment. Taffy Williams had the respect of his staff, was a superb feeder of horses and had a masterly feel for horses' legs – and it came as a bit of a blow when he had to retire early after a freak injury, and resulting illness, halfway through our time at Stanley House Stables. David (Ginger) Tyers, a hardworking and conscientious man, took over, and remained in post until I retired. Kevin Murrell, a cheery and charming fellow, who had been an apprentice with me, and ridden my father's Panda's Gambol to victory at Pontefract, becoming his deputy.

I had two fully fledged Assistant Trainers during my training career – both of whom had been successful jockeys. Mickey Greening was one of our best lightweight jockeys – and still went to scale at 7 stone 7lbs when he retired as my Assistant. Peter Boothman was Champion Apprentice in this country, before moving to Ireland, where he rode numerous winners. Mickey and Peter brought with them a wealth of racing experience, were much liked by my owners and staff, and were inspirational tutors to my Apprentice Jockeys.

Over the years, I also had a steady flow of Pupil Assistants – who, I must stress, were taught the basics of training by my senior staff and not by me. I have already made reference to Kazuo Fujisawa, who went on to be Champion Trainer in Japan for 14 years – to whom must be added the names of Oliver Sherwood, Simon Sherwood, Tom George, Sam Bullard, Ed Peate and Robert Cowell. I would like to take credit for employing Venetia Williams, a very talented trainer, in that capacity – but, in fairness, she was only my Secretary, her first job in racing – when Jean Short died very tragically.

I can honestly state that all my Pupil Assistants were hard working and very popular with my staff, fun to be with, and went on to succeed in their chosen careers. Oliver Sherwood was a very competent Amateur rider, winning on his father's Venture To Cognac at the Cheltenham Festival. He was an all-round horseman, who went on to be Assistant to Dan Moore and Fred Winter, before becoming a top-class trainer – with numerous successes including Many Clouds who won the Grand National for Trevor Hemmings.

Oliver, like all Sherwoods, had a mischievous sense of humour. His father Nat used to enjoy lunching at School Dinners, a notorious London Restaurant for fun-loving naughty boys, where the waitresses were all topless. And, if anyone dared to step out of line, he was reprimanded and beaten by the "Head Master", who always sat at the top of the table, waving his long cane. It was good clean fun, I might add!

At one of Nat's birthday lunches at School Dinners, Oliver and his great friend Kim Bailey had arranged previously for a surprise birthday cake to be brought to Nat's table. It was a coffee-coloured wobbling blancmange, in the shape of a girl's bottom – and, when Nat attempted to blow out the candles, Oliver and Kim, squidged and immersed his rather long, red nose into its midst. Childish stuff, but Nat and we all enjoyed it!

From day one, it was obvious that Simon Sherwood was going to be a very talented jockey. He was a "natural" on a horse, stylish, gifted and always in the right place in a race. He rode winners for me before going on to be a superb professional jockey, riding many other winners, the best of which was Desert Orchid, on whom he won the Cheltenham Gold Cup.

If it is possible, Simon was even more wayward and cheeky than his older brother – but did not have the same desire or inclination for Evening Stables, which he obviously found very dull and uninspiring. He would occasionally arrive on time at 4:15pm, still wearing his cap, always at a very jaunty and strange angle – which in smart Newmarket Stables was much frowned upon.

In desperation, Taffy and I banish Simon to the Bottom Yard for Evening Stables, on the basis that out of sight was out of mind – but I had to bite the bullet one cold December evening. Lord Derby was coming to Evening Stables to see his horses – all bar one of which were stabled in the Main Yard. The problem being that Asia Minor, whom Simon looked after, was in the Bottom Yard. In fear and trepidation, I enter Asia Minor's box with Lord Derby – where, to my joy and surprise, Simon was standing at the horse's head, arms outstretched, like an old-fashioned stableman, and minus his cap. I was relieved and thankful – until my eyes shifted to Asia Minor, looking immaculate, under a particularly bright lightbulb – but with Simon's cap perched on his head! Simon had cut out the horse's ear holes, very precisely. Lord Derby never uttered a word. To this day, I am not sure whether he noticed or not – or whether he was just being very diplomatic!

Some people have the right temperament to train horses – it can be a testing occupation as we know – others do not. Tom George definitely has! He was much liked by my staff, who were in awe of his laid back but very professional attitude to life – which has served him well, since he took out his Trainer's licence. I was delighted to give him his first ride at Fakenham – a just reward for his large contribution to my stable.

Many years afterwards, my youngest son Charlie was playing in a Colts rugby match for Radley College against Eton College, on the wing. By some strange coincidence, he was playing opposite Noel George, Tom's son, now a trainer in Chantilly, and their respective fathers watched the match together. Competition was intense and fierce between the two boys, and ten minutes before full time, they had a massive collision resulting in an unmerciful clash of heads, which could be heard 100 yards away. Both boys were badly shaken – Charlie suffering concussion. The game was abandoned, and Charlie was rushed to hospital in Oxford – but made a full recovery thank God.

Tom has trained National Hunt horses with great distinction from his stables near Stroud in Gloucestershire, for many years – and always has a string of winners every season.

I had a soft spot for Sam Bullard, from the first day that he came to be a Pupil Assistant after leaving the Army. He had an angelic face, and perfect manners – but, under that bright red hair, there was a rare twinkle, which harboured a dose of devilment and a wicked sense of humour. He rode well, performed his duties at Stanley House Stables with aplomb – and there was always a bright and breezy smile on his face, which was part of his charm.

Sam rode his first winner for me on Coral Harbour, owned by Lord Cadogan, at Fakenham – a very fitting and popular result, given that Sam's father Gerry, was Chairman of Fakenham Racecourse at the time. He went on to ride Dhofar to win the Past and Present Hurdle at Sandown's Grand Military Meeting. Surviving a torrid Stewards Enquiry, which also involved Timmy Thomson Jones, who had previously ridden winners for me, and was much more experienced and savvy in the Steward's Room.

One snowy winter, the gallops in Newmarket were frozen over for weeks on end, and Sam, very sensibly, suggested that our four jumpers – two of which were entered at the Cheltenham Festival – should be despatched to his father Gerry Bullard's lovely farm at Gressinghall in Norfolk, from where they could be boxed to Holkham under Sam's supervision every morning to exercise on the beach. This tactic worked very well, and Sam did an excellent job in charge of operations – but he became increasingly concerned that the trainer had not seen his jumping string, since they had been on vacation. He was right, my conscience pricked me, and it was agreed that I should go to Gressinghall one Sunday evening, enjoy kitchen supper, and watch the four horses canter the following morning. As one did, Coral and I had a lengthy Sunday lunch with friends near Newmarket – and did not return to Fairway till 6:30pm. To be reminded by the nanny that I was due to be at supper in Norfolk for 8pm. The roads were very icy and dangerous – and, very stupidly, I failed to take my map in the car. I lost my way on numerous occasions and as there were no mobile telephones in those days, was not able to contact Sam, to explain my predicament. Eventually arriving at Gressinghall at 10pm, now hugely embarrassed and apologetic. Gerry, and Sam's mother, Mally, were remarkably long suffering, understanding and diplomatic, given my uncalled for hopelessness and rudery – and we had a hilarious evening, going to bed in the early hours of the morning.

The next morning, Sam drove the horses in Gerry's horsebox – while Gerry very kindly took me in his car, a little later. After first lot, and breakfast in the Victoria Hotel, Gerry was eagerly awaiting the arrival of Mally, who was to bring Gerry's hunter, in her box, which he would ride, second lot. Now dressed impeccably in breeches, hunting boots, riding jacket and cap, Gerry looked excitedly from the dining room window of the hotel, as Mally's box came into view. We follow it, on foot, down the little lane at Holkham, that leads to the beach – Gerry enquiring very earnestly how his hunter had travelled. "We had the easiest and quietest journey possible, despite the icy roads," replies Mally, adding, "It was as if there was no horse in the box." How right she was, as it happens. When Gerry lowered the back ramp of the horsebox very carefully – there was no hunter inside. Post the confusion of our exceedingly late departure to bed, Mally had a slight misunderstanding with her very dependable resident groom and had driven off without Gerry's horse! Which in the circumstances, made me feel a lot better – and almost saved my bacon!

Sam's career then had a meteoric rise. After spending time with the redoubtable Irish Bloodstock Agent, Cormac McCormack, he moved on to Darley, where he has been Director of Stallions and Marketing for a number of years.

Ed Peate was a very competent horseman from the outset – and had been brought up with horses and on the hunting field in Sussex. His lovely mother and father had an extensive knowledge of horses, and Ed arrived at Stanley House Stables, possessing the basics of horse care and welfare, but eager to progress and learn more from my staff.

It was a pleasure to have Ed under my jurisdiction – and it came as no surprise to me that later in his career he went on to run a hugely successful Yearling Breaking Yard not far from Newmarket. He was renowned for his diligence and expertise, and it was not long before he attracted the attention of a number of leading Newmarket trainers, who continued to support and rely upon his skills and stable management. The yearlings always had the best possible start to their training career.

And there was an added bonus for me. The Peate family in Sussex were close friends of Simon Tindall – who, jointly with Michael Hesseltine, ran Haymarket Publishing in Hammersmith. Simon became a loyal and long-time owner of mine – and we spent many a happy day and evening together. He was a passionate follower of all sports, International Cricket and Rugby in particular – and a very generous host when we had days out at both Lords and Twickenham.

One could not fail to like Robert Cowell. He is charm personified, fun loving, a little vain and very entertaining – but a touch devious, below the surface, in the nicest possible way. He was very popular with my staff and determined to make a success of his career as an Amateur rider. At the time, Lord Cadogan had a very likeable but thus-far exceedingly moderate horse called Hidden Planet. Following some very disappointing runs, Lord Cadogan quietly confided in me that he would like to call a halt to his ownership, gift him to someone who would appreciate him, and find me a replacement to train. Robert, and his father Bob, were then looking for a sound, kind and suitable horse, to run in amateur rider races – and despite his apparent lack of ability, Hidden Planet fitted the bill, and the deal was agreed. To this day, I am at a loss to comprehend how or why – but in his very first race for Bob and Robert, he triumphed in an amateur riders race at Brighton, one cold, wet and miserable day. I was delighted for the family Cowell, but I daresay, a little embarrassed – but Lord Cadogan was genuinely thrilled for horse, owner and rider, and could not wait to congratulate them.

Robert went on to be Assistant to John Hammond in Chantilly – where he shared a house with Richard Gibson, Ian Williams, Jonny Portman and my son Rupert. He thrived on his job and life in Chantilly – but could not understand why John would not give him a ride in an Amateur Riders race in France. However, at long last the big day arrived. Robert was to ride Volcanic Dancer, for Cheveley Park Stud, in a race at Montier-en-Der, a little country track in the French Provinces. Volcanic Dancer was a hot, hot favourite, and Robert was mightily excited. As was my son Rupert, who was then Assistant to Criquette Head in Chantilly – the two travelling down together. As the horses are taking a turn behind the stalls, Volcanic Dancer jinks, whips round, and falls backwards into the river – which just happened to be very close by. Rupert, who was looking very intently through his binoculars, was horrified as was the unfortunate race commentator who announced to the unsuspecting crowd "Alors, il y a une catastrophe – le favori a tombé dans la riviere!" But all was not lost. Horse and rider remain united, Robert now steering his aquatic equine conveyance to the bank, having safely negotiated the sharp turn in the river. Clambering up the bank, trotting back to the start, joining the other runners –

and winning the race. I am often accused of fabricating my stories, but I can assure you that this is fact!

Robert has proved to be a masterly trainer, based in Six Mile Bottom, near Newmarket. He specialises in the preparation of sprinters, and is now much revered by everyone, in that particular division.

I was blessed and privileged to have a bevy of talented, competent and very charismatic young Assistant Trainers, who all, without exception, have gone on to enjoy hugely successful careers, later in their lives.

35.
Young Assistant Trainers in Newmarket

My parents always believed in the maxim that age should never be a barrier to friendship. And this was underlined, and accentuated, when I first went to work for my mentor, Harvey Leader. He was very fond of people, from all walks of life – the more so if they were female and pretty! He was a superb host, both at Shalfleet, and at Denston Hall. And opened his first bottle of champagne, when work was done for the morning, on the dot of midday without fail, inviting friends, family, owners, fellow trainers and notables from the town of Newmarket. He thrived on the company of others, and just wanted to have fun. His owners were always invited to stay with him and Miry at Denston Hall – where his cellar was extensive and stacked to the ceiling with cases of champagne and fine wine. Through Harvey Leader, I was introduced to a host of well-established trainers in Newmarket, many of whom would invite me to dinner or Sunday lunch. It was a different world in those days.

Once I was established as a trainer, I made a point of inviting my pupil Assistants to a weekday supper or Sunday lunch at Fairway, so that they could meet people and feel part of the team. As previously recorded, they were all charismatic young men, enthusiastic, well-mannered, with a good sense of humour – and added youth to the party. Through them, I also met their young Assistant Trainer friends in Newmarket, and we had many a jolly kitchen supper, where we were often joined by our resident nanny at the time – one of Julie Jarvis, Juliet Cursham or Willa Haggie. I got to know William Jarvis, William Haggas, James Fanshawe, John Ferguson and Paul Webber very well – and am delighted that they have all been so successful in later life in the world of racing. At the time, they were five little reprobates, dare I say, oozing charm and personality, and with a mischievous sense of humour – and I was often the butt of their well thought out and devilish jokes. Performing car wheelies down the drive and putting stink bombs through the letterbox in the front door at Fairway, when my owners were invited to lunch or dinner, were favourite pastimes, but one supremely devious prank will always stand out from the others.

It is a cold, wet and gloomy Sunday in January, and Coral and I have invited an assortment of our more prominent owners to have lunch in the dining room at Fairway. Coral's roast pork proves very popular, wine flows very freely, and all is going to plan. Then I see, out of the window, someone raking leaves in the far corner of the garden, beside the tennis court – strange, I think, on a Sunday afternoon. He is wearing a long brown smock, shabby boots, and an ancient trilby hat – and every now and again, he topples over as if the worse for drink. He lies prostrate on the ground, momentarily, before getting to his feet, and continuing to rake. I am not best pleased – but, luckily, darkness descends, and nobody appears to notice. Needless to say, I had my suspicions, as to the culprit, but no proof, of course.

No harm is done, I keep my thoughts to myself, and no accusations are made – but I suddenly have an inspiration, which tickles my fancy. Why don't I try the same prank on the lads at Stanley House Stables – in between first and second lot, when they are all having their breakfast in the Hostel.

The following Saturday morning, I put on a filthy old brown smock, which I had found in the box in the cellar, a grotty old hat, and a plastic mask depicting the face of a wizened old man, bought from the dressing up shop in Exning Road. I position myself in the circle of gravel, rake in hand, in the middle of the large grass lawn, in the Main Yard. I start my routine, as if the intruder at Fairway, but there is no reaction. Until I see, through the slits of my mask, my Assistant Trainer, Mickey Greening, who is walking up and down the yard, stopping periodically to stare in my direction, before striding over to me, in obvious disgust. "What the hell are you doing Guv'nor?"

he blurts out. "I know it is you. I could recognise your welly boots anywhere. If you want to get a better reaction, I would suggest that you go down to the Bottom Yard, where Billy Cahill is on his own lunging the yearlings. By all accounts, he had one hell of a session in the pub last night and is even more pissed than he normally is on a Saturday morning."

As advised by Mickey, I walk down to the Bottom yard, open the gate, and start raking leaves in the far corner. At first, Billy does not notice me, but through his drunken haze, something must have alerted him. He stops lunging the yearling, and brings it over to me and tries, with great difficulty, to work out what is happening. "What the 'f..k do you think you are doing?" he enquires, very confused. "I am looking for a job," I reply, in my best Liverpudlian accent. "Well you won't get one here" continues Billy. "The Guv'nor is a miserable bugger, and pays very little f.....g wages."

At that, I put down my rake and remove my mask and hat. Billy turns white, runs out the yard in total panic, leaving me with the yearling on the lunging rein, and locks himself in his little bedroom in the Hostel, not to be seen again for the rest of the weekend.

It was all very childish stuff, and not very professional on my part – but it made the rest of my staff laugh when they heard the story. But I don't think that Mickey ever forgave me!

36.

Ben Hanbury

Training racehorses was a competitive business, and, as young licence holders in Newmarket, we did our very best to outshine our peers. But there was still a deep rooted camaraderie between us – and, when the business of the day was done we would all congregate for supper, and a bottle or two of wine, in one of our houses. Johnny and Phillipa Winter, Jeremy and Sally Hindley, Michael and Pat Stoute, Ben and Chunky Hanbury were part of our coterie – as were Henry and Julie Cecil. The last named was one of the most hilarious people I have ever met – she had a razor-sharp wit and the most mischievous and outrageous sense of humour, and was adored by one and all.

I was, and still am, particularly fond of Ben Hanbury, despite the fact that he and I are total opposites in so many respects. Ben was a dashing, fearless and determined Amateur National Hunt jockey, riding 100 winners over fences and hurdles – and carried those attributes and experiences forward to his training career. He was a consummate horse and stableman and trained a stack of winners – notably Midway Lady, who won the 1000 Guineas and the Oaks. But he was not your run of the mill trainer – he was very much his own man, did things his own way, and couldn't care a stuff about what other people thought! He had impeccable standards and was always charming to meet – but impatient, impetuous and intolerant and prone to make decisive and instant decisions in his everyday life, which we all found very entertaining! Being a little vain, he was, and still is, very dapper and the trendiest of dressers – traits he no doubt inherited from his father, Captain Tom Hanbury, who had 80 pairs of shoes and 70 pairs of trousers in his dressing room in Letcombe Bassett – to which I can bear witness!

Ben and I had countless laughs and escapades together – nearly always as a result of the differences in our characters. Out of the blue during kitchen supper early one summer, Ben suggested that I should go with him to the Keeneland Yearling Sales in Kentucky – and the conversation went along these lines. "I have no reason to go, Ben, as I have no yearlings to buy there for my owners," I reply. "You don't need orders, Gavin, you silly arse," he continues. "I've been to Keeneland for the last five years with no orders and have always returned with five horses. All you have to do is stand at the exit to the Sales Ring, looking smart and knowledgeable and wait for one that has not been sold or failed to make its reserve. The wife of the American breeder will be in floods of tears as she rushes to console her pride and joy – you then put a sympathetic arm around her shoulders, tell her that you are in love with her yearling, that you cannot understand why it has not sold and offer to train it for her in Newmarket. It works a treat I can promise you."

I went with Ben to Keeneland, but unlike him came back with nothing. However, I did make the acquaintance of a charming and very wealthy American breeder, who later had horses in training with me.

Skiing is a wonderful sport and going on holiday with the Hanbury family was one of my favourite pastimes. Ben, Chunky, Coral and I were close friends, and on the same wavelength – while Emma and Amanda Hanbury and Rupert and Paddy were likewise. It was always cheap and cheerful – on this occasion in a tiny apartment in Val d'Isère. Being an insomniac, Ben was always up and about at 6am, way before the rest of us. Hair washed, he would then walk up and down the passage outside our bedrooms – dressed only in his brightly coloured Y Fronts with a hairnet over his black curly locks, swivelling a very noisy hair dryer back and forth. Shouting to everyone "time to get up". I like my sleep, and was adamant that I would not be up at "sparrow fart" on holiday, so that we could be the first on the piste at 7am. But that particular morning, Ben had other ideas. He thrust open the door of Coral and my bedroom and upturned our sofa bed into its upright daytime position on the wall. I clambered out bleary eyed and shell shocked only to be dragged by Ben to the downstairs locker room of our chalet, where our skis were kept.

Making no sense and shouted at by Ben, I put on what I thought were my skis – only to find, as we slip-slide down to the chairlift that they obviously belonged to someone else. Too late. I managed, with great difficulty, to get my backside onto the chairlift, now in motion – but, once airborne, and now twenty metres above ground, one of my skis falls off with disastrous results. An irate French male ski-lift attendant stops the lift and shouts up to me. "Sautez, Monsieur, immediatement." I understand what he had said but Ben does not. "What did he say?" enquires Ben belligerently. "He told me to jump off at once, but it is a very long way down, " I reply. In a flash, with no hesitation, Ben pushes me off the chairlift and I land in a large heap of freshly fallen snow, now badly shaken and exceedingly angry. I make my way on foot, skis on my back, past the chairlift and back the 200 metres to our apartment, exhausted and very unhappy.

Meanwhile, Ben arrives back at teatime, having had a blissful day on the mountain, oblivious to my troubles, casually asking me where the hell I had been!

Twelve months later, almost to the day, the Hanburys and P-Gs are due to leave for another skiing holiday in Val d'Isere, when the telephone rings as we are about to go to bed. It is Chunky – with the worst possible news. Ben would not be able to come. He is in excruciating pain and unable to travel. We are heartbroken – but, to our amazement, Ben is at the airport, to greet us, when we arrive, the next morning. No more is said and we have the most wonderful holiday as always. Ben, usually wearing his bright yellow 'canary' skiing suit, is the team leader on the slopes, despite being an erratic and unstylish skier – and takes the most phenomenal falls, which are the highlight of our holiday!

But things begin to deteriorate drastically on the morning of our last day. Ben and I are on a ridiculously long chairlift – I am sometimes accused of exaggerating but I assure you that it takes ten minutes. As we progress, Ben starts to groan, and shuffle from side to side in obvious pain. And it gets decidedly worse, just as we get to the point in our journey, when we are passing over a deep mountainous ravine, fifty metres below us. At this stage, Ben becomes delirious, grabbing me at random, eyes closed and now devoid of his senses. I struggle to calm him down, and restrain him, in vain – now terrified that the two of us will drop to our certain deaths in the ravine below.

However, by the grace of God, we reach the lift station intact. As the chair lift completes its 180-degree rotation, Ben falls flat on his face, and passes out unconscious. I am in a state of panic, but thankfully two uniformed ski paramedics are on hand and straight to their task. They carry and strap Ben to the nearby "blood wagon", the mountain emergency services sledge, put on their skis, and set off, at speed, back down to the village, instructing me to follow. In no time we are at the Medical Centre, where Ben is attended to by doctors – one of whom comes out to tell me that I should contact Ben's next of kin immediately. I take the cable car to the Mountain Restaurant, in which we had planned to meet for lunch – and wait for Chunky, who arrives half an hour later. Just as I am updating her about Ben's dramatic collapse and explaining that she is required urgently at the Medical Centre – we see a man skiing down past the restaurant, in a bright yellow "canary" ski suit. I think that it must have been a ghost – but, to our amazement, and relief, it is Ben!

It later transpires that Ben had been suffering from a very painful kidney stone prior to our holiday. Determined that this should not stop him skiing he had asked his local doctor to give him a very strong and expensive medication to anaesthetise the pain for the duration of the holiday. This then wore off as we were sitting together on the chairlift – and the timing could not have been more critical.

To complete the story, being brave, instantaneous and resourceful, Ben, when lying on the examination table, instructed the doctor to give him a repeat of his magical pain killing injection for which he must have paid a fortune. He did – and the rest is history.

Life with Ben Hanbury is never dull.

37.
Coral

To borrow a racing analogy, Coral was very true to her pedigree and indeed to her roots. Knowing a little bit about her father, Paddy Harbord – very sadly I never met him – but more about her mother, Leila, I can state with confidence, that Coral inherited her personality and her many attributes from her two parents. And these traits were further enhanced by being bred and brought up in the vibrant culture and delightful countryside of the County of Kildare in southern Ireland.

Coral was buoyant, bubbly and immensely energetic – and loved the company of others from all walks in life. She worried about them and cared for them – whatever their background or rank. She was always busy, active, never stopped working, and nothing was too much trouble. She had an infectious sense of humour – and the ability to make people laugh.

Above all, Coral was a wonderful mother to our sons, Rupert and Paddy. They came first in her life – and their health, welfare and happiness were paramount. She was strict with them and at pains to stress the importance of good manners – but was a permanent source of encouragement and always there for them, if something was amiss.

Paddy Harbord, who suffered at the hands of the Japanese in the Second World War, started the Curragh Bloodstock Agency in Newbridge – while Leila for her part was a trainer's daughter, sister to legendary National Hunt jockey, Aubrey Brabazon, and herself one of the most accomplished horsewomen in Ireland. So it was no surprise that Coral was a very competent rider, wanting to follow in their footsteps and involve herself in racing. She became the ultimate trainer's wife – brilliant with owners, but equally concerned with and considerate to my staff. She was a superb hostess, both at Shalfleet and Fairway, the invitations to breakfast, lunch, dinner or to stay, were like gold dust – and the perfect "mother hen" to my staff, overseeing the day-to-day running of the Hostel and responsible for the welfare and general requirements of our young apprentice jockeys. Our joint aims, as trainer and trainer's wife, were first, to have success for our owners – but secondly, to ensure that they enjoyed their overall owning experience. Coral rode out every morning with our string, travelled with me to the races, helped entertain the owners, and was there for the party, as well. It was essentially a partnership, and we had a load of fun and laughs along the line.

One day, we were driving to Yarmouth Races, very late setting off and stopped at traffic lights in Acle. Where there were two lanes, one for straight on, the other to turn right. As I look up from my newspaper, sitting in the passenger's seat, I notice that Coral is in the right-hand lane – and advise her quietly that there is a police car on our inside, ahead of five other cars, which should have been our point of direction. To my horror, as the lights turn to amber, Coral puts her foot hard down on the accelerator, leaving the police car standing, thus compounding her faux pas by far exceeding the 30mph speed limit in the village of Acle – and going even faster on the open country road ahead. No doubt mesmerised by Coral's antics, it takes the police car a couple of miles to catch us up, lights now flashing and sirens full on. I am now horror-struck , shouting at her to slow down – but Coral is oblivious to my advice, retorting defiantly "who is that bloody 'ediot' behind us, flashing his lights, I've not done anything wrong."

The car chase continues for another three miles, until the police car eventually overtakes us and steers us onto the hard shoulder of the road. To my further amazement, as the policeman exits his vehicle with intent, pencil and notebook in hand, Coral jumps from our car, and runs to confront him, gesticulating wildly, and shouting abuse.

As the confrontation ensues, the policeman appears to backtrack and accede, returning his pencil and notebook to his top pocket – at the same time looking closely at my tax disc on the windscreen and my Trainers' Car Park sticker beside. "Good Luck today at Yarmouth," he says with a smile, "I hope you have a winner."

As Coral gets back into the car, I enquire gingerly about her conversation with the policeman. "He asked me why I had been in the right-hand lane at the traffic lights, when actually intending to go straight on. I told him categorically that I was Irish, on holiday in the country for a week – and that there were no traffic lights in Ireland," she replied.

The luck of the Irish – they have a devil-may-care charm.

*

All horse related sports were close to Coral's heart and had precedence over any others. She took an interest in cricket and boxing, but professional football and rugby did not cut the ice. Not fathoming the ethos, rules and nuances of the two sports and bracketing the two together.

Violence at professional football matches in the Seventies and Eighties was rife, and very worrying – so, when I informed Coral that I was taking Rupert, then only six years old, to the England vs Scotland rugby match at Twickenham, she was angry, upset and in total disagreement. Being totally unaware that the International Rugby crowds were always good natured and that there was never any trouble. However, come the day, I am on edge, trusting that all would go to plan and deciding to arrive early when few people were about. Safely into the stadium, an hour before kick-off, I steer Rupert to the end of our row of seats where, to my horror, I spy this giant of a man, at least 6 foot 6 inches tall, who is scheduled to sit next to my eldest son. He is clad in tartan kilt, sporran and tam o'shanter, a bottle of whisky in one hand, and vodka in the other, swaying precariously, back and forth, very much the worse for wear. I introduce him to Rupert, in trepidation, and pray for a miracle. "Hello Rupert," he replies in his strong Glasgow accent. "It is great to meet you and your father – my name is Jock, and I am very drunk. I have been in London for the past two nights, and never been to bed. I have come here to Twickenham today to see the Scots put the English to the sword and to enjoy every minute of the massacre." Rupert turns pale, understandably terrified and fiercely indignant – but it soon becomes apparent that Jock has a heart of gold and a wonderful sense of humour. The two begin to chat and become friends, discussing at length the relative merits of the two teams, and the action that will shortly take place on the pitch. Minutes before the start of the match, Jock takes out his handkerchief and offers it to Rupert, remarking "You are going to need this young man, because when the boys in dark blue put the ball behind the England try line, you are going to cry." "Oh, no, I am not," replies Rupert. "You will want to use it more than me, because England are going to win."

It is a pulsating and high-scoring match, resulting in a 34–22 victory for England – the handkerchief passing relentlessly from Jock to Rupert, and back again, for the duration. Much to my relief. At the end of the match, I thank Jock for being so kind and attentive to Rupert, and explain Coral's concern that he might be trampled upon, and crushed, by the exiting supporters. Jock immediately picks Rupert up, puts him on his shoulders, and they make a triumphant descent to ground-floor level, together. Safely, thank God!

I will never forget that day – and nor will Rupert.

*

In today's world, safety, security and surveillance are vital at all international airports – and quite rightly so. We might curse about the long queues and tedious body searches but this has to be done, for sure. It was not the case in my day, when flying in a commercial aeroplane was a pleasure – you just handed your ticket and passport to the lovely girl at the departure check in, were shown to your comfortable seat, and given a three-course lunch!

Coral's paternal grandmother, Mitzie, lived in the latter years of her life in a retirement home near Sudbury in Suffolk. And, when she died, it transpired that she had left instructions that she should be cremated in Suffolk. But that her ashes should be buried in County Kildare, alongside the rest of her family.

Only days after the service in the crematorium, I am scheduled to fly to Ireland for the Yearling Sales and Coral asks me, very reasonably, whether I could take the casket of ashes with me in my luggage. I show my willingness immediately, wanting to give support at a sad time to Coral's family, and set off for Heathrow Airport, looking forward to four days of fun, at Goffs Sales. On arrival, I hand my suitcase to the girl at the check in desk – when to my horror, every alarm and siren in the building is triggered. Chaos reigns, and I am surrounded by a swarm of security men, who pin me to the nearest wall. It is a terrifying experience for me and probably for my fellow passengers – who now fear the worst. My suitcase is examined and ripped open – and there of course is the metal urn, with Mitzie's ashes inside, lurking innocently beneath my shirts, sweaters and underwear. I am dragged away, interrogated at length and given a severe reprimand, but, surprise, surprise, in hindsight, I am allowed to proceed to Dublin with the metal urn. That would not have happened today. I would have been arrested and locked up on the spot.

Mitzie would have laughed all the way to heaven – but for me it was disturbingly unfunny!

*

I consider myself to be quite proficient at geography, and to have an awareness of the massive range of daytime temperatures around the world but got it all very wrong in one particular instance.

It is mid-January and Coral and I are on a cheapy winter holiday in Barbados, when we are invited by Chris and Anne Hurt, generous owners of mine, to spend a night with them in New York on our way back to London. We accept with alacrity, having not thought things through, nor studied a map! It is 28 degrees in Barbados, when we leave, but as we land in New York it is minus 10 degrees! Our only holiday clothes are shorts, swimming trunks and t-shirts – and, to make matters worse, there is an ongoing "garbage" strike in New York.

Chris and Anne have very kindly arranged a very exciting evening schedule for us, and, having hurriedly purchased some cold weather apparel, we make ourselves at home in our fabulously comfortable high-rise hotel in readiness for the fray. We are treated to the latest production at the New York Opera House, much coveted by all opera fans and then taken to the world-famous 21 Club for dinner. It is a very spoiling experience and we go back to bed very happy on the 14th storey of the hotel at 1am.

Thirty minutes later, Coral jumps out of bed, shouting "I can swear that there is smoke in our room." I tell her to get back into bed, turn over and go to sleep. Not long after, Coral repeats her nocturnal acrobatics, and we turn on the bedside lights – and, lo and behold, there is smoke in the room and quite dense. I ring reception to be told that there is a fire on our floor, but that it is being dealt with, not to panic and remain in our room. I stumble, with difficulty, to the bedroom window and look down to street level, where there is a cavalcade of police cars, fire engines and ambulances, all congregated together. It is very frightening – and

Coral has a tendency to panic, in these situations. Her first concern is for her Irish passport, which I promptly stress is irrelevant in the circumstances – and she then proceeds to throw her towel in a bath of cold water, thinking that this might aid her escape, if covering her head. At this stage, now in desperation, she flounders her way through the smoke to the bedroom door, and opens it – and is immediately thrown back in by a very large yellow-helmeted New York fireman, who gives her very clear and firm instructions.

"Stay in your room young lady and do what you are told. We know what we are doing." It is now 2:30am and we are terrified. Half an hour later, Reception rings us, to say that the fire has been put out. So, there should be no further alarm. Despite this assertion, we cannot sleep, and as dawn breaks over New York we peer out of our bedroom door to see that the room next to us has been completely burnt out to a cinder.

Later that morning, as we are about to leave, we are approached by the Hotel Manager, who offers us his profound apologies for the nightmare scenario that we had experienced. Assuring us that every room in the hotel is self-contained, and that, in theory, a fire should not spread further. The only reason that smoke had filled our room was that it had escaped through the hot and cold water pipes that surrounded and serviced our floor of the hotel.

I have not been back to New York since and have no intention to do so. Those stench-ridden streets, piled up with garbage, large rats crawling over them, were not a good advertisement – nor was our night from hell in the high-rise hotel!

*

I have had numerous embarrassing experiences in my life, but this one must count as one of the worst.

I was asked to play cricket one July Sunday for Edmund Vestey, a long-standing owner of mine – who owned a large estate in Suffolk – at Ashdon, between Saffron Walden and Haverhill. His President's Eleven were pitted against the Village, who were notoriously enthusiastic cricketers. That evening, I had also been invited to give a talk about Racing to boys and their parents at Old Buckenham School, some distance east of Lavenham, and 30 miles approximately from Ashdon. It all looked perfectly feasible and I was looking forward to an action-packed day. Before accepting, I glanced briefly at my map, surmising that combining the two events should be no problem, despite the journey being all the way across country and being confined to small B roads.

Although mid-summer, it was a horrible, wet, filthy day – and, dare I say, had it not been the President's match, play might not have taken place. The wicket was sodden, the turf slippery, and the outfield under pools of water – not ideal, but the decision was made to play. The village batted first, and I fell over several times in a vain attempt to stop the village big-hitters from scoring yet more boundaries – my cricket trousers, shirt and boots now soaking wet and covered in mud. It was an all-day game, and late morning I was thrilled to see Coral arrive at the ground, in her little car, with Rupert and Paddy, whom she had collected from school for their Sunday out. They were excited and joined the two teams for lunch – a welcome change from school food, no doubt – and had fun and games despite the horrible weather.

Later in the day, when the President's Eleven batted, I asked Edmund if I could be one of the first to perform, given that I wanted to be sure of making a prompt getaway to drive to Old Buckenham. Coming to the wicket, after a dozen or so overs, when one of our two opening batsmen was dismissed, I am a very moderate batsman, but because I was now partnering a former county cricketer and superb batsman, who hogged the bowling, I faced very little of the bowling, and our partnership flourished. Which was good and also bad news, if you see what I mean – as by now time was ticking fast, and I had my eyes firmly on the pavilion clock. This rapidly became more of a concern – and, finally, a total disaster, when I saw Coral leaving the ground, with Rupert and Paddy waving a fond goodbye, but this time in my car. In which I had my dry clothes – blazer, shirt, tie, trousers and shoes – and my map, and vitally, my notes that I had made for the talk on racing at Old Buckenham. In desperation, I manage to run myself out, jump into Coral's car and drive – not having a clue where I am going, and unable to communicate with anyone, as there were no mobile phones in those days. And no sat nav, needless to say. It is the journey from hell. It should have taken one hour, but instead two – and I arrive at Old Buckenham, at long last, at 7:15pm. Having agreed to be there at 6:30pm. As I turn into the drive of the school, the Headmaster is waiting for me, fuming with rage and shouts out "Are you Gavin Pritchard-Gordon? if so you should have been here three quarters of an hour ago. There are 200 boys and their parents in the Sports Hall, all waiting patiently for you. Follow me." We hurtle up the drive, park and sprint across to the entrance to the Sports Hall. "What the hell do you look like, young man – you are a disgrace. I wish that I had never asked you to speak," he exclaims. He introduces me to the audience, now mightily surprised and angry, who stare, in astonishment, at their designated speaker, dressed in filthy white cricket trousers, shirt and boots.

I make a hesitant start, apologising for my appearance, and for being so late, trying to explain, without success, what had happened. Concluding that my only chance was to try and ad lib what I had previously prepared. Given the circumstances, it goes surprisingly well – but, after 15 minutes I come to a grinding halt, with no crib sheet to help me. My only "get out of hell" tactic being to ask the audience whether there are any questions, thus far. The saints are with me, hundreds of hands are raised, and I am back in the driving seat, confident that I could answer the majority of questions on what is supposedly my specialist subject.

My confidence, previously battered, begins to grow – to the extent that I keep putting to the back of the queue the little boy sitting right in front of me, with long spiky hair and thick spectacles, who has his hand up, without flagging, for ten minutes, waiting for his opportunity. "Have you heard of Baileys Horse Feeds, Sir, and do you give them to your horses?" he demands eventually with purpose. I respond in the negative, which turns out to be a serious mistake. "Well you jolly well should do, Sir, because my Daddy makes them. I will write to him tomorrow and tell him to contact you," he states very proudly.

It was a memorable and match-winning comment, for an eight-year-old boy, who exuded patience, self-confidence, business acumen, and devotion to his father and his business. It brought a smile to my face, against all the odds, on what had been a long and traumatic day.

There was always something going on in those heady days.

38.
Divorce

At that time everything at Stanley House Stables and Fairway appeared to be going with a swing – but, unbeknownst to me, large dark storm clouds were gathering, which would change the course of my life. It was a massive shock, and a bitter blow, when Coral told me that she was packing her bags, leaving the family home, and moving into a house on the other side of Newmarket with my friend and fellow trainer, Michael Stoute. Leaving two racing families living only 200 yards apart on the Bury Road distraught and in tatters. It was a very public divorce – not only did it stun the town of Newmarket – it also made headlines in the national Racing Press, and also in the gossip columns of Nigel Dempster in the *Daily Mail* and William Hickey in the *Daily Express*.

As a result, Stanley House Stables and Fairway had to go on the market, because for tax purposes, Coral was a partner in the business. Being a fine, prestigious and much sought-after property there was a great deal of interest – from Sheikh Mohammed in particular. However, being in a dejected frame of mind and aware that there would be vast capital-gains implications, I was very stubborn and difficult to deal with in regards to price. That did not endear me to the Maktoum family, or help my training career, once a deal with Sheikh Mohammed was done.

I was never the same man again – and my career as a trainer suffered enormously. I did my best to hold my head up high – but it was a very sad and difficult chapter in my life.

39.
Graham Place/Trillium Place

I have to admit, when Coral departed and Stanley House Stables were sold, I was in two minds about my future. Whether to carry on training or not? But, in the end, it was my pride and the input and support of my family, friends, staff and owners that persuaded me to continue. To make matters worse, there were no Newmarket Racing Stables on the market at the time – and, furthermore, any trainer who might be persuaded to sell would see me coming! Ultimately, it was Bill O'Gorman, who trained at Graham Place Stables on Birdcage Walk, who came to my rescue – and a deal was done. On the basis that he would build himself a new yard, on the Hamilton Road, on his departure.

The house at Graham Place was a decent size, attractive, and comfortable, and the yard in good condition – but there was still plenty to be done, if it was to be a suitable replacement for Stanley House Stables and Fairway. More boxes had to be built, along with accommodation for some of my staff – and I also considered a new covered Indoor Ride to be essential. This all took time to achieve – and I will always be eternally grateful to Jockey Club Estates who very kindly allowed me to stable my horses in the Racecourse stables at the Links in the interim.

Once the building works were complete, my horses were installed at Graham Place – which I renamed Trillium Place, in memory of my dear little first winner. I remember being told that this was unlucky but took no notice in the hope that this might have the opposite effect, given my predicament!

Needless to say, Trillium Place was a far cry from Stanley House Stables, but it presented a new challenge and was the beginning of a new chapter in my life. It seemed strange to be training on the other side of town next to the Rowley Mile Racecourse after being twice on the Bury Road, but we soon adapted. My horses, staff and owners were happy – and I was greatly heartened when Rupert and Paddy elected to live with me at Trillium Place when not away at boarding school.

*

Noalcoholic, Ardoon and Record Run were the best horses that I trained – but, the three for whom I have the most personal affection were Trillium, Gulfland and Shadow Bird. As my first and hundredth winner, little Trillium will always have a special place in my heart while Gulfland became an equine superstar in his own right. And a soft spot will be reserved for Shadow Bird.

Gulfland was a bargain basement chestnut yearling purchase at Doncaster for Lord Cadogan. By Gulf Pearl, and not fashionably bred, he was good looking, honest, with a very lovable personality. He was a fun horse for Lord Cadogan at two and three but injured himself quite seriously in his first race over hurdles at Huntingdon. He was very lame afterwards, having fractured a bone in his knee, and the prognosis for his racing future was not optimistic. My vet recommended an operation to remove the chip, but Lord Cadogan was not to be thus persuaded. Instead, he donated the horse to me to do what I wished – and gave me an order to buy a replacement. What a gentleman.

Against all the odds, Gulfland made a full recovery from his knee operation, and went on to win eleven races for me, in my colours, and my partners Sir John Mowbray, Peter Philipps and Lavinia Robinson. Gulfland gave four different riders their first ever winner. They were two of my apprentices, Mark Rimmer and Abigail Richards, Rupert P-G and the Princess Royal – and for the record, Abigail went on to ride Gulfland to win the Norwegian St. Leger in Oslo.

As you might expect, Rupert's first win on Gulfland, at Pontefract, was a red-letter day – a very long one for me, but worth every minute. At the time, Rupert was a boarder at Radley College, between Oxford and Abingdon, and only given permission by his Housemaster to be away from college for the day – so, my only option was to drive from Newmarket to Radley to collect him, take him to Pontefract and return him afterwards in time for his prep! Everything went to plan, Gulfland won in a photo finish – and Rupert was presented with his trophy by the then Lord (Stoker) Hartington. It was an enormously exciting, happy and emotional day. After the race, Rupert fell asleep in the back of my car and only woke up when I stopped at the motorway services on the M40 to give him a Coke and a sausage roll. "Thank you so much, Dad," he uttered, bleary eyed. "It has been amazing, riding my first winner on "Gulfie" in your colours. But who was that bald-headed old bugger who gave me the trophy?". "That was the future Duke of Devonshire, Rupert," I replied authoritatively. "And you will treasure that photograph, later in life."

I first met the Princess Royal when I was staying for the Cheltenham Festival with David and Dinah Nicholson in Condicote. In the course of conversation, she asked whether I could give her some rides on the flat, and I was happy to oblige. She came to Newmarket to ride out regularly at both Stanley House Stables and Trillium Place. She was very popular with my staff, always remembering their names, which meant so much to them. Already a consummate all-round horsewoman, the Princess Royal soon became an accomplished amateur rider – and her victory on Gulfland at Redcar was her first on a racecourse. It was also the first time that a member of the Royal Family had ridden a Flat Race winner since Charles II at Newmarket in 1674 – and that made headline news in all the national newspapers the following morning.

Wednesday the 5th of August. 1986, will go down in history – it was a very memorable day for everyone associated with Racing. We are so fortunate to be able to enjoy the Royal Patronage of our great sport – and long may it continue.

At the end of his long and distinguished racing career I gave Gulfland to the British Racing School in Newmarket – where he was loved, treasured and cared for by their loyal staff and many aspiring young jockeys alike. An honourable retirement and just reward for his many achievements.

Bred by Whitsbury Stud in Hampshire, Shadow Bird was a good-looking and very honest bay filly, who gave Paddy P-G the first of his twenty five Flat winners under rules. Paddy was also the first recipient of the Bollinger Trophy for Amateur Riders at the age of seventeen – no mean feat. It gave me enormous pleasure to train winners ridden by Rupert and Paddy – and one day at Ascot will always stand out from the rest.

I had two runners in the amateur riders race, the last on the card – Parking Bay, ridden by Rupert, and Shadow Bird, by Paddy. Parking Bay, owned by Lord Cadogan, who had won previously for Rupert at Haydock, is the favourite for the race – whilst Shadow Bird, who belonged to an enthusiastic syndicate in Norfolk, is one of the outsiders. It is a mile and a half race, and quite soon after the start, I realise that Parking Bay is making heavy weather and not going to win. I put down my race glasses in abject disappointment – when, just before the entrance to the straight, a friend standing next to me, gives me a nudge and exclaims excitedly "Paddy is going very well on Shadow Bird – see for yourself." Indeed he was – and despite our lowly expectations he wins the race to the delight of Andy Don and his jubilant team of Norfolk owners. Rupert is understandably despondent – but equally thrilled for his younger brother. After the joyous celebrations, I drive the two boys back to Radley, where they are greeted and treated as heroes by one and all.

Nurturing and supporting the respective riding careers of my two sons was the best possible tonic after a torrid time in my life – and it helped enormously to reignite and reinvigorate my enthusiasm for training racehorses.

40.
Yorkshire and Garrowby

Hand on heart, despite being Sussex born and bred, my most favourite county in this country is Yorkshire. I like everything about it – its cities, its varied countryside and its inhabitants. Yorkshire folks are friendly, down to earth, and not frightened to speak their minds, which is very refreshing. They adore their racing with a passion – and know about and understand horses.

For the record, if I had runners declared on any particular day at racecourses in Yorkshire and south of London, I always chose to go to the former. The courses were diverse and different in many respects – but had one common denominator. You were assured of a fun day out when a warm welcome, hospitality and competitive racing were a constant thread.

Pride of place will of course go to York, which is one of the finest racecourses in Europe. The atmosphere is electric, people go there to enjoy themselves and the racing is top class. One only has to see the hundreds of local enthusiasts walking on a race day from the centre of the city to the Knavesmire to appreciate how besotted Yorkshire people are about their racing. The Spring and August meetings are the pinnacle, but there are many others besides. In my day, John Sanderson was Clerk of the Course and a master of his craft. As a trainer, nothing was too much trouble for him or his staff – and I was lucky enough to be invited to stay sometimes in his house, close by the racecourse.

Doncaster is a magnificent racecourse too – and it was very handy to be able to combine racing with sales at DBS. "Donny" has its own atmosphere and charm – and, like York, its inhabitants are very proud of their racecourse. It is a very fair and galloping track, where the only Classic north of the Trent, the St. Leger, is staged every year.

However, I was equally happy to go to the smaller Yorkshire courses, which attracted a loyal and knowledgeable crowd of regular racegoers. Having trained three Zetland Gold Cup winners, I was made very welcome at Redcar – and Lord (Mark) Ronaldshaye (now Lord Zetland) became an owner of mine.

In my day, Lord (Christy) Grimthorpe was Chairman at Thirsk, and rang me, without fail, at breakfast if he saw that I had a runner. He invited me for lunch, and insisted that I sit next to him to find out whether my horses were fit and fancied and to have a wager, if so. That might have been frowned upon in today's world!

Ripon is a delightful little racecourse in stunning countryside – while trainers and their horses were very well cared for at Beverley, by the Clerk of the Course, John Cleverly. "Cleverly from Beverley" being his regular mode of introduction when meeting those who did not know him. As an aside, my digs for Beverley were with great friends, Bob and Mima Urquhart, at Hunsley House Stud, only a few miles away – where we had many a riotous night.

My record at Catterick, over the years, was not overly impressive, but I liked to have runners there if I considered that they would handle the notorious bends and undulations. And, to mitigate any disappointment, later in the day, lunch before racing at the Black Bull in Moulton was outstanding. An added attraction was a night spent with my loveable fellow trainer Billy Watts and his bubbly wife Pat in nearby Richmond, if I had a runner in Yorkshire, the following day.

Only weeks after I sold Stanley House Stables to Sheikh Mohammed, I was somewhat surprised to receive a telephone call from Lord ("Ernie") Halifax – congratulating me on the sale, and inviting me to stay with him and Lady (Camilla) Halifax at Garrowby, one of the finest houses, estates and stud farms in Yorkshire, for the following year's August meeting at York. Needless to say, I jumped at the opportunity – as it was an honour and a privilege to be included in such an illustrious house party and to experience the spoiling and splendour. It is not often that you have your suitcase unpacked for you by a valet!

Amongst my fellow guests were Ian and Emma Balding – and John Warren, then the Queen's Racing Manager at that stage, with his lovely wife Carolyn, herself an expert on all aspects of racing and breeding. Also part of our team at Garrowby was one Geoffrey Gibbs, a Handicapper for the Jockey Club – who, when not doing his "day job" was a talented garden designer, advising well-heeled members of the Jockey Club, when staying in their elegant houses, and partaking of their hospitality. Geoffrey was, and still is, one of the funniest men I have ever met – and can be totally outrageous at times. Quick-witted, opinionated and forthright, Geoffrey loves a good argument – and used to take delight in remonstrating on Sunday mornings with irate trainers, who rang to complain to him about their horse's handicap ratings. He only has one eye, which is off-putting to other people, but not to him – he just carries on regardless and cares not one jot.

It was a particularly hot and humid summer and that August meeting at York was a real scorcher. Every evening we had dinner, wearing black tie and dinner jackets, in the large dining room at Garrowby – at a long rectangular table, around which, at intervals, stood uniformed "flunkies" – referred to by the Collins Concise English Dictionary as "liveried manservants". On our second evening, the heat in the dining room became unbearable – and there was a passionate request from guests around the table for the gentlemen to be able to remove their coats. This was politely refused by Lord Halifax – but, at the third time of asking, and now with the support of Lady Halifax, our kind host relented, albeit a little disgruntled.

When the command was given, the gentlemen started this removal, helped now by the somewhat surprised flunkies standing behind them. Six of the seven coats were removed successfully – but Geoffrey's was not. As he swung his right arm rearwards with great gusto, there was a loud and ominous sound of a violent rip – as the sleeve of his very ancient dress shirt took leave of its body.

Geoffrey was not bothered in the slightest, now offering his second coat arm for removal. To our delight, there was an exact repetition – which left our hero, sitting in his shirt, his arms bared but totally oblivious to his plight. Perfectly happy to remain thus attired until his bedtime!

Happy memories of Yorkshire!

41.
NH Jockeys – The Bravest of The Brave

National Hunt Jockeys are the warriors of our great sport, risking their lives every time they are legged up to ride over fences or hurdles. In days of old, the likes of Terry Biddlecombe, Bob Champion, Stan Mellor, Jeff King, Josh Gifford, and David Nicholson were fearless riders – taking the most crucifying falls and giving their bodies an unmerciful battering. And they lived life to the full after racing. They were renowned party animals – and many were the times that they arrived at the course, next day, still feeling the effects of a late-night session. For the record, there was no testing of jockeys for alcohol, in those days – which, in hindsight, was a mixed blessing.

The next generation of National Hunt Jockeys were equally brave and fearless – but more regulated and aware of the risks they took on a daily basis. Amongst these were Johnny Francome, Peter Scudamore, Richard Dunwoody, Jonjo O'Neill and Steve Smith-Eccles.

I only trained four or five jumpers each year but loved every minute – in fairness, it was a lot more relaxed than the flat. From the outset of my training career, David Nicholson was my National Hunt jockey – but when he retired, and started training, I befriended Steve Smith-Eccles, who lived in Newmarket and rode for Tom Jones (Harry Thomson Jones), after David Mould and Ian Watkinson, to whom he had been apprenticed. Steve was never Champion Jockey, but always in the top flight of National Hunt riders – he struck up a memorable partnership with the hugely talented two-mile chaser Tingle Creek, for Tom Jones, and won the Champion Hurdle at Cheltenham three times for Nicky Henderson on See You Then.

From the start of his career, Steve, the son of a Derbyshire miner, was the ultimate professional, having been given a great start by

Tom Jones. He was polite, punctual, well dressed, with an astute brain, and very courteous with owners. He was not the most stylish of jockeys – but very strong and effective, especially in a finish. And also a very accomplished schooler of young horses. As a man, he was charismatic and flamboyant with a devilish sense of humour and fun. An avid party person – who considers himself to be very much the ladies man. When describing "The Ecc", the expressions "lovable rogue" and "cheeky chappie" come immediately to mind!

At Aintree, one year in the late Seventies, Steve was riding the second favourite in the Grand National, Classified, for which he was receiving a lot of media attention. He and his girlfriend, Di Haine, were staying at the Royal Hotel in Southport, and had dinner after racing on the Thursday night, when a host of owners, trainers and jockeys were in attendance. The party was soon in full swing – Di sensibly deciding to go to bed at a reasonable hour, locking her bedroom door, and leaving Steve to enjoy himself.

In the early hours of the morning, Steve stumbles his way back to his bedroom but soon twigs that he is locked out. The only option, he concludes, being to sleep the rest of the night in the back of his Mercedes, which is parked just outside the entrance to the hotel. In minutes, he is in the land of nod – but, not long after, he wakes up in shock and panic, in certain knowledge that his car is in motion, and travelling exceedingly fast, on a motorway, somewhere in the vicinity of Liverpool. Driven by a teenage Liverpudlian urchin, who unaware of his sleeping passenger, has gleefully hot wired Steve's pride and joy. He spies Steve in his driving mirror, thinks he has seen a ghost, slews the car off the motorway, onto the hard shoulder – and runs off into the open countryside never to be seen again.

Needless to say, Steve is in a hairy predicament – aware that no right-minded policeman is going to believe his story and that he has had a great deal to drink in the hotel during the evening. Knowing that he is now between a rock and a hard place, deciding that the lesser of the two evils is to drive himself back to the hotel in Southport – despite being totally unaware of his precise whereabouts. Luck is on his side, he returns safely to the Royal, slots back into his previous parking space, and sleeps the rest of the night in the back of the car, undisturbed.

On the Friday afternoon, Steve wins the first race at Aintree and is interviewed for the BBC by David Coleman – to whom his fellow jockeys have now recounted his infamous escapade. In truth, it is a brilliant story which makes headlines in every national newspaper on Saturday morning – but, sadly, there is to be no fairy tale ending. Steve finishes third on Classified – but this unthinkable experience now has its place in Racing's folklore.

42.
More about National Hunt Racing and SSE

In the Seventies and Eighties, the breeding of National Hunt horses was still geared more toward stamina than to speed. Breeders of National Hunt horses in this country sent their mares to stoutly bred stallions, the Irish provided us with a mass of similarly bred "stores", while French-bred jumpers were still in short supply. Flat-bred horses were considered to be more suited to two miles, over hurdles and fences – the pinnacle for National Hunt Horses still being the Cheltenham Gold Cup over three miles.

The tactic for my very small team of jumpers was to pick out a handful of scopey three-year-olds, and get them schooled in July, over railway sleepers and small hurdles on the Links Schooling Ground, which used to be the old National Hunt Racecourse in Newmarket. The facilities were top class, and it was only used by three or four of the trainers in town. For many years, Tom Jones had it all to himself and was extremely successful. If these "babies" showed an aptitude for jumping, we would then aim them at the early three-year-old Hurdle races in August and September – when the larger National Hunt stables were not fully tuned up. This proved to be a very rewarding ploy – King Pele, Corraggio, Peer Prince and Golden Vow being four of the best three-year-olds we ran over hurdles in those days.

For some strange reason, some horses that show very little ability on the flat, go on to excel themselves over hurdles if they prove to be natural and fluent jumpers. One such was a grey gelding, whose name escapes me, belonging to a young new owner, well regarded in the City of London. His form on the flat was moderate, but having schooled promisingly, I suggest that we should take him to

Fontwell for his first outing over hurdles, where he would be given a confidence boosting introduction.

Steve Smith-Eccles is booked to ride, and we travel down together to West Sussex, my county of origin, in my car, with a driver – on the assumption that we might return to Newmarket, via London, for a spot of dinner after racing. It is a lovely late August day, and, as we are going over the Dartford Bridge, I hear Steve in the back of the car on his telephone, obviously chatting to a lady friend. "Hello darling," says Steve. "Would you fancy a bit of lunch at Fontwell races this afternoon?" The answer must have been in the affirmative, as he then continues the conversation. "That's great, darling – catch up shortly. Make your way to the Owners and Trainers Car Park, and I will see you there. "

An hour later, as we park, a gorgeous looking blonde (let's call her Delilah), in an open-topped white Mercedes sport, pulls up beside us. We go for lunch in the Owners and Trainers Restaurant and have a fun time – until, after the fourth race, I quietly suggest to Steve that he goes to the Weighing Room to change into his riding gear for the last race. To which he replies, somewhat taken aback, "Well, okay, but I am not leaving Delilah with you!" But that is his only option in reality.

To our surprise and delight, our horse runs a blinder – beaten into second place in a photo finish. My wealthy young owners are jubilant, and we all retire to the bar – it is as if they have won the Grand National. It is a lengthy and very happy celebration – and, as we are about to leave the racecourse, my ecstatic owners invite Steve, Delilah and me to dinner in London. After which we go on to Tramp nightclub – Delilah still in tow, eventually arriving back at Trillium Place in Newmarket at 4am.

At this stage, Delilah is exceedingly concerned and agitated, understandably so – it transpires that she is an air stewardess, whom Steve had befriended the previous week at Plumpton, who lives in Brighton. And that she must be at Gatwick Airport, for her flight to Corfu at midday.

Purely by chance, Lady Luck comes to Steve's rescue. It suddenly dawns on me that I have a horse running that day at Brighton – and that Eddie, my Travelling Head Lad, is driving him there in our little horsebox. As Steve and Delilah leave the yard, I shout out "make sure that you are both back here at Trillium Place by 6:30am. Important."

Steve and Delilah return on the dot at 6:30am, just as Eddie is about to depart for Brighton, with our horse and its lad. "Hold on Eddie," I exclaim. "You have another passenger – with two legs and not four. Delilah lives in Brighton and would be extremely grateful for a lift home."

Everything goes to plan, and Delilah gets to Gatwick Airport on time – having completed a very swift turnaround in her little flat in Brighton.

It had been a whirlwind 24 hours – talk about tales of the unexpected.

43.
Racing at Perth

Lord Cadogan's London home was in Chelsea, where he had very extensive property and business investments – and he also had a magnificent house and estate, called Snaigow, near Perth. He was a very kind and generous man, and from the outset of my training career, I had an open invitation to go and stay with him in Perthshire if ever in the vicinity. This was always going to be a long shot, given that my travelling to racecourses took me the length and breadth of England – but only to Ayr, Hamilton Park and Musselburgh in Scotland. Racing north of Glasgow and Edinburgh was not usually on my agenda.

But this all changed one spring when Lord Cadogan suggested that we might run his four-year-old filly in a Novice Hurdle race at the Perth Spring Meeting – and to stay for a couple of nights at Snaigow. I booked SSE to ride the filly, and told him to find accommodation in the town of Perth – but, two days before setting off, he had failed miserably to make any arrangements, very cheekily suggesting to me that I might ask Lord Cadogan whether he could join me at Snaigow. I was not best pleased, but, against my will, acceded to his request – Lord Cadogan very kindly agreeing, and emphasising that he would be delighted to entertain my National Hunt jockey, on one of his rare visits to Perth, where he was Chairman of the racecourse.

Our filly finishes third in the second race, which is pleasing – but, as this is Steve's only ride of the day at Perth, he has plenty of time to down three or four drams of something strong, before he leaves the racecourse with me at 5:30pm. On arrival at Snaigow, I emphasise to Steve that he is to be on his best behaviour in such exalted company – but, to my horror, as we reach the top of the impressive flight of steps, leading up to the house, he gives a massive hug to Lady Cadogan, who was perhaps expecting a more formal welcome!

At dinner, in black tie and dinner jackets, when the great and the good of Perthshire are assembled, Steve and I are very honoured to be invited to sit either side of Lady Cadogan, at the top of one end of the table. After the first course, Lady Cadogan, a charming hostess with a wonderful sense of humour, turns to me and says "I just love chatting to Steve – he is such fun, and has let fly 24 F..ks already. Would you bet me that I can raise this to fifty by the end of dinner?"

This target is easily surpassed – and when our fellow guests either depart or go to bed, Lord Cadogan and Steve sit by the fire in the drawing room, quaffing their whiskies, putting the world to rights till the early hours of the morning.

Steve is incorrigible, I have to admit. He takes life in his stride, thrives in the company of others and can adapt to any environment.

44.

The Joys of Brighton

I was born and lived the first seven years of my life in Hove. But still consider that I am a Brighton boy, as the two towns are joined at the hip and always treated as one. It was an exciting place to spend one's childhood. For me, it had everything.

Our little house in Prince's Square was only a five minute walk to the sea, where the sea front had an array of attractions to excite youngsters of all ages and keep them amused and happy. There were two piers – the Palace and West – amusement arcades, funfairs, speedboats, an aquarium, pitch and putt and a miniature railway. And ice-cream and candyfloss stalls by the dozen.

In those days, Brighton and Hove Albion were based at the Goldstone Ground in Hove – and I became, and still am, a passionate fan. They played then in the lowly Third Division South – a far cry from the Premier League in which they thrive today. Sussex County Cricket Ground was also in walking distance from home – where I spent many a rapturous day, watching my cricketing heroes, amongst them England players like the Reverend David Sheppard, Hubert Doggart, Robin Marlar, Jim Parks and Alan Oakman. And, for good measure, Brighton Tigers were one of the best Ice Hockey teams in the country.

Brighton had some top-class five-star hotels, notably The Metropole, The Grand and The Albion – and for those in need of culture, there was the Pavilion, made famous by the Prince Regent, theatres, cinemas, and the Lanes, a district known for its antique shops and prestigious restaurants.

And, of course, there was Brighton Racecourse, high up on the Downs, overlooking the sea only a stone's throw from the town centre. Featured by Graham Greene in his novel *Brighton Rock*, about London razor gangs, intrigue and skullduggery. An oval track, the mirror image of Epsom racecourse, which has always been notorious for its undulations, bends and tricky cambers. And, for many years, it boasted a Derby Trial for Epsom – as did Lewes Racecourse, only 15 miles down the road. As a racecourse, it is not everyone's cup of tea – but does make for very exciting racing, where a horse's balance and manoeuvrability are at a premium.

Strangely enough, given my roots, I had very few runners at Brighton – but, on those rare occasions, it brought back happy memories and felt like coming home.

One visit to the racecourse of my birthplace will always come to mind. I had a fancied runner for a splendid lady, let's call her Mrs Chimneypot for now. From a noble family, she was no spring chicken but attractive nonetheless for her years, and she liked to live life to the full. She loved fun, a large drink and cigarettes – and was in fact a chain smoker. And this is why, until then, I refused to have her as a passenger in my car. I simply detested the habit having once been beaten at school for not smoking.

But, on this occasion, I relent – when Mrs Chimneypot promises faithfully, that, if needing a cigarette, we would stop for ten minutes for her to take a puff outside the car.

Our horse runs well, finishes a close second – and we decide to have dinner in the Lanes before returning to Newmarket. Being a Sussex boy, I suggest that we should take the scenic route – and we stop for Mrs Chimneypot's first cigarette of the journey, in a little clearing at the very top of the Sussex Downs. On her return to the car, Mrs Chimneypot is chirpy and upbeat, announcing "I've had a wonderful day, Gavin, thank you – but there is just one more thing I would like to complete it." "I'm very sorry Mrs Chimneypot but I have no chocolate in the car" I reply.

"That is not what I mean, Gavin – I feel like a bloody good F..ck." comes her summary request.

Taken aback, and at a loss for words, I thrust my car into gear, put my foot hard on the accelerator, and hurtle, at great speed, through the byroads of Mid Sussex, which, luckily, I know well.

The morals of the upper classes left much to be desired in that era – opportunism and infidelity went hand in glove.

45.
Pheasant Shooting – Not My Strong Point!

My father was passionate about driven pheasant shooting and very accurate, furthermore – as was his father before him. And so were my brothers Giles and Grant. But I was the odd-man-out and the exception to the laws of family genetics. I had no qualms about the killing of game birds – but was unable to hit the proverbial barn door from ten yards. This was not a problem when I was younger as my incompetence was taken for granted by my family and forgiven. They knew that I would still enjoy the ambience and jollity of the day – and the party afterwards.

However, this inability to shoot straight did me no favours, when I started training in 1972. The reason being that three-quarters of my lovely owners had smart shoots on their estates, to which I was frequently invited. Being kind and considerate people, they were at pains to assure me that my inaccuracy was of no concern to them – but I soon realised that it was of more consequence to their Head Keepers, who regarded me with disappointment and disdain. I had many an embarrassing day's shooting in their exalted company – but two in particular will always stand out.

I was invited to shoot by Lord Walpole at Wolterton Hall in Norfolk – a magnificent house and estate, steeped in the history of this country – and to stay the night before. On arrival, as I parked my humble little car on the sweep of the immaculate driveway in front of the house, I see what I imagine to be Lord Walpole standing at the top of the long flight of stone steps in evening attire. But I prove to be mistaken – it was actually the butler, who descended the steps to greet me. "Mr Pritchard-Gordon, I presume," he announces, "I am delighted to meet you. On behalf of Lord and Lady Walpole, welcome to Wolterton Hall." At this juncture, he proceeds to look closely into my car, before continuing "Mr Pritchard-Gordon, where are your dogs? Guests are expected to bring them when invited to shoot at Wolterton Hall. And, furthermore, a kennel has been made ready, at the rear of the house, which will not now be needed, sadly."

This is not the best start to my overnight stay at Wolterton Hall, but things improve after a few glasses of champagne, with fellow guests before dinner – and a fun but formal feast in their beautiful dining room. As one might imagine, I am now very apprehensive about the next day's shooting – and with good reason as it transpires. The shooting at Wolterton Hall is let to a syndicate of local dignitaries and enthusiasts – but one gun is retained each day by Lord Walpole. He no longer shoots but uses the days to entertain his guests.

At the first drive, standing in the middle of the line of guns, I am bombarded by a multitude of pheasants – likewise at the second, third and fourth drives before lunch. My percentage of birds shot to cartridges expended is abysmal to say the least. It also occurs to me that Lord Walpole might have kept the best gun positions for his trainer – which frustrates, maddens and enrages his syndicate members of course given that they are paying handsomely for their sport.

To make matters worse, my misery is compounded when we go for lunch, again in the dining room at Wolterton Hall. The syndicate members have brought bottles of beer and sandwiches, which they eat sitting around the dining room table – while Lord Walpole, Lady Walpole and I are treated to a three-course lunch with wine, served by the butler at the top of the table.

I could not wait for the day to end to return to the normality of life in Newmarket, and to see my two dogs – which were blissfully unaware of the purgatory that I had endured!

However, this tale pales into insignificance, when I think back to my second shooting nightmare – which started with a telephone call, whilst I was having a drink with my Head Lad and Travelling Head Lad in my office at Trillium Place, after Evening Stables. It is the Princess Royal. "Good evening, Gavin – I hope that you and your horses are well. I would like to invite you to shoot at Sandringham on Wednesday of next week, and very much hope that you can come." I am caught totally unawares, lost for words and terrified – doing my best to resist and pleading my lack of shooting prowess. But to no avail. "No worries, Gavin, we look forward to seeing you at Sandringham next week. 9am, and please do not be late," comes the royal retort.

I am in a state of confusion and panic for the next few days – in dread and fearing the worst. I book into bed and breakfast near Sandringham the night before, and arrive as bidden at the appointed time.

By chance, I draw peg number 9 at the first drive, a walking gun, and nothing flies out of the wood in my direction! At the second drive, I am positioned in the middle of a little thicket, where I am hoping that nobody can see me. How wrong I was. As I retreat from the thicket having missed practically every bird that came over me, I am met by a very stern Head Keeper, who berates me for my incompetence in his broad and deliberate Scottish accent. "I saw you in the thicket, Mr Pritchard-Gordon – you were not very good. Things can only improve as you are now number 5 at the King's Drive here at Sandringham."

I am now quaking in my boots, there for everybody to see. Members of the Royal Family and their distinguished guests looking on in anticipation. At this stage, I must emphasise that it is a "cocks only" day at Sandringham, that the wind is blowing a gale, and that the sun is shining very brightly – in my eyes, needless to say. An avalanche of pheasants hurtle over my head, flying at breakneck speed. A speck on the horizon, at first glance, but behind me and out of range in seconds – my biggest concern being not to shoot a hen bird on a cock's only day. It is sheer purgatory.

At the end of the drive, my new-found friend, the Head Keeper, approaches and says "Mr Pritchard-Gordon, have you anything to be collected – I don't think so." By then, I am distraught, having made an utter fool of myself in front of royalty. At the next drive, where the guns are placed in close proximity to each other, I am determined to shoot the first cock bird that comes over my head, come what may. But, to my horror, I get it wrong – yet again. In my confusion and despair, picking upon an unsuspecting hen bird – which falls stone dead at my feet. As he passes by my peg at the end of the drive, the Head Keeper looks me in the eye and delivers his final flourish. "Well, Mr Pritchard-Gordon, there is not a lot more that I can say – enjoy the rest of the day."

At lunch, in the Log Cabin in the woods, I was honoured to sit between the Queen Mother and the Princess Royal who were absolutely charming putting me at my ease throughout. At the outset, the Queen Mother enquired tenderly whether I had enjoyed a "wonderful morning", which confounded me completely. Keeping my nerve and lying through my teeth, I replied in the affirmative, all the while praying to God that I would be forgiven for my sins.

46.
Midwood

I am lucky to have lots of friends – not just from the world of racing but many from other walks of life. Being one of five P-G siblings, I started with a wide-ranging family network – and this grew when I started training as I travelled round the country, meeting and staying with different people, not just with my owners.

One of my best and closest friends is a man called David Midwood, a larger than life character, who lives and farms in the village of Wickhambrook, ten miles from Newmarket. By description, I would liken him to "a big cuddly bear". Generous and hospitable by nature, he is a jolly, genial and very noisy man – and I start laughing as soon as I see him. We banter with each other incessantly and share the same very silly and simple sense of humour – and always try to see the funny side of life. However, he can be very bossy and dictatorial – and has a short fuse when things go wrong, or not according to his plans. We have had many an adventure together – and, when I started this book, I vowed to write one brief segment about him, for three valid reasons. First, because he was the only owner of mine, who had just one horse in training with me that won six races. Secondly, because I wanted to recount one or two tales, relating to various nefarious exploits in which we both participated. And thirdly to cause him a little aggravation. I know that he will be delighted that I am writing about him, thereby spreading his notoriety – but, conversely, very displeased that he will have to suffer in silence. And have no recourse to a written reply.

From now on, I will just refer to him as Midwood.

Midwood's father Ralph had several horses in training with Harvey Leader, amongst them top-class performers Dites, Exchange and Bringley – and his grandfather owned the winner of the Grand

National, Shaun Golin in 1930, but it was not till 1991 that Midwood himself ventured into the realms of racehorse ownership. In consultation with and advised by his bloodstock agent David (Minty) Minton, he bought a chestnut yearling filly by Sharrood, later named Farmers Pet, for 5000 guineas at Doncaster Sales, and kindly sent her to me to be trained. It soon became apparent that Farmers Pet, a big rangy filly, bred to stay, was not going to shine as a two-year-old. That did not please Midwood, who being new into racing, was expecting some instant action. I formulated a plan, which needed some persuasion, to run the filly a few times at the back end of her two-year-old season with a view to realising her true potential at three. A sound strategy in theory, which put a great deal of pressure on the trainer – but, which worked in this instance. Running initially off a particularly lenient handicap mark, and benefiting greatly from a measurable increase in distance, she went on to win six races as a three and four-year-old, and became a very useful handicapper.

Farmers Pet's first success was at Wolverhampton, then a grass track, over 1 mile, six furlongs as a three-year-old – when the trainer's plan, skill and reputation came under the microscope. She won very easily at 11–1, and, spurred on by his trainer, Midwood had a £50 each-way bet. That day before racing, I booked a table for lunch en route to Wolverhampton at a little restaurant near Rugby – and this set a precedent for all future races. Lunch before racing was to be a prerequisite and de rigueur. Further victories were recorded at Yarmouth (twice, when she was ridden by both Frankie Dettori and Walter Swinburn, respectively), Warwick, Newcastle and Doncaster. At the last named, she was ridden by my second son Paddy, and thereby hangs a tale.

Thus far, all Farmers Pet's races had been at afternoon meetings – but at Doncaster, the amateur riders race was part of an evening fixture. I presumed that lunch would not be on the agenda, but was swiftly overruled by my owner, who had already booked a table at the Ram Jam Inn, on the A1, an hour from Doncaster.

Lunch is a marathon session, which suits Midwood, but not poor Paddy, now a competent Amateur rider, who is confined to very light helpings and sparkling water. On arrival at Doncaster Racecourse, Paddy and I set off to walk the course, as previously agreed – the race is over two miles, and the weather is unbelievably hot. Midwood insists on joining us, which proves to be a faux pas. We stop at the entrance to the straight, as the first race of the evening, over five furlongs, is about to begin. After the race, Midwood is pouring sweat and looking very pale – so, being very concerned about my owner, I flag down the ambulance, as it passes by, and ask the medic driver to take him back to the First Aid room in the stands, for a check-up. He makes a swift recovery, thank goodness – and Farmers Pet wins the race. It is a magical moment. David hugs me, and standing with Jane, tears of delight run down their faces – and I am hard-pressed to remove them from their position on the stand, to go and greet horse and rider in the Winners' Enclosure.

Sadly, Farmers Pet broke down in the Moet & Chandon Stakes at Epsom, her next race, ridden by a very dejected Paddy P-G – and this was the end of her very illustrious racing career. She made 15000 guineas at the Tattersalls December Sales, later that year, and went on to produce a number of foals – having given Midwood, Jane and their family, enormous pleasure.

Midwood came to Wickhambrook after serving with pride in the 1st Battalion Grenadier Guards and became a very capable and successful farmer. We soon became pals, and our friendship grew, as a result of our joint obsession for International Rugby. In those days, he had a debenture seat at Twickenham, alongside fellow rugby enthusiasts Mark Coley, Simon Taylor, David Dobbie and Robert Bigland – and I was often invited to join them. At a later date, Midwood's brother-in-law, Sir Anthony Pilkington, sponsored the Six Nations Championship for five years, and we were very kindly given seats at Twickenham amongst rugby's hierarchy – and also for away Six Nations International matches. We were blessed and privileged and had some hilarious weekends in that duration. Celebrating England's first ever Six Nations match against Italy in Rome was a momentous occasion – whilst International matches in Paris and Dublin became very dear to our hearts.

One rugby weekend in Paris will live long in the memory. On the Friday night, we party into the early hours – and continue our festivities on the Saturday morning at the Deux Magots café in the Latin Quarter, a favourite of many rugby fans. The metro down to Parc Des Princes is jam-packed, and I am crammed around one of the metal hand poles in the carriage, immediately opposite my friend Midwood. As is his wont, he is giving instructions to our party, in a loud voice, about the number of stops before our final metro station – and I am unaware that he is tying the toggles of my Puffa jacket to the pole. As the others leave the carriage, bubbling with excitement, I try to follow – but the toggles of my jacket tighten into a very small and vicious knot, and I am left swinging around the pole, powerless to escape. But Lady Luck is on my side, for once. As a 19 year old, I had spent six months of my life in Paris, and it dawns upon me that there is a loop at the end of the Ligne Austerlitz, which then returns swiftly to the Porte D'Auteuil, our scheduled station of departure and close to the rugby stadium.

However, I am well and truly knotted by now – my only option being to beseech any unsuspecting passenger, and ask, in my best French "S'il vous plait, avez vous un canif?" Not the wisest of moves in that part of Paris.

To my relief, a very large, swarthy and frightening looking Frenchman obliges, and cuts my toggles, very neatly. Now clutching my match ticket given previously to me by Midwood in the café, I rush from the Metro station and gallop, at great speed, to the ground at Parc des Princes. And I am sitting in my seat, feeling very smug, when my so-called friends arrive.

*

As a lover of the Emerald Isle, I treasure every opportunity to return to Dublin – to my mind, the most vibrant, friendly and fun-provoking capital in Europe – especially when England are playing Ireland there in the Six Nations Championship! At this particular renewal, our gang of reprobates are staying at Jury's Hotel, very close to the stadium at Lansdowne Road – and I am sharing a bedroom with Midwood. A large one, thank goodness – with two separate beds.

As always, Friday night in Dublin is magnificent, Guinness flowing freely – and we return to the hotel at a late hour, feeling no pain, to join the enormous crowd of Irish and English rugby fans, who are gathered in the large, long and extensive hotel bar. The noise levels are full decibel, Irish country music is blaring – and the floors of the bar are two inches deep in beer, cream and water. It is one hell of a party. I make the casual acquaintance of a jovial middle-aged Irishman, who has obviously enjoyed his evening to the full. He is perched upon a high bar stool, rocking gently backwards and forwards, in front of a massive pile of beer glasses, which are being carefully washed and dried by a contingent of resident barmen.

Midwood leaves the bar quite soon after our arrival – which surprises me, given that he is usually the last to retire to bed. Muttering to me as he goes "I will leave the bedroom door ajar with a shoe, Gavin – just in case you get lost." I carry on chatting to my new found friend, until he lurches violently forward and headbutts the pile of glasses, which crash to the floor in smithereens. All hell lets loose; pandemonium reigns. A platoon of irate barmen leap over the bar, grab my miscreant friend and are about to seize on me. Sensing imminent danger and disaster, I run headlong from the bar, up the stairs, and along the long corridor of bedrooms. Thanking my lucky stars that Midwood has kept his word, and placed a shoe outside the door as promised – which I slam shut firmly behind me.

To my surprise, he is sitting up in bed and watches me intently, as I undress with great difficulty and fall into bed. But, even in my inebriated stupor, I twig that something is amiss. The top sheet has been double backed, and my feet are unable to fathom the bottom of the bed as intended. A wry smile appears on Midwood's face – and he starts to rock with laughter. Like a naughty little school boy, he has made me an "apple- pie bed" – and wanted to witness my reaction.

By this stage, I too am in convulsions of laughter – and, as neither of us can sleep, we decide to go for an early breakfast in the hotel dining room at 6:30am. And have our first Bloody Mary of the day.

Truth to tell, I have much enjoyed penning these jaunty little jottings – and am now ready for reprisals from you know who.

47.
Billy Cahill at The Police Station

Billy Cahill has been a constant thread, throughout my memoirs, and quite rightly so. He was the most brilliant man with horses, especially yearlings, with whom he had a very special empathy. He was also a legend, in his own right, with a larger-than-life personality – and was the source of relentless fun and entertainment for others.

He figured prominently at Shalfleet and Stanley House Stables – and at Trillium Place, as well. One evening after Evening Stables, I am sitting at my desk, minding my own business, when the telephone rings. It is the Chief Superintendent of Newmarket Police. "Good evening, Mr Pritchard-Gordon" he begins. "I have something very important to discuss with you but this cannot be dealt with on the telephone. I would like you to come down to the Police Station, immediately. If you have had more than a couple of drinks, I will send someone down to collect you."

"Can I ask you whether this might involve a member of my family?" I reply immediately now in dread. "No it does not, I can assure you – but all will become apparent when I see you," he states.

I jump into my car in haste, having only just poured myself my first drink – and go straight to the Police Station, where I notice at once that everyone is wearing flak jackets and carrying guns – which is very worrying. I am ushered into the Chief Superintendent's office, where three more senior policemen are sitting, ready for my interrogation.

"I believe that you have an Irishman called Billy Cahill in your employment, and that he lives in one of your staff houses in Doris Street, in the town," he starts. I nod and he continues. "We have it on very good authority that he is harbouring a member of the IRA (which was very active in the UK, at the time) – and we are going to storm his house and arrest him later this evening."

I plead Billy's innocence, knowing full well that this cannot be true, but the Chief Superintendent is adamant. "Could you please describe to us the layout and room plan of the house as this will be crucial to our strategy this evening." This is almost impossible, as I have only been in it a couple of times, but I do my best.

"Thank you Mr Pritchard-Gordon, that has been very helpful," continues the Chief Superintendent. "We will be evacuating Doris Street, and erecting arc lights – and will make a forced entry, if necessary, at 11pm. Please do not contact Billy Cahill, or be anywhere near Doris Street later this evening."

I leave the Police Station totally bewildered and in panic – very concerned for Billy's safety – but also confident that Newmarket Police have got things very wrong. My last advice for the Chief Superintendent being, "You will be wasting your time if you enter the house in Doris Street at 11pm – it is Friday night, and Billy will still be in the pub with his housemates and countless friends having a very boozy time."

I had been invited to dinner locally, but excuse myself and leave early – determined, contrary to instructions, to monitor developments in Doris Street, come what may. Doris Street is only five minutes' walk from Trillium Place, and, as I approach, I see a large group of very disgruntled residents, furious that they have been evacuated from their homes, at such a late hour. 11pm passes, then 11:30pm – and, needless to say, there is no sign of Billy. Just after midnight, Billy and his mates can be spied, walking drunkenly from side to side down Doris Street – into the arms of a gaggle of heavily armed police officers. Billy is arrested, thrown into a police van and rushed to Newmarket Police Station for interrogation. Lights flash, sirens blare.

Sunday morning's national papers are full of the story – Billy's name – and mine – are plastered all over the pages – given the national prominence of the IRA at the time. There is no sign of Billy till Evening Stables – when to my relief and joy he marches into the yard at Trillium Place as if nothing has happened. I leave him to do his work but, as he is leaving, tell him to come to my office to apologise and explain himself.

"I am very sorry Guv'nor," he explains in his lilting Limerick brogue. "There has been a big misunderstanding. The police have apologised and everything is fine. And, what is more, I have made you even more famous than you were before. Those stories in the papers were hysterical, and it was all great craic!"

You can see why I loved Billy.

48.
Giles William

Lord Cadogan and my brother Giles were the only two owners of mine who had horses in training with me when I started training in 1972 and retired in 1994. They deserved long service gallantry medals. The large majority of Harvey Leader's owners, whom I originally inherited, had died by then. I've already made various references to Lord Cadogan, always in glowing terms – but, thus far, I've not written about Giles. I wanted to leave the most intriguing and influential person in my life till last. He was not only my younger brother, but also my closest friend and confidant – there to support, advise, cajole and criticise – whichever was appropriate at the time. In particular, when I was a trainer.

Giles Revel William Pritchard-Gordon burst into this world in Hove on Thursday the 22nd of May 1947, 18 months after his elder brother. But the young Giles was like a comic-book cheeky boy, a sort of *Just William* character. He was naughty, tricky, obstinate, single-minded, but enchanting, from day one. He caused incessant heartache and anxiety to his mother (Sec) and elder brother – despite being fond of both. From his earliest days, he was bold, determined and tough – with an ounce or two of stubbornness and truculence, thrown in for good measure. He craved everything physical and sporty – and was particularly keen on tree climbing. As soon as he was old enough to move from a cot to a bed, Giles and I shared a bedroom and a lifelong brotherly relationship was firmly cemented.

Giles was a frequent presence at Hove Hospital's A&E. He visited so often that Sister knew him personally and would greet him with the words, "Not you again Giles – what is it this time?" One particularly busy week saw Giles at A&E three times. The first visit was to address a massive gash at the back of his head, following a very boisterous game of football with Manager on the upstairs landing at 3, Prince's Square. Visit number two occurred two days later, on a busy Sunday morning, when Manager was driving us back from Brighton and Hove Golf Club. As a treat, he would often slide back the sunshine roof of his little Austin 10, and allow Giles and me to stand on the front seat, and stick our heads and shoulders through the opening, as we hurtled down the steep hill into Hove. On this particular morning, a bumblebee, going the other way, collided with Giles, diving down his shirt and stinging him very badly. Fortunately, Hove Hospital was very close by. Incident number three happened in the back garden at 3 Prince's Square. Manager was digging his potato patch, when picking up a large fork, and attempting to copy his father, Giles drove the fork through his flimsy Wellington boot, pinning his little foot to the soil. So back again to A&E in Hove!

With brother number three, Grant (always known to us as Badger) on the way, the decision was taken that an au pair girl was required to help our dear pregnant mother to manage her two boisterous boys. Gauda, a very pretty 22-year-old Dutch blonde soon arrived. While in theory a sound plan, in reality it turned sour, when Gauda quickly developed a crush on Manager. Despite our youth, aged only six and four and a half at the time, Giles and I sensed the gravity of the threat and quickly came up with a plan. In those days, the virtues of fresh air could not be overstated, and every morning, after breakfast, we were taken for a walk, but riding our bicycles, along the seafront in Hove. This was a responsibility which Sec, now heavily pregnant, quickly delegated to the flirtatious Gauda. Giles and I soon identified and seized our opportunity. One morning, out on the seafront, we bolted, managing to lose Gauda, and returned home unaccompanied, wailing that we had got lost. When Gauda eventually returned to Prince's Square, an hour later, breathless and in a state of panic, Sec understandably sacked her on the spot for being so irresponsible. Mission accomplished!

When Giles was six and I was seven and a half, our little family moved 25 miles north to Hill House in Turners Hill, West Sussex. Manager wanted to give his children a rural upbringing, and follow his own yearning for country pursuits.

Village life in 1953 was a much calmer and quieter affair than the hustle and bustle of Brighton. There were very few cars, and good neighbourly behaviour and community spirit were part of the package. People talked to each other in the street, as a matter of course, and the church was filled to capacity every Sunday morning – where our spirits were lifted by our inspirational vicar, the Reverend Gilbert Foss. There were three pubs in the village that were packed every evening – and the Bakery and Central Stores supplied everyday culinary needs. The village doctor, Dr Palmer, was on duty both night and day – and Bert, the village policeman, patrolled his patch with military precision. Sport was part of the community package – every weekend there were two teams for football or cricket, with fierce competition for places in the First Eleven.

Initially, Hill House was taken on a lease, but things changed when Manager went to work for Clarksons, in the City of London, where he would remain. The move came with a pay rise commensurate with his increasing business experience, which allowed him to purchase the freehold of Hill House. In 1957, mortgaging Hill House to the hilt, Manager bought the two-hundred-acre Fen Place Farm, which adjoined the paddock at Hill House. The farm buildings, a mile and a half away, had not been used for a number of years, and were in an appalling state of filth and disrepair. The cowsheds were 3ft deep in cow dung. They smelt horrific, and had attracted an army of rats. Manager instructed George Streeter, the gardener at Hill House, a loyal and reliable man devoted to the P-G family and their pets, to clean out the cowsheds. And suggested to Giles and me that we should help him, to earn a little pocket money.

After a week of hard labour, the rats had largely been exterminated – and we only had one very small bit of the large cowshed to clear. We were in the process of making our final digs, when out popped the most gigantic doe rat imaginable. Cornered, it attempted to escape, but met a wall of legs and forks. In panic, it ran up George's left trouser leg! He fell to the floor, shrieking, clutching crazily at the rat in his midriff, as it writhed around his nether regions. Giles and I were beside ourselves with fear, as we looked on helplessly, riveted by this horrendous scenario, which appeared to be unending. After a five minute battle, poor George succeeded in pinning and throttling his ferocious assailant. He stood up, exhausted, and very badly shaken – even Giles had turned white with terror.

Despite this woeful experience, Giles thrived on country life and pursuits – and it was here in Turners Hill, where he first developed his passion for farming, livestock, cattle and shooting.

School for Giles was one long jape – an excuse to make friends, play sport and have fun. He was naturally bright but only did the minimum of work to get by. This was evident first at Fonthill Lodge, near East Grinstead; then at Mowden School in Hove; and finally at Radley College, between Oxford and Abingdon, which Giles loved from the outset. It was when he moved from adolescent to young adult, excelling at rugby, cricket and boxing, gathering a lifelong group of friends around him – namely Quentin Wallace, Charlie Carter, Philip Beck, John Garnsey and Chris Thin. Betting on horses, drinking, partying (later to be known by Giles as "roistering"), became enduring passions in his life. He had a general disregard for rules that he considered pointless and being the most fun person at the party.

Once his school days were behind him, Giles's mindset and attitude to life changed. He set his sights on following Manager into the ship-broking business and making money. And this meant starting at the bottom – sound advice from Manager, needless to say.

He was sent to work as a welder in a German shipyard in Kiel for six months – and was then given a position with Norwegian Shipping Company Fearnley and Egger, working in the engine rooms, as a greaser, being paid the princely sum of one Kroner a day. He disembarked after six months in Hong Kong, and secured a one-way passage to Australia, where he worked on a sugar cane estate and played professional Rugby League for Proserpine.

By the time he returned to England, Giles was a rounded, battle hardened, mature and resourceful young man – and this stood him in good stead, when he joined Clarksons as a trainee ship broker. He impressed his employers immediately with his quality of hard work, determination, intelligence, overall knowledge of the industry and of the world, and his ability to get on with people. And soon became their youngest Director and star broker. But, despite being highly paid with an expense account larger than his salary, Giles made the momentous decision to leave Clarksons and go out on his own aged twenty-six. He told his very surprised father, "I am fed up with making money for other people – I want to make it for myself."

It was at this juncture that Giles met Lou, daughter of Epsom trainer, Ron Smyth, in London. They shared the same interests, soon became inseparable, and were married on the 19th of November, 1970. Settling down to married life in Delvino Road in Parsons Green – which was to become HQ for Giles W. Pritchard-Gordon (Shipbroking) Ltd. Giles's business thrived, and grew from day one, and not long afterwards moved to its first real office in Stratton Street, Mayfair. It later diversified into ship owning – and for over forty years, Pritchard-Gordon Tankers has been one of the largest privately owned ship owning companies in the UK. An incredible story.

As Giles's career in shipping flourished, so did his ability to pursue his passions for racing and farming. Giles knew that he wanted to bring up his family in similar surroundings to those he had enjoyed as a child, which was also Lou's philosophy, and they moved from Parsons Green to Ludwell, a small cottage near Ardingly in Sussex, four miles south of Turners Hill. Following in Manager's footsteps, Giles quickly added some acres to his property, and started his own herd of Sussex cattle – and this is where Giles's daughters Ali, Emily, Lucy and Eliza were brought up, enjoying a blissful childhood.

As the family grew, and Giles became more established, he purchased the Slaugham Park Estate, just a few miles further west from Ardingly. This parkland house and setting, surrounded by woodland, and with sensational views of the South Downs, was to be the family home for the rest of Giles's life, the base from which Giles grew his property empire, drove forward P-G Tankers, continued to breed his Sussex cattle, and set up Slaugham Park Stud, which was to give Giles, Lou and the family so much interest, satisfaction and success. Slaugham Park was to become the backdrop to a warm and social Pritchard-Gordon family life, as Ali, Emily, Lucy and Eliza grew from young children to teens, and then into adults. Friends came and went incessantly, and Slaugham Park parties were legend.

Giles and I were introduced to racing, and racehorses, when we went to stay, as very young boys, with our step grandfather, Tom Corrie, and our wonderful grandmother Doodie, at Leighton Hall in Shropshire, ten miles from Shrewsbury. Uncle Tom farmed a large estate, and also trained a small stable of racehorses, with a great deal of success. Giles's early passion for horses and betting grew and flourished, in parallel to his work as a shipbroker – inevitably aided and abetted by his father-in-law, Ron, following his marriage to Lou. Horses – both the racing and breeding – were something Giles and Lou did together. Everything was shared, from the choosing of their colours – cerise and white hoops (Radley 1st Fifteen colours) with light blue and white quartered cap – to deciding which horses to buy, what to call them, and which to try and breed from, and when.

Their first success as owners came soon after the wedding, when Lucky Run stormed home as a two-year-old at Wolverhampton. Kyrios was another multiple winner – but their best horse, trained by Ron, was Heaven Knows, bought as a yearling for little money, which proved to be a very useful two-year-old. At three there was much excitement at Giles's local track, when Heaven Knows won the Lingfield Oaks Trial, Group 3. Her very best performance was as a four-year-old, when she won the Earl of Sefton Stakes, Group 3, at Newmarket.

Being a loyal brother, Giles supported me instinctively, when I started training in 1972 – his first winner, of many with me, being the aptly named Brokers Folly, who carried his colours to victory as a two-year-old at Lingfield. And also at Yarmouth, where she won the first running of the Harvey Leader Memorial Nursery Handicap. Which gave us all enormous pleasure.

Giles loved his horses and took an immense interest in their careers, from foals to the end of their racing and breeding days. He planned his mares matings in infinite detail, nurtured his young stock personally with Lou at Slaugham Park, and followed their progress avidly, when they came into training. He came regularly to Newmarket to see his horses and attend and buy at Tattersalls Sales. He was hugely popular with my staff, who were fascinated by his candid opinions and his unusual approach to the training of racehorses. Being brothers, we had a very close and productive owner–trainer relationship – but this could become a little tempestuous at times.

Giles had a passion for Deauville. He just loved everything about the place. The stylish hotels, restaurants, racecourse, sales pavilion, nightclubs and casinos had an elegance, ambience and allure that appealed to his inner soul. Racing in Deauville for Giles was a pleasure. As an owner, he was treated with respect, courtesy and hospitality. Lunch in the Owners and Trainers Restaurant on the racecourse was an uplifting experience, served with refinement, in exceedingly comfortable surroundings. The perfect aperitif to an afternoon's racing was his customary mélange of the best local seafood and an ice cold bottle of his favourite vin blanc.

Given this, in 1992, Giles decided to take a Slaugham Park yearling to the Deauville Yearling sales, a very likeable bay colt. Giles fancied a gastronomic few days in Normandy and wanted to prove to potential French buyers that English-bred yearlings could compete comprehensively with their best.

Regrettably, his master plan backfired and his equine pride and joy failed to make his reserve. But Giles was as resilient as ever, already formulating Plan B. He called me later that evening from his hotel. "Gavin, do you want the good news or the bad?" I elected for the latter. "The bad news is that those ignorant bloody French fellows did not like my horse. The good news is that you are going to train him – AND we are going to win their big race, the Challenge D'or Piaget, confined to graduates of the sale, next August in Deauville!"

Later that year, the yearling, now named Prince Babar, came into training with me in Newmarket. He promised to be special from day one. As a two-year-old he won his maiden and then came second in the Lanson Champagne Stakes at Goodwood in July. He was now on track for Deauville. I found out about the opposition in Deauville from my close friend Julian Wilson, BBC TV Racing Correspondent, who told me that Prince Babar would start as 2–1 favourite. Concerned that Giles would become overexcited, I played down his chances. The next morning, I had a call from Giles telling me that he was sending a small plane to collect me and Paddy from Newmarket. The plane would then pick up Giles and Lou in Shoreham and fly on to Deauville. As planned, our party arrived at the Normandy Hotel where we were all staying.

As I had feared, overexcitement did follow. Joined by racing friends at the Hotel Bar, Giles then took everyone out for dinner in Trouville. We called into several bars on the way home, ending up in Regines Nightclub. We finally got to bed at 4:30am.

As a result, the following day, we were very tired, hungover and jaded. We made our way to the racecourse on foot with difficulty. It was unbelievably hot with both owner and trainer suffering big time. Lunch was declined. Race time approached, and a young Frankie Dettori (claiming 3lbs) entered the paddock to receive his riding instructions. Jockeys mounted, horses went to post, and the excitement built. Our hopes were fulfilled beyond their wildest dreams. Prince Babar won the race at 11–1 on the Tote, beating a horse of Sheikh Mohammed's, netting a massive €179,211 for his ecstatic owner, who had also had a substantial wager.

Without doubt this was one of the happiest days of our P-G life. The more so given that it was Manager's Birthday, 21st of August. Prince Babar was the hero, and Giles had taught the French a lesson. Agincourt, Waterloo and now Deauville, to add to the history books.

A week or so later, Giles confided to me why he had decided that we should party quite so hard that night in Deauville. "As you were so unexpectedly confident, I thought we should celebrate the night before the event. Just in case something went very wrong on the day!"

What a man!

*

Giles was a perceptive, strong-minded and very candid man. When he felt something strongly he spoke his mind. To be honest, my training career was taking a downward slide at Trillium Place. Coral was not there, most of our original owners had died, the Maktoum family were not sending me horses, and my zest for training was not as before. I was still training plenty of winners, but my position in the Trainers Table was dropping. One evening, in the summer of 1994, I had a call from Giles. "I would like to come and stay at Trillium Place tomorrow night and take you out to dinner. Important." We drank a great deal of wine, much more than usual – and returned to Trillium Place for a nightcap. "Pour yourself a very large whisky, Gavin – I've something to tell you that you will not like. I've given this some serious thought, and I'm adamant that you must stop training at the end of the season." I looked at him in amazement, rocked by this bombshell, telling him in no uncertain terms that he was wrong. A fierce argument ensued, tempers became frayed – but I was finally silenced, when he delivered his broadside. "You are being very stubborn and unrealistic, Gavin. If it makes it easier for you to understand the gravity of the situation, I would like to tell you that I will remove my three horses, and send them elsewhere, if you continue to protest." That was game, set and match. End of story. I agreed then and there to take heed of Giles's advice. It was a crucifying blow to me – but, in my heart of hearts, I knew that he was right.

The following evening I told my staff. And afterwards my family and owners. And two days later the Racing Press. They were all shocked and stunned by my decision and I was heartbroken. Training horses had been my life – and this was now the end of an era.

When I retired, Giles sent his horses to be trained by Jack Banks in Newmarket, Richard Fahey and Mick Easterby in Yorkshire, and my son Rupert in Chantilly – and had fun and success with all of them. He struck up a wonderful friendship with Mick Easterby – they were two very loveable rascals together.

Giles was very fond of my two sons, Rupert and Paddy – and loved having horses in training with Rupert in France. They had many winners together – the best being Arvada, well bought as a yearling, and named after the local town in Wyoming where the P-Gs owned their ranch. She was a winner at two, and showed top class form at three – when third in the Prix St Alary Group 1, at Longchamp. This encouraged Giles to send her to New York, to be trained by Bobby Frankel. She then proceeded to win La Prevoyante Handicap, a Grade 2 race in Florida and the Glen Falls Handicap, Grade 3 at Saratoga. She was later sold at the 2004 Keeneland Breeding Stock Sales for $700,000, a not inconsiderate sum, to leading Japanese Breeder, Katsumi Yoshida.

In 2000, Giles was very proud to be named Small Breeder of the Year by the Thoroughbred Breeders Association. Just reward for his large contribution to the British Bloodstock Industry.

When Giles fell ill for the second time with cancer, all the qualities that had been evident throughout his life were apparent in death as in life. He lived to see all his four daughters married. And treasured his latter days in Slaugham, at his house in Seaview, in the Isle of Wight, his ranch in Wyoming, his two estates in Australia, and his beloved Scotland.

He died on the 15th of October, 2011, at Slaugham Park. His funeral was held a week later at Slaugham Church, which was packed to the rafters with some 600 people – family, friends of all ages, who had known and loved him.

Giles was a remarkable person. Hugely successful in so many spheres – but, first and foremost, a family man.

49.
The End of My Training Career

I was at a very low ebb at this point, understandably. Training racehorses had been my life for twenty-four years, and this was a seismic shock to the system. In my heart of hearts, I knew that Giles had made the right call, but it was very difficult to come to terms with reality. My pride was hurt, my self-confidence shattered – and my future as a fifty-year-old former trainer more than uncertain.

My family, friends and owners were both understanding and supportive – and the racing media, taken unawares by my knee-jerk retirement, were very complimentary about my achievements as a trainer and the contribution I had made to racing.

My first priority was to make sure that my staff found alternative employment, either in Newmarket, or further afield. They had been very loyal to me over the years – and six of them had been with me for the full duration of my training career. I was also at pains to see that my owners found suitable trainers to whom they could relocate their horses.

I made the decision to rent out my yard, but to retain the house at Trillium Place, to which I had become very attached. Newmarket had been my home for thirty years, and this is where I wanted to remain.

Against all the odds, however, there came a glimmer of hope, from an unexpected quarter. Lord (Stoker) Hartington, now the Duke of Devonshire, then Senior Steward of the Jockey Club, rang me out of the blue, expressing his surprise and disappointment at my decision to retire, and asking whether I would like to join his fledgling team in the establishment of his new brainchild, the British Horseracing Board, which morphed later into the British Horseracing Authority.

Within days, I was at a meeting in the BHB's offices, which adjoined those of the Jockey Club, at 42, Portman Square in London – and it was agreed that I would be part of the BHB's Marketing Department, working closely with Lee Richardson, the recently appointed BHB Marketing Director. Under the direction of Tristram Ricketts, who had moved from the Horseracing Betting Levy Board to become BHB's Chief Executive.

This was indeed manna from heaven, and I will be eternally grateful to the now Duke of Devonshire for coming to my rescue at a time of need. Very soon afterwards, I swapped first lot on Racecourse Side for an early morning train commute from Newmarket Station to Kings Cross, via Cambridge. And soon became absorbed in and fascinated by my new role in Racing.

And something else happened which raised my spirits, only days later, when my life was still in disarray – which necessitated a great deal of thought, planning and consideration, on their part. I had a call from Gay MacRae, Harvey Leader's daughter, inviting me to Sunday morning drinks at her lovely house in Stradishall, near Newmarket – and to look at her yearlings on the stud. Initially, this sounded strange, given that I had just announced my retirement from training, but I accepted with alacrity, nonetheless. On arrival, it was eerily quiet. No cars in the driveway and absolutely no sign of anyone. "Come and have a glass of champagne," announced Gay, opening the doors of the drawing room with aplomb. I was flabbergasted, lost for words – forty of my owners, past and present, were gathered there sworn to secrecy and silence, till I entered the room. It was a magical and memorable experience – everybody thanking me for my contribution, as their trainer, reminiscing about fun, successful and happy times past and wishing me well for the future.

This was followed by a superb lunch in the dining room, at which Lord Cadogan spoke, with warmth and sincerity, on behalf of all, having travelled down especially for the occasion from Scotland – and I was presented with a magnificent silver salver, inscribed beautifully with the signatures of a host of my owners, who had contributed to the outlay.

Giving up training was a wrench – but it was very gratifying to know that I had been appreciated.

50.
BHB

I thoroughly enjoyed my six months at BHB in Portman Square – it was a new experience, another challenge, and my first taste of working in an office in London.

From the start, I had the greatest respect and admiration for the then Lord Hartington, both as a person, but also as the Chairman of BHB. He was hands on, charming, hugely enthusiastic – and above all a listener and a people person – all attributes that have served him so well since he has been custodian of Chatsworth House in Derbyshire, as Duke of Devonshire. He encouraged a strict work ethic, and a unified team spirit – but there was always time for occasional jokes and hilarity as well in the course of our daily chores. Most mornings, he would come into my office and sit on my desk to discuss Racing in general and the BHB in particular. And I learnt a lot.

Tristram Ricketts was a superb Chief Executive with a brilliant brain. He was a born administrator, dedicated to his many responsibilities and he had a profound knowledge of the structure of Racing, and its finances. He was very popular with the staff at BHB – and very considerate to me as an office newcomer. His objectives as Chief Executive were to streamline the administration and governance of Racing – and to forge lines of communication between Racing and Government, which he handled with consummate tact and skill.

My association with Lee Richardson worked very well. He was a very professional and experienced marketeer, but knew very little about Racing. For my part, I only had a very limited knowledge of marketing – but had been at the grassroots of Racing for 30 years. It proved to be a rewarding arrangement, which was mutually advantageous to us both.

I very soon realised that life at BHB was all about meetings – where it was always the politics of Racing that were discussed, much more than the horses themselves. This surprised me somewhat but that was the nature of the beast.

Meetings were structured and taken seriously, and strong opinions were expressed – given that all the individual associations involved in Racing were usually represented. And this could be entertaining, needless to say.

I remember one particular meeting of the BHB Industry Committee held in the bowels of 42, Portman Square. It had a long, narrow rectangular table, which could seat twenty people. There were also five doors leading from it, dotted at various intervals – and this proved to be the problem that day. The Chairman of the Racehorse Owners Association, a rather intimidating man, with considerable experience in big business, felt particularly strongly about one specific item on the agenda, and took objection to the equally robust views from the representatives from his fellow organisations, who were in total disagreement. Eventually in disgust, slamming his agenda papers into his briefcase, and storming out of the room through what he thought was the door to the corridor outside. Regrettably, for him, it turned out to be the broom cupboard, where he remained incarcerated like a church mouse, till the end of the meeting to save his embarrassment, only finally making his exit, when everybody else had left.

To those who knew the layout and geography of 42, Portman Square, and the Committee Room, in particular, this was hilarious of course.

During my sojourn at BHB, I became acquainted with a number of knowledgeable people, passionate about Racing, who gave their time freely for the betterment of our Sport. One of these was Rhydian Morgan-Jones, who was about to become the Chairman of the Thoroughbred Breeders Association. He informed me that the TBA were looking for a new Chief Executive and asked whether I might be interested. I took this as a compliment and jumped at the opportunity, accepting his invitation very quickly. Having cleared this first with the BHB's Chief Executive.

My time at the BHB had been a massive learning curve and very rewarding – but this was a far greater challenge, which would give me more recognition and responsibility on the administrative side of Racing. And, furthermore, the TBA's offices and HQ were at Stanstead House in the Avenue, in Newmarket – and only ten minutes' walk from Trillium Place.

51.
TBA

When I started my job as Chief Executive of the TBA, I have to admit that I had only limited knowledge of Thoroughbred Breeding, and the Thoroughbred Breeding Industry as an entity. It might sound strange, but the training of racehorses and the breeding of thoroughbreds, differ in so many ways despite dealing with essentially the same product. From the outset, my Chairman, and his TBA Council, made me aware that the administration of Stanstead House, communication with TBA Council Members and the TBA Membership and the promotion of the British Thoroughbred Breeding Industry were my chief responsibility. And that I could call upon TBA Council Members and the TBA's Veterinary Advisor for any advice on all breeding and veterinary related issues at any time. Charles Frank, initially, and later Richard Greenwood, two affable, experienced and much-respected Veterinary Surgeons, kept me on the straight and narrow for the duration of my time at the TBA and became firm friends.

I was much looking forward to my first day at Stanstead House – but things did not materialise quite as I had expected. On arrival, I was introduced to the seven lovely girls, who would comprise my team at Stanstead House – each of whom were allotted an individual responsibility, be that Membership, Accounts, Stud Staff training, National Hunt, Marketing and Promotion, Receptionist or Personal Assistant to the Chief Executive. I then immersed myself in the various TBA files on the bookshelves in my office and the pile of correspondence awaiting me on my desk.

It was not long before the office telephone rang, and the call was put through to me, by one of the girls. "Gavin, there is somebody on the line, who wants to speak to you about balloons," came the message. To which I replied, without hesitation, "Well, tell them to ring back later – it is obviously one of my troublemaking friends, causing mischief, on my first day in the office." But the girl was adamant. "Gavin, this is a genuine call, from a distinguished and now irate TBA member, who wants to speak to you immediately." It soon becomes apparent that a squadron of low flying hot air balloons had passed over his Stud Farm, terrifying his prized and very valuable broodmares, causing two of them to abort their foals. I promised the Stud Owner that I would contact Charles Frank as a matter of urgency – and he was very soon on the case. This was indeed a baptism of fire but, by the end of the week, I was feeling more confident about the challenges that lay ahead.

The TBA was in my day, and remains, a very structured and efficient organisation, in effect the Trade Body for Thoroughbred Breeders in this country. From Stanstead House, it services and advises TBA members on a daily basis – and represents them in the complicated world of Racing's governance and politics. It promotes the British thoroughbred, both in this county, and abroad.

Rhydian Morgan Jones was my first Chairman – to be succeeded by Nigel Elwes, Philip Freedman and Kirsten Rausing, in the time that I was Chief Executive. They were all diligent and dedicated and very knowledgeable about the Thoroughbred Breeding Industry.

My first TBA President was Sir Michael Oswald – followed by David Oldrey and Michael Goodbody. All three were supremely supportive, had a wonderful sense of humour, were greatly respected in the industry, and became close friends.

In my time, we were fortunate to have some outstanding TBA Council Members, who were always there to help and advise me. We had a Council meeting every month, which was always very well attended, focused and very productive.

The TBA National Hunt Committee met regularly to promote British-based National Hunt stallions, and the ownership of British bred National Hunt mares.

For best practice, the TBA was divided geographically into eight regions, each with a Regional Representative. Every region had one Regional Day per year, when we visited local trainers and stud farms, to which I always went. It gave me, and my staff, an opportunity to meet TBA members, throughout the country.

The TBA AGM was held in the first week in January, usually in London – to be followed by the Annual Awards Dinner.

As one might imagine, my Chairman and I had to attend numerous industry meetings, most of which were in London. The former was a member of the BHB Board, and I sat on the BHB Industry Committee – the meetings mostly taking place at 42, Portman Square.

As the TBA, we were members of the European Federation of Thoroughbred Breeders Association (EFTBA) and attended an AGM every year, in one of the participating countries. This was an excellent opportunity to exchange notes with our European counterparts and to sample their culture. With Tattersalls and DBS, we went on Trade missions to Hong Kong, Bangalore and Dubai, encouraging them to attend our sales and invest in our Bloodstock.

However, the jewel in the crown was the International Breeders Meeting, held every two years – on my watch in Lexington, Tipperary, Deauville, Newmarket, Rome, Melbourne and Tokyo. Valuable international friendships were made, business was done – and I will always have particularly fond memories of our trip to Japan.

The conference was staged in Tokyo, but the Japan Racing Association very generously flew all delegates to the island of Hokkaido for two nights to visit their magnificent stud farms at the epicentre of the Japanese Breeding Industry.

We also went racing back in Tokyo, for the Japanese Derby. This was a fascinating experience – made more so, when, during lunch on the racecourse, I was handed by a liveried waiter, on a silver salver, a handwritten letter addressed to me from my former Assistant, Kazuo Fujisawa – for many years Champion Trainer in Japan. It was an invite to come to the Paddock for the Japanese Derby, in which he had three runners. The Paddock was crammed with distinguished Japanese people, and I only picked out Kazuo because he was surrounded by so many members of the Press and TV cameras. On seeing me, he gesticulated with authority, urging me to join him and his bevy of owners. People immediately stood back, in reverence to Kazuo, allowing me to pass by – a scene reminiscent of the biblical parting of the Red Sea. As I approached, Kazuo walked towards me, and hugged me, exclaiming to me in English. "Everything I have done in racing is because of you and Mrs Coral." It was a magical moment, which I will always treasure. Kazuo is a very special human being – and a brilliant trainer.

That evening, every conference delegate was invited to a smart and lavish dinner in Tokyo – where I was more than lucky to be seated next to Terya Yoshida, a hugely successful breeder and owner in Japan, and President of the JRA. It was indeed an honour, which made my fellow international delegates extremely envious of course. I got on very well with my distinguished host, who then invited me to join him, and his friends for Karaoke, in a private room in the hotel, after dinner. I accepted with alacrity and joined the party – giving an alcohol-fuelled rendition of Tom Jones' "It's Not Unusual", if my memory serves me rightly. But, at 4am, I suddenly had a horror realisation. I was due to be picked up at 4:15am, by a taxi, to be driven to the airport, for my return journey to the UK. Now in a state of panic, I thanked my kind host profusely, apologising for my hurried departure – rushed to my room and threw my clothes and belongings randomly into my suitcase. But, alas, I did not have time to change out of my black tie and dinner jacket.

On arrival at Tokyo Airport, I joined the very long queue for Premier Economy – noting that there were no passengers checking in for First Class. And that the attractive Japanese stewardess, in charge of First Class was looking at me in disbelief – eventually coming over to introduce herself. "Please forgive me, sir, " she says very politely. "But I think you are in the wrong line. You are so immaculately dressed, you must surely be travelling First Class." I mumbled something incoherently in reply – whereupon, I was immediately upgraded to First Class. To this day, I count my lucky stars and have a passion for Karaoke. I slept all the way back to London, in the most comfortable bed, waited on hand and foot. A luxury I had never experienced before – and never will do again.

I emphasise that my life as Chief Executive of the TBA was not all "beer and skittles", and that there were hardships as well. But I still loved every minute. I met some wonderful people, gave it my best shot – and think that we achieved a fair amount at Stanstead House while I was in situ.

When I retired in 2010, I was over the moon to be presented with the Dominion Trophy, at the TBA Annual Awards Dinner. "In recognition of your outstanding contribution to the British Bloodstock Industry." That made me exceedingly happy, as you might imagine. And was a heart-warming finale to my 14 years at Stanstead House.

*

To back track for a moment – it was during my last year of training at Trillium House that I first met Romana Morton, through mutual friends, James and Lucy Barrow. We gelled immediately, and our relationship blossomed, while I was working for BHB in Portman Square and she still lived in London. Love was in the air, at the same time I was leaving BHB, to start with TBA, and we got engaged shortly afterwards. Towards the end of the year, we were married quietly in London and started our lives together at Trillium Place. We had two lovely children, Rosanna and Charlie – but, very sadly, Romana, who was missing her life in London, became disenchanted with Newmarket. We moved to a house in the country, near Wickhambrook, ten miles from Newmarket, but this was not the answer. We drifted apart, and Romana finally returned to London, when Rosanna and Charlie were teenagers. I then sold the house in Wickhambrook, and moved to Kentford, three miles east of Newmarket – and the two children commuted between us.

Looking back, it was all very regrettable for and tough on our children. But there has been a saving grace, thank God. Both Rosanna and Charlie are thriving and happy – and Romana and I are very proud of them. Rosanna left school, and went straight to Business School in London, before spending six and a half years with Savills in Richmond, latterly as an Associate, before starting work for a Property Developing Company in Mayfair. Charlie went to Bristol University, where he achieved a 2.1 in Engineering. He has now started work as a graduate for Atkins, the leading engineering company, in London.

They both now live in London, have numerous friends, work and play hard, and are making the very best of their lives.

52.
Walk Up Memory Lane in Newmarket

I am now spending most of my time in Leicestershire, within a stone's throw of the Vale of Belvoir – and also the town of Melton Mowbray, made famous through its Royal association with fox hunting, and home to the prestigious Leicestershire pork pie.

Now in my late seventies, I have been blessed to find a wonderful soulmate, consider myself to be very lucky, and have found happiness again. She calls a spade a spade, which suits me; we share the same sense of humour; and make each other laugh. She has boundless energy, charm and determination – and is loved, admired and respected by everyone in the counties of Leicestershire, Nottinghamshire and Lincolnshire, and much further afield. I just pray that she keeps my P45 safely tucked away in the pigeonhole of her neatly arranged bureau.

But I still have a bolt hole in Newmarket, which has been my spiritual home for 56 years. I am renting a small flat in the Chambers of the Jockey Club Rooms, where I can remain in contact with all my Newmarket friends, go racing and attend Tattersalls Sales.

This morning I am planning to go for a walk 'up memory lane' – a slight variation on the norm, in this case – as I will take a right turn out of the Jockey Club car park, and walk north, not south, along Newmarket High Street. It is early March, and winter is almost over, and the town is coming to life again, after the ritual slumbers of post-Christmas and New Year in January and February. The start of the turf Flat Race season is in sight.

The bar is set high, as almost immediately, I am smitten by the statue of Hyperion. Standing majestically now, in his own little cobbled courtyard, between the Coffee Room of the Jockey Club

Rooms and the High Street pavement. It is the first ever life-size bronze of a thoroughbred, fastidiously created by the legendary sculptor John Skeaping. I am reminded of the four hours I spent, in his admiration, at the behest of Harvey Leader, when the statue of this remarkable racehorse held sway along the Snailwell Road, before his move to the High Street.

Within strides, I am at the entrance to what was the Subscription Rooms, where trainers, jockeys and local dignitaries used to gather for drinks before lunch, and a game of cards or snooker, afterwards. It was then home to the Racing Museum, which is now based at Palace House in Palace Street, where Sir Jack Jarvis and Bruce Hobbs used to train. It is magnificent, a treasure trove of Racing's history and memorabilia over the centuries.

I then pass by what for many years has been Golding of Newmarket, bespoke tailors and outfitters for all hunting, shooting and racing enthusiasts, with a fine reputation. It is a rare gem today on Newmarket High Street and long may it remain.

Continuing on my way to what was Musk's – now Nationwide – the renowned local butcher, where Sir Winston Churchill's chauffeur was dispatched to collect his sausages, every week, without fail. At this stage, I bump into Grand National winning jockey Bob Champion, who is in conversation with Edmund Mahony, and Jimmy George, respectively Chairman and Marketing Director of Tattersalls. And Jim Wordsworth, Chairman of Anglo Hibernian Bloodstock Insurance Services. We chat about the upcoming Cheltenham Festival, prospects for the Flat Racing season, and the state of the world Bloodstock market.

Shortly after this, I am thrilled to meet Kevin Murrell and Graham Buckley, two of my senior lads, and reminisce about the good old days, laughing a great deal, needless to say.

I wend my way past the Rutland Arms Hotel, the scene of many a late-night party over the years – particularly when the Irish were in Newmarket for the sales and racing. And over the Clocktower Roundabout, up the Bury Road, of which I have so many happy memories. I pass Heath House Stables, on my right, Sir Mark Prescott's immaculate yard – and stop to watch the strings of William Haggas and James Fanshawe, as they cross the road, in single file, on their way to exercise on Bury Hill.

I am soon abreast of the delightful St. Agnes Church, originally commissioned by the Duchess of Montrose, where all four of my offspring were christened. I chuckle to myself when recalling Rosanna's Service. It was conducted by a charming, loveable but very elderly vicar, who had a very bad stutter. At the font, as he held Rosanna in his arms, and crossed her forehead with holy water, he struggled to pronounce her Christian name – only able to utter the first of three syllables, for an agonising few minutes. This was too much for her two godfathers, David Midwood and Malcolm Wallace (who formerly commanded the King's Troop Royal Artillery, is a close friend, and one of the best raconteurs, I know) – and my brother Giles, all three having to dash to the door of the church, to conceal their laughter.

On then past the garage flat at Ballybrack House that I rented with the rascally Jean-Michel de Choubersky, as a Pupil Trainer, from Wing Commander Tim Vigors, a brave fighter pilot in the Second World War, whose family was steeped in Racing History. And Boyarin Lodge, home in those days to the hugely charismatic Lady Bruce, and her party-loving offspring, Marianne, Lauretta and Jamie.

Two hundred yards further on, I come to Mesnil Warren, home of course to Teddy Lambton (and his wife Pauline), whose life I saved, purely by chance, through my own adversity – and soon afterwards to Abington Place, where Derby winning trainer Geoff Wragg and his wife Trish lived, when Geoff's trainer father Harry died. I was very fond of Geoff and Trish and became a close friend.

By now I have almost reached the traffic lights at the end of the Bury Road, where there is a fork. Straight on for Mildenhall, Thetford and Norwich – and bearing right for Bury St. Edmunds and Yarmouth, and Charlie Appleby's magnificent training complex at Moulton Paddocks, a mile and a half from the centre of town.

In the vast triangle of grass, between these two roads, is the Lime Kilns, probably the most famous training gallops in this country. Beautifully tended and manicured by generations of conscientious and meticulous Jockey Club Heath staff, this is sacred ground. A cushion of turf, which never becomes firm, even in the hottest, driest of summers. Beyond the Lime Kilns is Waterhall, used by trainers in the spring of the year. This mile gallop runs next to and parallel to the railway line, before swinging right handed to the Gypsy Boy's Grave. A well-known Newmarket landmark.

Now making a 180-degree turn, I walk down the opposite side of the Bury Road, back towards town – passing by Clarehaven Stables, now base to the all-conquering Classic-winning trainer, John Gosden and his son Thady – and formerly to Alec Stewart. And then Freemason Lodge, made famous by Captain Sir Cecil Boyd-Rochfort, one of our greatest post-war racehorse trainers – and another Royal trainer, Sir Michael Stoute, whose training career continues to be an ongoing story of success.

The stables of the astute Roger Varian at Carlburg come next – where Clive Brittain, one of Newmarket's most popular trainers, plied his trade with distinction.

Soon afterwards, I cross the Cambridge to Ipswich railway line, which runs through a tunnel, under the Heath, from close to Newmarket station, emerging on the Bury Road. The station today is busy at rush hour, not otherwise, and unmanned – the old station buildings converted to offices and storage. How strange to think that the old station was a thriving and hugely important hub from where Newmarket trained horses were transported by train to racecourses all over the country, before the advent of motorised horse boxes.

The railway line forms the northern perimeter of what was in my day, Stanley House Stables, now Godolphin Stables, home to Saeed Bin Suroor, which I had bought from Lord Derby and where I had the privilege to train for ten years. A stables locked into racing history, which will always remind me of my best horse, Noalcoholic.

Next door to Stanley House Stables is Shalfleet, which will forever have a special place in my heart. Where I was first a young Pupil Trainer with Harvey Leader, before taking over the licence, when he died in 1972. It is a lucky little yard, where I had my first winner, Trillium – and later Record Run and Ardoon. Happy days – enhanced by the close proximity of our great friends Johnny and Philipa Winter and their children, Nicky, Emma, and Johnny Jnr, who lived at Highfield Stables, the other side of what we referred to as the 'Berlin Wall'. Paul Kelleway and Jeremy Noseda followed me at Shalfleet – and Sean Woods, who did so well as a trainer in Hong Kong previously, is there now.

On the other side of Shalfleet is the Bedford Lodge Hotel, once a racing stable, and now very popular with visitors to Newmarket, especially during racing and sales weeks. It adjoins Bedford House Stables, where Luca Cumani, another Classic-winning trainer, saddled countless winners – and where Charlie Fellowes trains today.

Beyond Bedford House Stables stands Bury Hill, my first digs in Newmarket, then owned and run by Bunty Richardson, mother of Jeremy, and his three sisters, Patsy Anne, Judith and Jo Jo. The ambience and relaxed atmosphere of Bury Hill was much loved by young people aspiring to make careers in the Racing and Breeding Industry, who appreciated a party after a long day's work in stables or on stud. Camaraderie was nurtured, lasting friendships were made – and stamina, mixed with a sense of humour, were a prerequisite. In my days at Bury Hill, in addition to the Richardson family, Danny Mellen, Tote Cherry-Downes, Tim Preston and Tom Collins were in residence – as was Anne (Scrivvy) Scriven, the doyen of Racing in Newmarket, who first came to town in 1952 to be Racing Secretary to Captain Sir Cecil Boyd Rochfort, and afterwards to Sir Noel Murless, Sir Henry Cecil and Geoff Wragg.

Bury Hill overlooks the Severals, a large expanse of grass dear to the hearts of Newmarket people – with a horse track, running through it, used on a daily basis by strings of horses on their way to and from exercise on the Bury Hill gallops.

Very soon, I am back at the Clock Tower Roundabout, where, to my right, on the Fordham Road, when I first came to Newmarket, Tom Jones, John Oxley, Ryan Jarvis, Teddy Lambton, and Walter Wharton used to train. And later Michael Jarvis, Jeremy Hindley, Mark Tompkins and Chris Wall. Today, Ed Dunlop, William Jarvis, Tom Clover and William Haggas are in residence – whilst James Fanshawe and Marco Botti are within spitting distance, on the Snailwell Road.

At this point I head back down the High Street, but on the opposite side past Cartwrights, the electricians, one of the town's oldest surviving shops – and then The Waggon and Horses pub, where many a strong pint has been pulled, a story told, a romance started.

Not far away is Barclays Bank, which has been closely associated with the Racing and Breeding Industry in Newmarket, since its inception – but sadly closed recently. I will always be extremely grateful to their affable, genial and very professional Manager, known affectionately to us trainers as "Mr Scattercash", who enabled me to buy Shalfleet from Harvey Leader in 1972. And was equally supportive when I made the bold step to purchase Stanley House Stables from Lord Derby, six years later.

Close by is Tindalls, once a thriving book shop, specialising in the sale of racing and breeding publications but now only a shadow of its former self. And Whipps, formerly the fishmongers, which had a countrywide reputation but closed long ago, sadly.

At this juncture, I come across Paul Tulk, still very sprightly in his eighties, who was a popular and very capable Newmarket-based jockey in his prime – and whose father Fred worked for Harvey Leader. He reminds me of the day he rode in a mile maiden race at Leicester in the early Seventies, when there were no stalls, and races were started by a flag. A field of 16 runners were taking a turn at the start, when another horse lashed out with his hind legs, and caught Paul with a vicious blow on his left knee. Now in agony, blood gushing from a very deep wound, Paul loses consciousness, falls to the ground, and his horse is withdrawn. There is no First Aid man at the start, so after the race an ambulance is dispatched to the start to attend to the now stricken Paul. On arrival at the start, the ambulance driver pulls up beside Paul, jumps out of his driver's seat, has one look at Paul's blood covered leg – and faints. By all accounts, the Stewards had to request another ambulance to take Paul and the original ambulance driver to Leicester Infirmary!

I am still in fits of laughter, as I make a brief detour down Market Street, which leads to the Guineas Shopping Centre – constructed for the purpose, when Geoffrey Barling's Primrose Cottage Stables were demolished, nearly 50 years ago. To recount Paul's story to my jovial hairdresser and friend Buster, who knows everything about everyone in Newmarket – and which horses are fancied by connections to win on a daily basis. He is very much amused – as is the gallant Alison Hayes, long-time News Editor of the *Newmarket Journal*, whose offices adjoin Buster's busy and popular salon.

Beyond the former offices of Rustons & Lloyd, solicitors who used to specialise in legal work relating to the Racing and Breeding Industry, is Beaufort Cottage Stables – from which Rossdales, the Veterinary Surgeons used to operate. Their business thrived and they have since relocated to a state-of-the-art clinic in Exning.

I am now outside the White Hart Hotel, which has been part of the Newmarket scene for ages – besides which was De Niro's nightclub which thrived for many years but has since closed. For the record, it was originally a cinema, The Doric, when I first arrived in Newmarket. The town's second cinema, the Kingsway, was on the other side of the road, beside the Post Office.

From here, the road rises – and halfway up this incline was in my day the veterinary practice of Reynolds, Leader, Day and Crowhurst. It has changed its name periodically, dependent upon the partners, who were in situ – amongst them, two good friends of mine, David Ellis and Richard Greenwood. It has now moved to a magnificent premises, just beyond the National Stud Roundabout, on the Cambridge Road, and is called The Newmarket Equine Hospital.

Mention must be made here of the notorious Fountain Restaurant, situated on the corner of Fitzroy Street close to Michael Bell's Fitzroy House Stables. Under the genial and hospitable proprietor John's expert guidance, "The Fountain" has been in business as a Chinese eatery for over forty years – and continues to flourish – especially during racing and sales week.

I have now reached the top end of town, and, having passed the Daniel Cooper Memorial, another well-known Newmarket landmark, am heading up Birdcage Walk towards Trillium Place, where I spent the last eight years of my training career. Happy recollections of Rupert's first winner, Gulfland, at Pontefract; Paddy's memorable victory on Shadow Bird at Ascot; and Prince Babar's sensational win in Deauville, for my brother Giles. And, when I retired from training, the births of my two younger children, Rosanna and Charlie. David Simcock now trains very successfully at Trillium Place.

At the junction of Birdcage Walk and Hamilton Road, I stop to gaze at and admire the Rowley Mile and July Racecourses. Standing majestically, enveloped by those immaculate Racecourse Side Gallops. Between them, two Classics and several other Group 1 races are run there every year – and so many famous racehorses have graced their hallowed turf.

In the late Sixties, Hamilton Road was but a quiet thoroughfare – a handful of attractive houses on one side, stud paddocks on the other, leading to Hamilton Stud, and the Jockey Club Shoot. Today it hosts a bustling community of trainers, following the Jockey Club's decision to build a number of training yards on the other side of town, and a concrete horse walk through town, servicing trainers on both sides of Newmarket Heath. Over the years, amongst many others, Alex Scott, Lester Piggott, Ben Hanbury, James Toller and David Ringer trained numerous winners there – and today, the likes of Stuart Williams, William Knight and George Boughey continue to fly the flag for Hamilton Road.

Now turning left into Hamilton Road and before crossing the busy Cambridge Road, I look back in admiration, at the bronze statue of our late Queen Elizabeth II, standing contentedly, with mare and foal, sculpted by Charlie Langton and Etienne Millner. It is superb and perfectly placed on an expanse of grass at the top of Birdcage Walk, there to greet all those driving into Newmarket from London and Cambridge – and for all the townspeople of Newmarket to be proud of. It is a lasting and very appropriate memorial to our dear late Queen, who was so passionate about the thoroughbred, and loved her visits to the Headquarters of Racing and Breeding in this country.

On the other side of the Cambridge Road is Newmarket Cemetery, where so many of Racing's great and good are buried. Including the legendary Fred Archer, one of the most distinguished jockeys of all time. There with them is Coral P-G, who now lies at rest, looking out over the town, the gallops and its rolling stud land of which she was so fond.

I now head northwards back towards town – but take a right turn by Queensberry House, once owned by Jockey Club member Lord Wolverton, then offices for the British Bloodstock Agency, and now converted into much sought after apartments for Racing enthusiasts. Into the quiet of Queensberry Road and past the Sales Paddocks of Tattersalls – the leading Bloodstock sales company in this country, and indeed the world. It is a vast and widespread complex of 46 acres, amazingly, right in the middle of Newmarket. Comprising a magnificent Sales Pavilion, 900 boxes, exercise paddocks, lunging rings, restaurants, offices and extensive parking space for both horseboxes and cars. These mind-blowing Sales Paddocks are beautifully maintained, universally admired, and one of Newmarket's finest hidden treasures.

I am now into the final furlong of my journey – walking downhill past Gibsons, racing equipment specialists, whose staff have been painstakingly crafting racing saddles since the 1900s. And still have the warrant for the making of racing silks for the Royal Family.

And, finally, at the bottom of Queensberry Road, close by its junction with The Avenue to Stanstead House where I spent 14 very contented years as Chief Executive of the Thoroughbred Breeders Association and latterly as Executive Director of British Bloodstock Marketing. Despite being a Racehorse trainer by trade and at heart, I loved my time at the TBA. Meeting breeders, the length and breadth of this country; getting to know the many challenges that they faced on a daily basis, and having the opportunity to travel to many parts of the world, observing the status of the International Breeding Industry and meeting many of the key players.

Within minutes, I am back in the busy High Street, standing by the gate to the Jockey Club – my mission accomplished. It has been a very rewarding and cathartic experience – and highly enjoyable. Revisiting some of Newmarket's well-known landmarks, some of my favourite old haunts – and going back in time over the history of the Racing and Breeding Industry in Newmarket.

But, there is one caveat, which saddens me. Like so many other market towns in this country, Newmarket is not the place it once was – and the High Street has deteriorated markedly. The vast majority of those wonderful old shops have disappeared – to be replaced by a proliferation of betting shops, cafes and fast food outlets. But, I must emphasise, it still retains its charm and its individuality. And, despite the continuous forebodings of today's wretched woke-mongers, the rich history of this magical town cannot be changed nor re-written.

It is now time to quench my thirst, celebrate my "walk up memory lane" and raise a large glass of wine to the town of Newmarket, which has been my spiritual home for 56 years and to the sport of Horseracing.

And I know exactly where I am heading!

53.

The Epilogue

Forward planning has always been of importance to me. It is Friday, when there is a weekly lunch, throughout the year, at the Jockey Club Rooms – for members and their guests, which is always well attended and very congenial. So this morning, I have agreed to meet a quorum of my old friends, who have figured prominently in my life and in these memoirs. Tim Preston, David Midwood, Ben Hanbury, Jeremy Richardson, Steve Smith-Eccles and Anne (Scrivvy) Scriven make up our lunch party. Peter McCalmont, Hon. Secretary of the Jockey Club Rooms, is at the next door table with fellow Old Farts Sam Sheppard, Will Edmeades, Philip Mitchell and Dick Fowlston.

The Jockey Club Rooms is a magnificent building, parts of which date back to the mid 1750s befitting the Headquarters of the Jockey Club. It is classic in style, lovingly maintained, and houses one of the finest collections of equine art in this country. Its long and impressive hallway is brim full of stunning paintings of famous horses; distinguished owners, trainers and jockeys; and other dignitaries involved with our sport over the years. Those depicting Sir Noel Murless, Sir Henry Cecil, Sir Anthony McCoy, Sir Mark Prescott, Lester Piggott, Dick Hern with Sir Gordon Richards, Sir Winston Churchill, and our late Queen Elizabeth, amongst many others, are displayed very prominently.

The magnificent Dining Room in the Jockey Club Rooms has some eye-catching paintings by German artist Emil Adam – but the jewel in the crown, hanging imperiously in the Drawing Room, has to be Stubbs' exceptional painting of the mighty Eclipse. Standing proudly on Newmarket Heath, the Rubbing House beyond, and worth many millions of pounds.

Lunch is superb, many stories are told, reminiscences shared, and banter abounds throughout. And as my long-time friends depart, I wander down the "Rogues Gallery" of the Jockey Club Rooms, to which it is referred, on my return to the flat. A long corridor, portraying, on both sides, the photographs of every elected member of the Jockey Club, since 1815. Some being pen portraits, in those early days, before the science of photography was perfected. It is a fascinating experience – and very satisfying to pick out those former Jockey Club members who have played a part in my life. My owners Lord Willoughby de Broke, Lord Cadogan, Lord Derby and Lord Vestey amongst these. And many others who have featured in my memoirs – in addition to some more recent members, who are now friends of mine.

Back in my flat, I take delight in my own much treasured memorabilia – of my family and of horses that I trained. I look lovingly at photographs of my dear father and mother, my siblings, Giles, Badger, Tessa and Panda – and my four wonderful offspring, Rupert, Paddy, Rosanna and Charlie. And those photographs taken of Trillium, Gulfland, Shadow Bird, Record Run, Ardoon, King Pele, Do Justice – and of course Noalcoholic.

It makes me very happy and proud – and I start to reflect on my life since leaving school at the age of 18. It has been action-packed, never dull – but sometimes unpredictable.

In my early days as a trainer, Rupert and Paddy, as young children loved going racing with me. Particularly to Yarmouth, where we would watch our horses run and then drive the short distance into the town of Yarmouth afterwards, to enjoy the amusement arcades, the pier and the ice-creams – and their favourite of all, the funfair at the far end of the seafront, which was superb. I too was mad about the funfair and its many attractions – which I often think could be regarded as an analogy of my life in racing. Strange to relate.

The merry-go-round carousel, with its bib-bobbing brightly coloured horses, sets the scene from a trainer's perspective. The near misses, bumps and collisions of the dodgems equate to one's everyday life in racing. And the big dipper rollercoaster ride epitomises the last fifty five years of my life. The thrills and spills, the ups and downs, the highs and lows – but, at the end of this daunting challenge, a feeling of elation, satisfaction and achievement.

In summary, I will always be eternally grateful to that Dean of Christ Church College in Oxford, who identified, so quickly, the paucity of my academia, despite the grief it caused me at the time. To Bill Hicks, the Sports Editor of the *Daily Mail*, for his sound advice and for steering me towards a career in Racing, albeit in journalism. And to my mentor, Harvey Leader, who was kind enough to give me the opportunity to train racehorses and pursue my passion for Racing.

Hindsight tells me that being a bumbling barrister in Biblinghampton, or a sedentary solicitor in Slivery Camden would have been as dull as ditch water in comparison and not my cup of tea!

*

Harvey Leader

Taffy Williams and Gavin

Harvey Leader with Taffy Williams

Gavin, Paddy, Coral and Rupert

Staff at Stanley House Stables

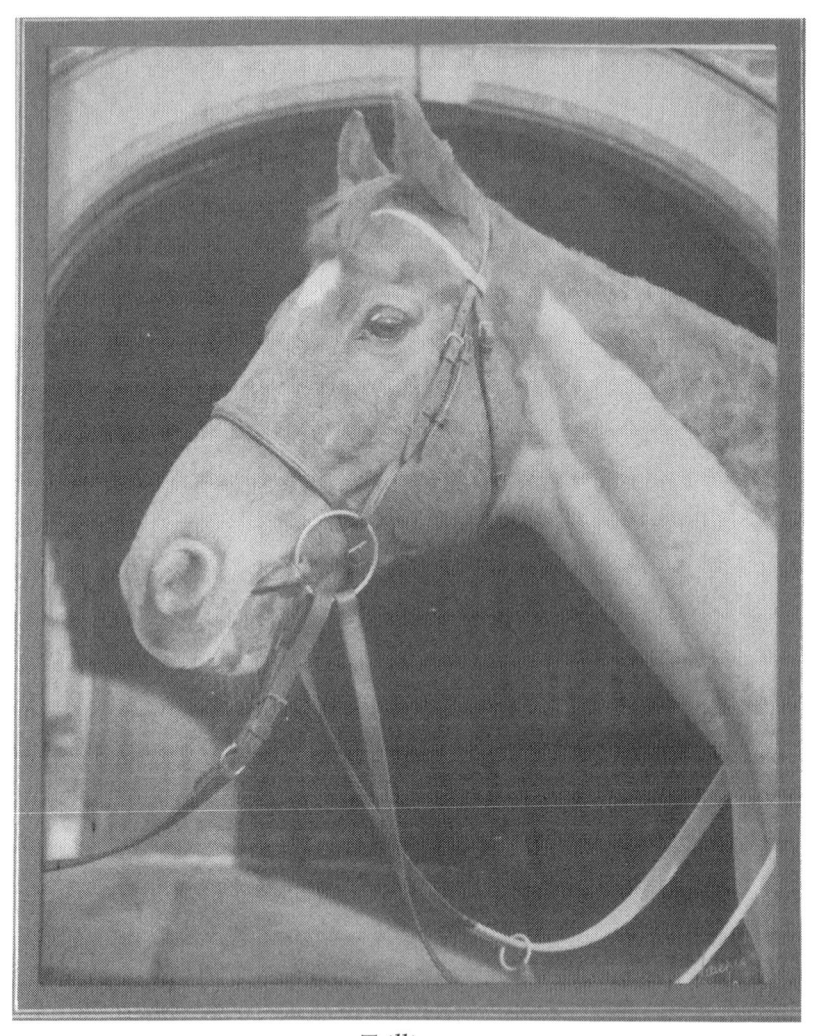

Trillium

Brian Taylor

Mill House

Deep Run - the stallion

David Nicholson on Do Justice

Ardoon at Ascot

Record Run at Ascot

Noalcoholic at Goodwood

Noalcoholic wins Sussex Stakes

Desert Orchid with Simon Sherwood

Rupert and Gulfland at Pontefract

Gulfland at Redcar

Paddy on Shadow Bird at Ascot

Rupert with Lord Hartington (now the Duke of Devonshire)

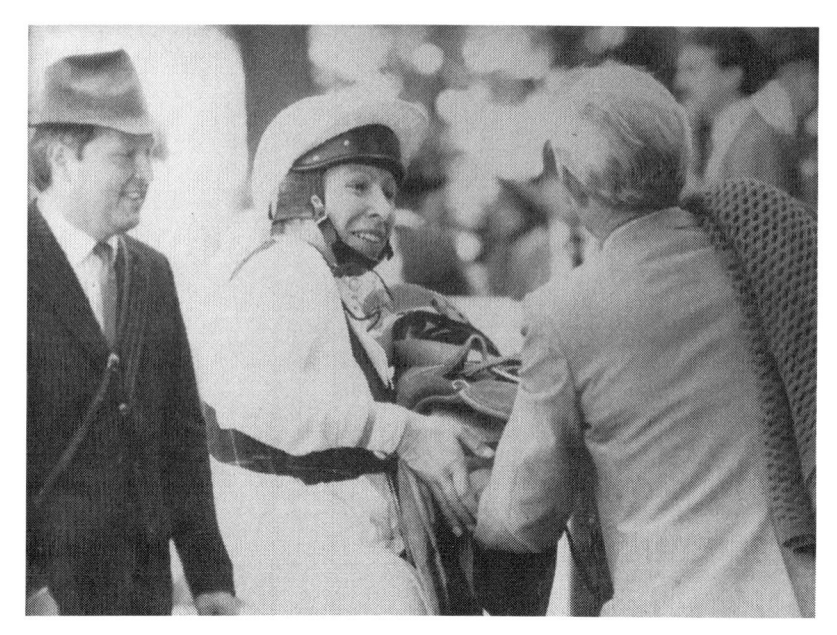

The Princess Royal with Gulfland

King Pele

Prince Babar's win at Deauville

Billy Cahill

Julian Wilson

Lord Willoughby de Broke (John)

Peter Walwyn

Steve Smith-Eccles

Lord Vestey (Sam)

The Earl Cadogan (Bill)

Minty, Gavin and Pam Sly

An outstretched Minty

The Earl of Derby (John)

John Garnsey (on left) in party mode

Sam Bullard with William Buick

Sir Mark Prescott

Sir Noel Murless

Ben Hanbury

Oliver Sherwood

Midwood

Family P-G at Hill House

Bill P-G

Lesley P-G

Bill P-G

Hill House

Boom Patrol at Leicester

Lesley P-G, Ros and Michael Meacock

Lou and Giles P-G

Brokers Folly

Rosanna and Charlie

Rosanna

Paddy and Rupert

Charlie

Gavin and Diana (Billy)

GAPG

Index

Adam, Emil 271
Aintree Racecourse 16, 214–215
Aird, Emily (P-G) 242
Alexander, Hamish 150, 152–153, 156
All Systems Go 21, 101, 132
Andrew, Rob 165
Anglo Hibernian Bloodstock Insurance Services 261
Angus, Nigel 148
Anne, HRH The Princess Royal 205–206, 226–227, 288
Appleby, Charlie 263
Archer, Fred 269
Ardoon 102–103, 132, 205, 264, 272, 282
Armstrong, Sam 52
Asmarine, Societe 21–22
Ayr Racecourse 5, 83, 88–89, 148–149, 219

Bailey, Kim 178
Baileys Horse Feeds 202
Balding, Emma 211
Balding, Ian 165, 211
Banks, Jack 246
Barling, Geoffrey 52
Barrow, James 259
Barrow, Lucy 259
Batten, David 164
BBC 22–23, 25, 125, 134, 165–167, 215, 244
Beaumont, Billy 167
Beck, Philip 137, 240
Bedford Lodge Hotel 39, 264
Beeby, Harry 150
Beeby, Henry 150
Bell, Michael 267
Bengough, Sir Piers 84
Benson, Charles 138

Beverley Racecourse 124, 210
Biddlecombe, Terry 213
Bigland, Robert 230
Billy the Cob 51–52
Bin Suroor, Saeed 264
Boothman, Peter 177
Boss, Ron 172
Botham, Ian 161
Bothway, Colin 116
Botti, Marco 265
Boughey, George 268
Boyd-Rochfort, Arthur 159
Boyd-Rochfort, Sir Cecil 44, 52, 263
Brabazon, Aubrey 60–61, 64, 193
Brearley, Mike 161
Briscoe, Moira (Frisky) 67
British Bloodstock Agency 53, 94, 155, 269
British Horseracing Authority 248
British Horseracing Board 248
Brittain, Clive 263
Brooke, Geoffrey 52
Brown, David 161
Bruce, Jamie 262
Bruce, Lady 262
Bruce, Lauretta 262
Brudenell-Bruce, Dana 160
Buckley, Graham 261
Bullard, Gerry 180
Bullard, Mally 181
Bullard, Sam 177, 180, 298
Buster, hairdresser 266–267

Cadogan, Earl of (Bill) 77, 81, 83–84, 180, 182–183, 205, 207, 219–220, 237, 249, 272, 295
Cadogan, Lady (Bunny) 220
Cahill, Billy 6, 98–99, 187, 234, 235, 289
Carson, Willie 125, 168
Carter, Charlie 240
Cartwrights, Newmarket 265

Catterick Racecourse 69–70, 143, 210
Cecil, Julie 188
Cecil, Sir Henry 188, 265, 271
Champion, Bob 213, 261
Channon, Mick 168
Charles, Rowe 54
Cheveley Park Stud 183
Christ Church College, Oxford 273
Churchill, Sir Winston 261, 271
Clayton, Jack 52
Cleverly, John 210
Clover, Tom 265
Cohen, Leslie 87
Coleman, David 215
Coley, Mark 230
Collins, Tony 148
Conway, Chris and Yvonne 129
Cooper, Henry 130
Cooper, Jilly 164
Cooper, Leo 164
Corbett, Ronnie 141–143
Corrie, Helen (Doodie) 155, 242
Corrie, Sarah 155
Corrie, Tom 155, 242
Cottrill, Humphrey 52, 170
Cowell, Bob 183
Cowell, Robert 177, 182
Crapnell, Dick 54–56
Crowhurst, Leader and Day 31, 53
Crump, Neville 83
Cumani, Luca 264
Curragh Bloodstock Agency 53, 64, 132, 155, 193
Curragh, The 53, 56, 58, 60–64, 68, 75, 86, 90, 132, 155, 193
Cursham, Juliet 185
Cusworth, Les 167

Day, Reg 52
Deauville Racecourse 48, 95, 96, 102, 243–245, 256, 268, 289
de Choubersky, Jean-Michel 262

Deep Run 62–63, 280
Dempster, Nigel 203
Derby, Earl of (John) 46, 118–119, 120, 141–143, 179, 264, 266, 272
Derby, Lady Isabel 141
Desert Orchid 109, 178, 285
Dettori, Frankie 229, 245
Dobbie, David 230
Doggart, Hubert 221
Don, Andy 207
Doncaster Bloodstock Sales 150
Doncaster Racecourse 29, 31, 45, 63, 83, 85, 91, 97, 103, 124, 150–151, 153, 205, 209, 229, 230
Driscoll, Tony 67
Duffield, George 101, 133, 142, 175
Dunlop, Ed 147, 265
Dunlop, John 147
Dunn-Gardner, Miry 30
Dunwoody, Richard 213
du Pont, Bill 132–133
Dymock, Peter 23

Easterby, Mick 246
Eddery, Pat 79, 85, 102
Edwards, Eddie 77, 82, 101
Eldin, Eric 139, 152–153
Elizabeth, HM The Queen Mother 227
Elizabeth II, HM The Queen 143, 268
Ellis, David 159, 267
Elwes, Nigel 255
Emburey, John 161
Epsom Derby 42–43, 143
Eykyn, Mrs W. 106

Fahey, Richard 246
Fanshawe, James 185, 262, 265
Fauresson, Philippe 21
Featherstonhaugh, Brud 61

316

Feeney, Frank 102–103
Feilden, Major General Sir Randle 160
Fellowes, Charlie 264
Fellowes, Robert 54, 157
Fenwick, John 146
Ferguson, John 164, 185
Finch, Tim 116, 168
Finn, Mrs 77
Fontwell Park Racecourse 217
Formby, George 129
Forster, Captain Tim 70
Foss, Reverend Gilbert 239
Fountain Restaurant, Newmarket 267
Fowlston, Dick 271
Francome, Johnny 213
Frank, Charles 254–255
Frankel, Bobby 247
Freedman, Louis 69
Freedman, Philip 255
Freeman, Keith 48
Freud, Sir Clement Freud 135
Fujisawa, Kazuo 94–95, 177, 257

Garnsey, John 137–138, 240, 298
George, Jimmy 261
George, Tom 177, 179
Gibbs, Geoffrey 211
Gibson, Richard 183
Gibsons, saddlers 269
Gifford, Josh 213
Gifford, Macer 156
Goffs Auctioneers 54, 124, 150, 197
Goldings, Newmarket 53
Goodbody, Michael 255
Goodwill, Arthur (Fiddler) 127
Gorvin, Peter 104
Gosden, John 263
Gosden, Thady 263
Gower, David 161
Graham, Clive 17

Grand National 16, 29, 103, 109, 178, 214, 217, 228, 261
Grant, Commander Kenneth 89
Greening, Mickey 78, 177, 186
Greenwood, Richard 254, 267
Gregg, Tessa (P-G) 174, 272
Grey, Sidney 33, 102, 103
Grimthorpe, Lord (Christy) 210
Gulfland 205–207, 268, 272, 286, 288

Haggas, William 136, 159, 164, 185, 262, 265
Haggie, Willa 185
Haine, Di 214
Halifax, Earl of (Ernie) 79, 160, 210–211
Halifax, Lady Camilla 79, 211
Halsey, Jock 31, 39, 77
Hammond, John 183
Hanbury, Amanda 189
Hanbury, Ben 159, 188–189, 192, 268, 271, 301
Hanbury, Captain Tom 188
Hanbury, Chunky 188
Hanbury, Emma 189
Happy Valley Racecourse 42
Harbord, Derna 64
Harbord, Lelia 61, 64, 72
Harbord, Mitzie 197
Harbord, Paddy 64, 193
Harrington, Johnny 64, 71
Hartington, Lord (now Duke of Devonshire) 206
Hastings-Bass, William (now Lord Huntingdon) 163
Hastings, Colonel Robin 94
Hastings, Gavin 165
Hastings, Scott 165
Hayes, Alison 267
H. Clarkson and Company 14, 21
Head, Criquette 183
Helaissi, Mr A. S. 112

Hemmings, Trevor 178
Henderson, Nicky 213
Hernandez, Dr Juan 122
Hern, Dick 271
Hesseltine, Michael 182
Hickey, William 203
Hicks, Bill 16–20, 31, 36, 38, 273
Hills, Barry 160
Hindley, Jeremy 158, 265
Hindley, Sally 188
Hobbs, Bruce 261
Holding, Michael 158
Hollingsworth, Dick 160
Hotel Pretty 21, 22
Howard de Walden, Lord 69
Humble Duty 75
Hurt, Chris and Anne 198
Hyperion 46, 120, 260

Jakobson, Tony 158
Jarvis, Julie 185
Jarvis, Michael 265
Jarvis, Ryan 52, 139, 155, 165, 265
Jarvis, Sir Jack 52, 261
Jarvis, William 159, 164, 185, 265
Jockey Club Rooms 46, 260, 271–272
Joel, Jim 41
Joel, Solly 161
Joel, Stanhope 102, 161
Johnson Houghton, Fulke 62
Johnstone, Captain Andrew 79
July Racecourse 32

Keane, Lucy (P-G) 242
Keane, Moss 167
Keeneland Sales 189
Kelleway, Paul 121, 264
Killer Shark 83–84
King, Jeff 213
King Pele 97, 102, 104, 216, 272, 288
Knight, Billy 268

Ladbrokes 144
Laing, Ray 67
La Linea 90, 91
Lambton, Pauline 262
Lambton, Teddy 52, 111–112, 262, 265
Lambton, The Hon George 120
Langton, Charlie 268
Lauder, Harry 49, 50, 51
Lawlor's Ballroom, Naas 58
Leader, Harvey 29–37, 39–43, 45–52, 54–56, 59, 75–78, 83, 85, 89, 94, 100, 104, 127, 129, 163, 185, 228, 237, 243, 249, 261, 264, 266, 273, 275, 276
Leader, Ted 52
Leicester Racecourse 175, 266, 307
Lewis, Geoffrey 151
Lewis, Noelene 150
Liem, Mr S. 139
Limekilns Gallop 84
Lindley, Jimmy 41
Lingfield Park Racecourse 132, 243
Lloyd, Andy 161
Loder, Sir Edmund 59
Longchamp Racecourse 21, 247

Macauley, Willie 150, 156
MacRae, Gay 249
MacRae, Mac 104
Magnier, John 62
Mahony, Edmund 261
Maitland, David 102
Maktoum, Sheikh Hamdan 171
Maktoum, Sheikh Mohammed 203
Mariti, Walter 134
Marlar, Robin 221
Mason, David 116
Mason, Tim 117
McCalmont, Major Victor 64
McCalmont, Mrs Dermot (June) 69
McCalmont, Peter 271
McCormack, Cormac 182

318

McCormack, Matty 67
McCoy, Sir Anthony 271
McFarlane, Michael 43
McKeever, Peter 64, 71
McKeown, Terry 97, 103
Meacock, Alexander 55
Meacock, Michael 147, 308
Mellen, Danny 265
Mellor, Elaine 72
Mellor, Stan 72
Mercer, Joe 41, 168
Mid Sussex Times 18-19, 21
Midwood, David 228, 262, 271
Midwood, Jane 230
Midwood, Ralph 228
Millan, Jack 23
Mill House 74-75, 279
Millner, Etienne 268
Minton, David (Minty) 104
Mitchell, Philip 271
Moore, Dan 178
More, Lady 149
Morgan-Jones, Rhydian 252
Morton, Romana 258
Mould, David 213
Mowbray, Sir John 205
Murless, Beryl 58
Murless, Sir Noel 43, 53, 150, 265, 271, 300
Murless, Stuart 56, 59
Murray, Tony 81-82
Murrell, Kevin 177, 261
Musk's, butchers in Newmarket 53, 261
Myerscough, Cyril 54
Myerscough, Philip 54

National Horseracing Museum 54, 261
Nelson, Peter 42
Newbury Racecourse 23, 24
Newcastle Racecourse 88, 132, 152-153, 229

Newmarket 9, 12, 17, 25-31, 35-36, 39-40, 43-47, 49-50, 52-58, 62, 64, 70, 75-78, 85-86, 88-90, 92, 94, 97, 99-100, 102, 106, 108, 110-112, 114-119, 121-124, 126-128, 130, 133, 136, 139, 141-142, 144, 146, 148, 149, 155, 158, 159-161, 163-164, 165-166, 168-174, 179-182, 184-185, 188-189, 203, 204, 206-207, 213, 216-217, 222, 225, 228, 234-235, 243-244, 246, 248-249, 253, 256, 259-268, 269-271
Newmarket Equine Hospital 267
Nicholson, David 97, 159, 168, 213, 281
Nicholson, Dinah 106, 206
Nicholson, Frenchie 85-86, 97, 103
Noalcoholic 132-133, 205, 264, 272, 284-285
Northern Dancer 62
Noseda, Jeremy 264

Oakman, Alan 221
O'Brien, Aiden 61
O'Brien, Vincent 61
O'Gorman, Bill 204
O'Gorman, Paddy 52
Oldham, Gerry 50
Oldrey, David 69-70, 255
Oliver, Ken 150
O'Neill, Jonjo 213
O'Sullevan, Peter 17, 24
Oswald, Sir Michael 255
O'Toole, Mick 61
Oxley, John 52, 54, 159-160, 265
Oxx, John 61

Paine, Terry 168
Palmer, Dr 239
Parks, Jim 221

Peate, Ed 177, 182
Perth Racecourse 219
Philipps, David 23
Philipps, Peter 205
Pick, Charlie 153
Pick, Sandy 154, 156
Piggott, Lester 40, 88–89, 105, 113–114, 268, 271
Pilkington, Sir Anthony 230
Player, Peter 167
Plumpton Racecourse 20, 175, 218
Pontefract Racecourse 175, 177, 206, 268, 286
Portman, Jonny 183
Powell, Jim 54
Powell, Paddy 62
Prendergast, Kevin 61
Prendergast, Paddy Jnr 61
Prescott, Sir Mark 142–143, 170, 262, 271, 299
Preston, Rossie 88
Preston, Tim 30, 44, 88, 132, 265, 271
Price, Ryan 16, 42, 88
Pritchard-Gordon, Charlie 179, 180, 259, 263, 268, 272, 311
Pritchard-Gordon, Coral 61, 64, 71–72, 76, 78, 81, 84, 86–87, 90–94, 104, 106, 109, 119, 123, 129, 133, 139, 141, 143, 169, 180–181, 186, 189–190, 193–201, 203–204, 245, 257, 269, 277
Pritchard-Gordon, Giles 237, 309
Pritchard-Gordon, Grant (Badger) 174, 238, 272
Pritchard-Gordon, Great Uncle John Pritchard-Gordon 92
Pritchard-Gordon, Lesley 174, 305, 308
Pritchard-Gordon, Lou 174, 241–244, 309

Pritchard-Gordon, Paddy 105, 109, 174, 189, 193, 200–201, 205, 207, 229–230, 244, 247, 268, 272, 287, 311
Pritchard-Gordon, Rosanna 259, 262, 268, 272, 310
Pritchard-Gordon, Rupert 92, 105, 107, 109, 165, 174, 183, 189, 193, 195–196, 200–201, 205–207, 246–247, 268, 272, 277, 286–287, 311
Pritchard-Gordon, William 174, 304, 306

Radley, Clive 161
Ratcliffe, Robin 163
Rausing, Kirsten 255
Record Run 102, 205, 264, 272, 283
Redcar Racecourse 90, 91, 102, 127, 206, 210, 286
Reynolds, Richard Jnr 59
Richards, Abigail 205
Richardson, Bunty 30, 44, 264
Richardson, Jeremy 44, 159, 163, 271
Richardson, John 104
Richardson, Lee 249, 251
Richards, Tim 23
Ricketts, Tristram 249, 251
Rimell, Fred 63
Rimmer, Mark 205
Ringer, David 268
Robertson, Ian 165
Robinson, Lavinia 205
Roger, Baroness 22
Rogers, Tim 61
Roper, George 104
Rossdales, Veterinary Surgeons 267
Rowley Mile Racecourse 26, 29, 115, 126, 168, 205, 268
Royal Ascot 102–103, 115, 118, 120, 133

Rudolf, Arno 101
Rutland Arms Hotel, Newmarket 262

Sanderson, John 209
Sangster, Robert 61, 148
Sassoon, Sir Victor 43
Scott, Alex 268
Scott, Brough 9, 95
Scriven, Anne (Scrivvy) 44, 55, 265, 271
Scudamore, Peter 213
Severals, The 30, 131, 170–171, 265
Shadow Bird 205, 207, 268, 272, 287
Sheppard, Reverend David 221
Sheppard, Sam 271
Sheridan, Panda (P-G) 174–175, 177, 272
Sherwood, Nat 107, 157
Sherwood, Oliver 115, 177–178, 301
Sherwood, Simon 177–178, 285
Short, Jean 31, 39, 76, 77, 177
Shortt, Francis 62–63
Sieff, Sir David 103
Simcock, David 268
Skeaping, John 261
Slattery, Fergus 167
Sly, Derek 156
Sly, Pam 155, 296
Smith-Eccles, Steve 84, 171, 175, 213, 217, 271, 293
Smyly, Mark 70
Smyth, Ron 241
Sobers, Gary 158
Sparkman, John 132
Stewart-Brown, Ian and Jane 146
Stoop, Eliza (P-G) 242
Stoute, Sir Michael 23, 25, 158, 203, 263
Streeter, George 239
Suggett, Colin 168
Swinburn, Walter 229

Tattersalls Sales 243, 260
Tavistock, Lady Henrietta 103
Taylor, Brian 33
Taylor, Simon 230
Thatcher, Margaret 135
Thin, Chris 137
Thirsk Racecourse 210
Thompson, James (Tonk) 137
Thomson Jones, Harry 52, 170, 213
Thomson Jones, Tim 180
Thoroughbred Breeders Association 247, 253, 256, 269
Tindall, Simon 182
Tindalls, Newmarket 266
Titmus, Fred 161
Toller, James 159, 268
Tompkins, Mark 159, 265
Trillium 79–81, 94, 125, 205, 264, 272
Tulk, Fred 266
Tulk, Paul 266
Tyers, David (Ginger) 129, 177

Urquhart, Bob and Mima 210

Van Cutsem, Bernard 118
Varian, Roger 263
Vestey, Edmund 200
Vestey, Lord Sam 106
Vigors, Wing Commander Tim 262
Vittadini, Dr Carlo 47

Waggon and Horses, pub 265
Wales, John 169
Wallace, Malcolm 262
Wallace, Quentin 137, 240
Wall, Chris 265
Wallis, Tommy 103
Wallis, Viv 103
Walpole, Lord (Bobby) 224, 225
Walwyn, Fulke 74
Walwyn, Peter 64–76

Walwyn, Virginia (Bonk) 65, 67, 69, 71–72, 74
Warden, Colonel Dick 141
Warren, John 211
Warwick Racecourse 39, 71, 79, 80–81, 84, 104, 229
Watkinson, Ian 171, 213
Watt, Peg 61
Watts, Billy and Pat 210
Waugh, Jack 52
Waugh, John 52, 77
Waugh, Tom 52
Webber, Paul 185
Weld, Charlie 61
Weston, Garfield 59
Wharton, Walter 265
Wheeler, Peter 167
Whelan, Dermot (Boggy) 99
Whipps, fishmonger 53, 266
White Hart Hotel, Newmarket 267
Wilcox, Joe and Kevin 96
Wilcox, Paula 96
Williams, Colin 56
Williams, Ian 183
Williams, Stuart 268
Williams, Taffy 31, 34, 39, 51, 56, 77, 94, 129, 177, 276
Williams, Venetia 177
Willis, Bob 161
Willoughby de Broke, Lady Rachel 79
Willoughby de Broke, Lord 26, 29, 39, 79–80, 89, 94, 272, 291
Wilson, Jim 156
Wilson, Julian 23, 25, 125, 134, 159, 160, 168, 244, 290
Wilson, Robin 156
Wingfield Digby, Ali (P-G) 242
Wingfield Digby, Nick 159
Winter, Fred 16, 178
Winter, Johnny 92
Winter, Philippa 92, 109
Wogan, Sir Terry 165

Wolfson, Lord (David) 103
Wolverhampton Racecourse 39, 81, 96, 97, 103, 127, 175, 229, 243
Woods, Sean 264
Wolverton, Lord 269
Woodward, Clive 167
Wordsworth, Jim 261
Wragg, Geoff and Trish 50, 54, 262, 265
Wragg, Harry 50–52, 97

Yarmouth Racecourse 48, 87–88, 117, 126, 167, 194–195, 229, 243, 263, 272
York Racecourse 79, 80, 118, 135, 148, 209, 211
Yoshida, Katsumi 247
Yoshida, Terya 257

Zetland, Lord (Mark) 210

Acknowledgements

There are a number of people I would like to thank for their contributions to this book, which have been hugely appreciated.

First, Brough Scott, for encouraging me to finish the book, once half way through; and for kindly writing a foreword.

Car Colston Hall Stud for their generous sponsorship of the book – and Jockey Club Estates in Newmarket for all their support, in different respects.

Tom Jackson for putting the book together – and to Colin Mackenzie for his wise counsel and sound advice re publication, and for introducing me to Tom in the first place.

Alison Hayes, Editor of the Newmarket Journal for correcting my punctuation, and some of the factual content of the book.

Susan Oakes, for her painstaking secretarial and computer skills – and my niece Annie Pritchard-Gordon, who collated all the photos, and recreated them in the required jpeg format.

They have all been remarkable.

Printed in Great Britain
by Amazon